# Content and Workflow Management for Library Web Sites:

## Case Studies

Holly Yu
California State University, Los Angeles, USA

 **Information Science Publishing**

Hershey • London • Melbourne • Singapore

| | |
|---|---|
| Acquisition Editor: | Mehdi Khosrow-Pour |
| Senior Managing Editor: | Jan Travers |
| Managing Editor: | Amanda Appicello |
| Development Editor: | Michele Rossi |
| Copy Editor: | Maria Boyer |
| Typesetter: | Rachel Shepherd |
| Cover Design: | Lisa Tosheff |
| Printed at: | Yurchak Printing Inc. |

Published in the United States of America by
 Information Science Publishing (an imprint of Idea Group Inc.)
 701 E. Chocolate Avenue
 Hershey PA 17033
 Tel: 717-533-8845
 Fax: 717-533-8661
 E-mail: cust@idea-group.com
 Web site: http://www.idea-group.com

and in the United Kingdom by
 Information Science Publishing (an imprint of Idea Group Inc.)
 3 Henrietta Street
 Covent Garden
 London WC2E 8LU
 Tel: 44 20 7240 0856
 Fax: 44 20 7379 3313
 Web site: http://www.eurospan.co.uk

Library of Congress Cataloging-in-Publication Data

Content and workflow management for library websites : case studies / Holly Yu, editor.
 p. cm.
 Includes bibliographical references and index.
 ISBN 1-59140-533-5 (h/c) -- ISBN 1-59140-534-3 (s/c) -- ISBN 1-59140-535-1 (ebook)
 1. Library Web sites--United States--Case studies. 2. Library Web sites--Design.
3. Online databases. 4. Electronic information resource searching. 5. Electronic
reference services (Libraries) I. Yu, Holly.
 Z674.75.W67C66 2004
 025.04--dc22
                                                    2004022153

British Cataloguing in Publication Data
A Cataloguing in Publication record for this book is available from the British Library.

All work contributed to this book is new, previously-unpublished material. The views expressed in this book are those of the authors, but not necessarily of the publisher.

# Content and Workflow Management for Library Web Sites:
## Case Studies

# Table of Contents

# Preface

Web content management (WCM) as a branch of content management (CM) gained importance during the Web explosion in the mid-1990s. However, the concept of utilizing content management solutions to manage library Web sites has only just started to emerge. More and more library Web administrators are coming to the same conclusion: that Web content needs to be managed throughout the content life cycle, that static HTML pages are time consuming to maintain, and that a lot of Web content in libraries can be re-purposed effectively. Additionally, rising demands from users for customized Web functions, as well as from library staff for easier and more streamlined internal workflows, are all calling for more effective solutions to Web content management. Content management solutions therefore seek to make content more usable to the user community, and to streamline the process of creation and publication of library Web pages, thereby reducing the time and cost of content management.

Content management can be simply defined as a process of collecting, organizing, categorizing, and structuring information resources of any type and format so that they can be saved, retrieved, published, updated, and re-purposed in any way desirable.

The ultimate goal of publishing Web content through the use of a WCM system is to automate the entire process of writing and publishing content by integrating easy-to-use Web authoring tools with a large database of information resources, while ensuring that library users receive well-managed and current information with a consistent look and feel. These databases are designed to allow easier management and retrieval of the resources and incorporation into a variety of Web presentations.

# Current State of Library Web Content Management

Using WCM tools or systems to manage increasingly diverse Web content and to streamline workflows is a solution recognized in libraries today, although the field of Web content management in libraries is in its infancy. Libraries are increasingly aware of the need, and many find themselves currently in the planning stages to implement such a solution. However, limited library Web content management models and funding constraints prevent many libraries from purchasing commercially available WCM systems. Rather, libraries typically are utilizing database-driven methods to manage portions of a library Web site, such as subject guides, lists of electronic resources, calendars, and the like. In many libraries, WCM applications are developed to resolve a particular challenge existing in library Web site development. And the lack of much-needed technical expertise in building in-house WCM applications also presents a great challenge for libraries of all types.

Currently in many libraries, the tools and methods used to maintain Web content are not meeting the demands and expectations of library users. Libraries are still struggling to provide current, consistent, up-to-date information on their Web sites using only the primitive tool of HTML. In many libraries, the hands-on nature of Web content management is still a mainstream situation. A typical example is the management of subject pathfinders or electronic resources lists. Most Web editors agree that the process of producing subject pathfinders using basic HTML coding is tedious, labor intensive, and in many ways repetitive because many subject areas contain identical resources, descriptions, and links. As both the electronic collection and print collection develop, these pages need to be updated constantly. Updating these pages requires repetitive and tedious editing, as every single one of these occurrences has to be updated. In many cases, HTML-coded Web content has become unmanageable.

Libraries are facing a situation where demand for dynamic access and online delivery of information is growing rapidly. Add to that an increasing amount of content being generated for Web sites and other publications by a variety of authors, some with little or no Web expertise. In many large academic and public libraries, Web content is created by a roster of authors, including professional librarians, staff members, student assistants, and interns. As a result, the question of how to streamline the workflow and publish easily and consistently has become a critical issue. The Webmaster model is still employed by many libraries as a primary means to manage its Web site, but has been proven to be inefficient in an environment where a team of developers and editors contribute to the Web site. The changing nature of Web authorship and user demands is necessitating change in how libraries manage their Web sites.

# Discussion in the Literature

In researching this preface, the author found that the literature is relatively scant on the overall management of Web content in libraries, but rather extensive in business. Most articles on the management of library Web sites dealt with the design of the site and the evaluation of it. As well, most of the literature on administering library Web sites finds librarians discussing the creation and usability of the site (Shropshire, 2003). There is very little research on the ongoing content management of library Web sites. The fact that the majority of librarians creating Web pages are self-taught means that little attention has been given to defining the roles of library workers regarding Web site content management, and that librarians have not been discussing the processes and workflows associated with running an academic or large public library Web site. Being self-taught also suggests that librarians are sharing the technical know-how without formally examining the processes required to maintain the content of a Web site.

In large part, the library literature has omitted library Web content management and workflow quality control. Issues surrounding library Web content management did not come to view until 1999 when Antelman (1999) points out that "library Web sites have grown in size and complexity over the last several years without a corresponding growth in the sophistication of the underlying technology." Antelman argues that the primitive tool of HTML is no longer sufficient to deliver information with multiple access points and via user-defined displays. The Webmaster model is proving to be increasingly inadequate due to the increase in number of people involved in Web development and the sheer volume of HTML pages being created. User expectation of tailored displays and personalized selection of resources adds another layer to the problem.

In terms of reviewing and choosing WCM solutions, the literature is also deeper in business environments. Many of the articles on WCM for libraries only give a layman's guide to the process, with a few notable exceptions appearing in the last two years. In her first article, "What Is a Web Content Management Solution?", Kim Guenther (2001), a librarian writing from a corporate approach, defines the WCM product classes and familiarizes readers with some required WCM vocabulary. She also discusses in a second related article the necessary planning leading up to a review and selection of a content management solution, while providing and exhorting readers to examine and plan workflows and business strategies.

In contrast to the lack of formal research on the topic, there are a large number of conference proceedings, presentations, informal papers, listservs, and Web sites that provide library Web developers with information on various tools on Web site management. However the author has found no systematic investigation of library methods and tools in terms of WCM. Given the light treatment of the topic in the literature, it is timely that this volume appears. Much that has been learned in the business environment can be applied successfully to the library setting, particularly academic libraries. Both Shropshire and Guenther, among others, strongly encourage libraries to examine their business strategies to ensure that the content that appears on the Web site is meeting the needs of the user group. In her article, "Library Web Site Administration: A Strategic Planning Model for the Smaller Academic Library," Susan M. Ryan (2003) argues for a systematic approach to Web site development that ties into the library strategy for delivery of services.

The advent of the library Web portal has also developed to provide patrons with a customizable interface to information resources. The library literature reflects this new trend. Articles are appearing that cover a variety of related topics, including the history of Web portals and their development in libraries (Zhou, 2003), a philosophical discussion on personalized library portals as an organizational culture change agent (Lakos & Gray, 2000), as well as methods and approaches in creating Web pages without HTML coding (Bills, Cheng & Nathanson, 2003) and creating discipline-specific portal to periodicals (Womack, 2003). The MyLibrary portal (my.lib.ncsu.edu), which allows customized access, is a pioneer in the library world. Following the implementation of the MyLibrary portal at the 1999 American Library Association (ALA) mid-winter meeting, the MyLibrary model was deemed as one of the key future trends for library Web content management and dynamic display solutions. Six years have passed since the inception of the first library portal, yet we have not seen the anticipated large-scale acceptance of the library portal model in libraries. Users of the portal also tend to be small in number, but active in their use. Eric Morgan (2003), creator of the MyLibrary portal, notes the fact "that a small number of users makes up a large part of the system's usage." Crawford (2002) echoes and cites other problems that may have impacted the use of the library portal, such as solipsism—where a user's narrowly defined profile limits the full use of library resources—and differential service—where users who did not set up a portal profile receive low-quality service. While user behavior may have been one of the major reasons why the MyLibrary kind of portal model has not been embraced by many libraries, time and energy spent in maintaining the application, keeping up with new technology, and changes in organizational culture also further impeded the success of portal applications in libraries.

The real motivation that pushes libraries, especially academic libraries, to start creating home-grown database-driven applications is the challenge they face in creating subject guides or pathfinders. Bills, Cheng, and Nathanson (2003) have the same observation as mentioned earlier that the process of producing subject guides was tedious, repetitive, and labor intensive, and it required librarians to become proficient at the intricate task of Web-page creation. Recording the information in a database allows the information to be entered or updated once, and propagated to as many pages as one desires. Early home-grown database-driven applications mainly utilized Access database, ASP, Java, or CGI, with ColdFusion Express, PERL, SQL, XML, and PHP coming into play around the turn of the century.

In most cases, while library Web portals that automate Web content management for the entire Web site do not seem to serve the best interests of the library user, a new trend is emerging in Web content management—that is, to embrace open source software products to manage portions of library resources and services, namely, subject guides, online resources, library news, online tutorials, and more.

The possibilities of widely used open source software (OSS) in libraries are investigated by Morgan (2002), who summarizes the discussions that have appeared on OSS4Lib (Open Source Systems for Libraries), and lists the main threads as: national leadership in the form of institutionalized support, mainstreaming of OSS in the areas of enumerating the advantages and disadvantages of OSS, and promoting and marketing OSS as a viable means for implementing sustainable OSS applications. Discussions of open source software applications in libraries appear in the literature early in 2002. David Brethhauer (2002), in his article "Open Source Software, a History," provides a historical account of the sophisticated movement of OSS. Roy Tennant (2003) classifies open source software for libraries into two categories: complete systems that handle all of the tasks related to a service (e.g., portal system), and tools that perform specific tasks that can be integrated with other components to create new services. The benefits of open source software for Web content management stem from its unique features—cross-platform simplicity and an easing of licensing restrictions. However, there are drawbacks, as Cervone (2003) observes. In many cases, the support costs for OSS can be more than the costs for equivalent commercial software. Installing and maintaining OSS applications generally requires a higher level of technological sophistication than that required for commercial software. Nonetheless, because libraries are free to run, copy, distribute, study, change, and improve the software, more and more of them are using the software as a tool for Web content management.

In general the library literature presents great possibilities in using open source solutions. What is lacking is how these tools can be integrated into the process of Web content management and to provide various models that can be applied by many libraries.

Using Web content management solutions to manage increasingly diverse Web content and to streamline workflow is a solution recognized by many libraries. However, limited library Web content management models and the lack of much-needed technical expertise in building home-grown WCM applications both present great challenges for libraries of all types. Any solutions that involve programming skills take time to develop, especially where technical expertise is lacking. For example, some solutions involve migrating the existing data into new database management software, such as MySQL, which requires a learning curve for those who are not familiar with the software.

# Organization of the Content

This book provides practical and applicable Web content management solutions through case studies. Following an introduction to needs and challenges in library Web content management in Chapter 1, and a discussion of available methods and tools used for Web content management in Chapter 2, there are eight case studies. These case studies contain successful database-to-Web applications as employed in a variety of academic libraries, all with their own unique environments. The applications vary in scope and cover a range of practical how-to-do-it real-life and cost-effective examples: database-driven Web development for dynamic content delivery; locally created Web content management applications; systems for distributing content management responsibilities, quality control, and open source tools. Issues and challenges associated with the development process are discussed. Authors also discuss the detours and missteps necessary in a real learning experience.

Holly Yu, in Chapter 1, "Library Web Content Management: Needs and Challenges," explores the notion that rising demands for user-centered and customized Web functions and streamlined workflows are the major motivation for better solutions to WCM. This chapter begins by defining the content and scope of Web content management. Needs and benefits are addressed based on aspects of library WCM from content creation, updating, delivery, look and feel, and re-using data to more administrative functions including workflow management, quality control, and cost-benefit. Issues and challenges associated with implementing a Web content management solution—including strategic planning, selection of WCM tools, and the impact of new features and organizational culture—are also discussed.

In Chapter 2, "Methods and Tools for Managing Library Web Content," Johan Ragetli provides a comprehensive overview of the tools and methods currently available to libraries that are seeking a WCM solution for their Web sites. Solutions for managing a wide variety of materials and contributors range from enterprise-wide content management systems to home-grown solutions utilizing open source products. Increasingly collaborative software such as blogs or wikis have also found their use in delivering library content easily and consistently by librarians without detailed knowledge of Internet protocols and coding. Regatli notes that current trends indicate that libraries are developing a variety of custom tools and systems that tackle content challenges on a case-by-case basis, often featuring a distributed architecture that favors flexibility and supports a group of contributors with varying technical skills. This kind of development also allows for a greater sharing of resources, allowing more libraries to capitalize on efforts and gains made by other libraries. This trend is already taking hold in many libraries as system librarians try their hand at programming and database creation, whether it is a blog, a wiki, or a searchable collection of classified links in a relational database.

In Chapter 3, "Developing a Distributed Web Publishing System at CSU Sacramento Library: A Case Study of Coordinated Decentralization," Juan Carlos Rodriguez and Andy Osburn outline the steps that were undertaken at the California State University Sacramento Library in moving from a centrally managed, static, and disjointed Web site, to a efficient, collaboratively managed, database-driven Web site utilizing an easy-to-use, customized Web content management system developed by the library. The case discusses the decisions and actions taken during the various stages throughout the design and implementation of the Web publishing system. Rodriguez and Osburn present the methods used, including some of the Web-based technologies, and discuss the issues encountered and how they were addressed during the development and implementation of the locally created Web publishing system.

Chapter 4, "Indiana University Bloomington Libraries Presents Organization to the Users and Power to the People: A Solution in Web Content Management" by Diane Dallis and Doug Ryner, describes how the Indiana University Bloomington Libraries created a database-driven Web system that enables librarians and staff to publish content to the libraries' public Web site that maintains a consistent design and places the content into a logical and consistent structure. The system is composed of the libraries' public Web site interface, the content manager (CM) administrative interface, and an intranet. Dallis and Ryner provide the process of how the new Web system was designed to replace a decentralized process that was previously followed in maintaining a large Web site of 8,000+ static HTML pages. The new system made it possible for their large, decentralized library system to present a unified and well-designed public interface on the Web. The authors also describe the technical and conceptual development of the content management aspect of the system.

In Chapter 5, Laura B. Cohen, Matthew M. Calsada, and Frederick J. Jeziorkowski of University Libraries, SUNY-Albany, describe the planning, development, and implementation of a quality management tool—in their case, "ScratchPad: A Quality Management Tool for Library Web Sites." The case explains the impetus for the project, presents the rationale for developing the tool, and describes the system components. The tool balances the needs of Web contributors with the assurance of a professional presentation of the organization's Web site by offering a systematic workflow from development to production, with appropriate quality control prior to public posting. Implementation outcomes are discussed, especially as they relate to staff engagement and solving post-production issues.

In Chapter 6, "Website Maintenance Workflow at a Medium-Sized University Library", Michelle Mach indicates that more than half the library staff at a medium-size academic library maintain large numbers of static Web pages, using Web editors rather than content management tools. While not optimal in the technical sense, this process does maximize the individuals' creative contributions to the site. Because of this flexibility, feedback about this process has been primarily positive at an individual level. However, a growing number of challenges in the areas of content, priorities, technical skills, and workflow exceptions have cast doubt on this system's long-term prospects. The case discusses the balance between individual and group needs, and the true cost of a purely technical solution to the problem of Web maintenance.

In Chapter 7, Michael D. Whang introduces the design of a PHP and PostgreSQL content management system as a means of maintaining content within a library's online subject guide collection in his case, "PHP and PostgreSQL Web Content Management Systems at Western Michigan University Libraries." The author argues that the content management system, combined with distributed authorship, provides an efficient and effective way to manage a large growing body of content that changes frequently. Furthermore, Whang hopes that understanding the process of building a content management system, from system and data requirements to database design and content display, will not only inform librarians and technical staff of good system design practices, but also assist in the understanding of a content-driven library Web site.

In Chapter 8, Stephen Sottong from California State University, Los Angeles (CSULA), in his case, "Database-Driven Web Pages Using Only JavaScript: Active Client Pages," describes the process of how one university library decided, as part of an overall redesign of its Web site, to use a database-driven Web application. Sottong discusses how a new method of creating the database-driven pages without the necessity of special servers was devised. The resultant Web pages use JavaScript arrays to simulate a database and embedded JavaScript programs to provide the dynamic content for the library Web site.

In Chapter 9, Anne Marie Donovan and Michael Nomura study the development of the Tactical Electric Power Digital Library (TEPDL), a special-purpose document repository and information resource Web site. Their case is entitled, "Tactical Electric Power Digital Library." The discussion focuses on content management considerations and their effect on project planning, Web site design, and maintenance. Also described are the process and challenges associated with implementing the content management and content delivery features of TEPDL. The case study is intended to highlight the importance of addressing content management issues early in the digital library Web site planning and design process, and to illustrate how a content management needs analysis can be translated into the selection and development of specific content management tools and processes.

In Chapter 10, "Developing Committees to Create a Web Content Management System," Sarah Robbins and Debra Engel examine the use of committees to develop a Web content management system at the University of Oklahoma Libraries. The case explains the process undertaken to move from an HTML to a database-driven Web site and the issues involved with using committees to steer such projects. Creating a framework in which librarians use locally developed content management tools to control Web site content, while the systems office retains control of the presentation of content, is also discussed. Another aspect of the case study includes the evolution of Web committees in the organization and the development of a system-wide philosophy.

These cases provide insights into each library's path to accomplishing their projects and offer a road map for anyone about to embark on similar projects. Approaches, tools, models, and codes found in this book can be applied immediately. For librarians who have been involved in WCM projects and wish to learn more, for librarians who have not been involved in such projects but anticipate or plan to do so, and for those who are aware of the need and are in the planning stages for implementing a solution, this book will provide a learning process going from strategic planning, through process development , and up to final delivery.

*Holly Yu*
*Editor*

# References

Antelman, K. (1999). Getting out of the HTML business: The database-driven Web site solution. *Information Technology and Libraries, 18*(4).

Bills, L., Cheng, R.J., & Nathanson, A.J. (2003). Subject Web page management without HTML. *Information Technology and Libraries, 22*(1).

Bretthauer, D. (2002). Open source software: A history. *Information Technology and Libraries, 21*(1).

Cervone, F. (2003). The open source option. *Library Journal netConnect,* (Summer).

Crawford, W. (2002). Talking 'bout MyLibrary. *American Libraries, 33*(4).

Guenther, K. (2001a). What is a Web content management solution? *Online, 25*(4).

Lakos, A., & Gray, C. (2000). Personalized library portals as an organizational culture change agent. *Information Technology and Libraries, 19*(4).

Morgan, E.L. (2003). Putting the "My" in MyLibrary. *Library Journal netConnect,* (Fall).

Ryan, S.M. (2003). Library Web site administration: A strategic planning model for the smaller academic library. *Journal of Academic Librarianship, 29*(4).

Shropshire, S. (2003). Beyond the design and evaluation of library Web site: An analysis and four case studies. *Journal of Academic Librarianship, 29*(2).

Tennant, R. (2003). Open source goes mainstream. *Library Journal, 128*(13).

Womack, R. (2003). Bel Jour: A discipline-specific portal to periodicals. *Information Technology and Libraries, 21*(2).

Zhou, J. (2003). A history of Web portals and their development in libraries. *Information Technology and Libraries, 22*(3).

# Acknowledgments

Many people have contributed to the writing of this book over the past few years. My original thought of using a database-driven solution to resolve issues in library Web content management and workflow streamlining was inspired by Kristin Antelman's article "Getting out of the HTML Business: the Database-driven Web Site Solution" in 1999. At that time, I worked with my colleagues at the Pasadena Public Library to look into the feasibility of creating subject pathfinders utilizing MS Access database. We all agreed that database-driven Web content management was the right way to go for the development and management of such library resources. Due to our lack of technical expertise and perceived lack of models to follow at the time, our discussions did not lead to fruition. Nonetheless, these initial discussions contributed to a better understanding of the need for a more effective Web content management solution.

As I took on the responsibility as library Web administrator at the University Library, California State University, Los Angeles (CSULA), the pressure to effectively manage library Web content and to streamline workflows in the creation, maintenance, and updating of Web content was mounting. In 2001, the Library Web Team embarked on an overall redesign of the Library Web site, of which streamlining content management workflow was a major concern. A decision was made to implement a database-driven solution to resolve content development and update issues for external users, internal Web content contributors, and the Web Team members maintaining the Web site. The goal was to redesign the Web site as a dynamic resource that patrons would use in a highly individualized way, and to ease the content management workload. Since various obstacles prevented the Library Web Team from using Active Server pages (ASP) and SQL server to execute our plan, a JavaScript constructed data source was chosen, and it in large part achieved our defined goal. For this process, I'm indebted to my colleagues serving on the Web Team. I would like to take this opportunity to thank Scott Breivold, Paul Bui, Barbara Case, Doug Davis, Yvonne Hasegawa, Chad Kahl, Ken Ryan, Romelia Salinas, and Stephen Sottong for their creativity, patience, and perseverance. Particularly, my thanks go to Stephen Sottong for his initiative and testing in developing the JavaScript constructed Web content management structure.

This process urged me to seek out other successful or alternative models in managing library Web content. Around the same time, I received an invitation from Dr. Mehdi Khosrow-Pour to edit a book on a subject of my choice. My prospectus on library Web content and workflow management was well received and was deemed to be worthy for publication. From the inception of this project to final publication, I received guidance and continuous support from Dr. Khosrow-Pour and his staff at Idea Group Publishing. Special thanks go to Dr. Khosrow-Pour, whose enthusiasm motivated me to initially accept his invitation for taking on this project. Further thanks go to Jan Travers, Senior Managing Editor, for her support throughout the project. I would also like to thank Michele Rossi, Development Editor, and Amanda Appicello, Managing Editor, who always timely responded to my email inquiries regarding the progress of the project. Jan, Michele and Amanda kept the project on schedule.

A very special "thank you" goes to all of the authors for their exceptional contributions, dedication and commitment to this book. I have learned from and been inspired by their research results, insights and practical solutions.

Several of the authors of this book also served as referees for articles and cases written by other authors. Thanks go to all those who served as reviewers and who provided constructive, critical and comprehensive reviews. Among them, Carlos Rodriguez, Director of Library Information Systems, California State University, Sacramento, provided very comprehensive and insightful reviews despite a very busy schedule. Stephen Sottong, then Technology, Engineering and Computer Science Librarian at CSULA; Sarah Robbins, Electronic Services Coordinator at University of Oklahoma; and Michelle Mach, Digital Projects Librarian at Colorado State University, offered their constructive opinions on the cases they reviewed. A special thanks also goes to my long-time friend and colleague, Johan Ragetli, Information System Analyst, Peterborough School Board, for his encouragement and insightful suggestions throughout the process.

This book would not have been possible without the generous support from my colleagues, mentor, and supervisor at CSULA who offered their invaluable perspectives during the process, and served as reviewers. A special thanks goes to my mentor Ken Ryan. I value his detailed copyediting, insight, and most importantly, his willingness to help whenever I asked. Barbara Case, the former library Web administrator, inspired me to do my best through her enthusiasm and dedication toward her work. Doug Davis, the University Librarian, provided his invaluable perspective on many issues that I had puzzled over. I appreciate very much for their support, opinions, and encouragement.

Last, but not least, I must express my heartfelt appreciation to my husband, Alex, for his patience with my turning our living room into a study hall filled with mountains of books, papers, and notes for the duration of almost a year. My thank you and love also go to our dearest daughter, Judy, for her sparkling smile, lively comments and endless energy.

# Section I

---

# Introduction to Library Web Content Management

Chapter I

# Library Web Content Management:
## Needs and Challenges

Holly Yu
California State University, Los Angeles, USA

## Abstract

*Rising demands by library users for customizable Web function and by library Web administrators for streamlined workflows call for better solutions to Web content management. This chapter begins by defining the content and scope of Web content management. Needs and benefits are addressed based on aspects of library Web content management from content creation, updating, delivery, and re-use to the "look and feel," workflow management, quality control, as well as cost-benefits. Issues and challenges associated with implementing a Web content solution including strategic planning, selection of Web content management tools, impact of meta-searching, and the organizational culture of the library are discussed.*

# Introduction

This chapter discusses the needs of and challenges to libraries of all types and sizes in developing Web content management strategies and solutions. Rising demands for user-centered and customized Web functions, and streamlined internal workflows call for better solutions to Web content management. The entire life cycle of the Web site from its initial definitions of content requirement, tool selection, workflow management, and rollout, to ongoing updates and upgrades involves content management. The author believes that successfully addressing these challenges will significantly contribute to developing user-centered Web sites and more effective workflow for internal Web site management.

# What is Web Content Management?

## Definition of Content Management

Content management, or CM, can be simply defined as a process of collecting, organizing, categorizing, and structuring informational resources of any type and format so that they can be saved, retrieved, published, updated, and repurposed or reused in any way desirable. Today's content management solution is either a sophisticated software-based system or a database-driven application. A full-featured content management system "takes content from inception to publication and does so in a way that provides for maximum content accessibility and reuse and easy, timely, accurate maintenance of the content base" (Warren, 2001).

Theoretically, content management encompasses a broad spectrum of areas such as document management (DM), knowledge management (KM), records management (RM), electronic content management (ECM), financial content management (FCM), and Web content management (WCM). Web content management is one of the branches of content management.

Content management gained importance during the explosion of Web sites in the mid-1990s. The Web has dramatically changed the way published content is used. The value of published material goes beyond its finished physical form, and the true added value of content becomes evident "if it can be re-purposed continually and profitably" (Kartchner, 2001). Miller and Manafy (2003) assert that the true power of content management "may actually lie in its flexibility to change shape to fit each new business problem before it." Consequently almost every organization or library comes to the realization, sooner or later, that it needs a system to manage its content for Web publication and other forms of publication.

## Scope of Web Content Management

The scope of WCM includes combinations of WCM systems and WCM tools or applications. A fully featured Web content management system includes the process from content inception to publication, in a system that allows Web administrators to streamline workflows and to enable all content contributors to easily edit, update, and publish Web content without in-depth knowledge of HTML. Many libraries have utilized WCM applications to create or maintain portions of their Web content, such as subject guides or bibliographies, online electronic resource lists, and library personnel rosters.

Boiko (2001) categorizes Web content management systems, or WCMs, into four levels: nominal WCM systems, database-driven or dynamic Web sites, full WCM systems, and enterprise CM systems.

- Nominal WCM systems are those tools like Microsoft's Notepad, FrontPage, and Macromedia Dreamweaver. These tools provide basic Web management mechanisms such as page templates to all authors to create standard page layouts across a Web site, site outlines and link managers to verify that all links are working properly, and a publication manager that allows Web managers to upload newly created or modified pages to Web servers. These tools are suited for creating and managing small and single Web sites.

- Database-driven or dynamic Web sites, in a strict technical sense, are not WCM systems, but are rather Web-based applications. A dynamic Web site is a "system for producing Web pages 'on the fly' as users request them" (Boiko, 2001). Usually, the application contains a data source stored on a Web server. The data source can be built using a relational database, or XML structure, or a structure constructed by other scripting languages, such as JavaScript. The data source contains the content in response to a user's queries when a user clicks on a link. There is a template page that connects the data source and the user, and there are HTML codes and programming scripts or objects in the template page that can interpret the user's request, activate the data source, and send appropriate content to the user's Web browser as an HTML page. Dynamic Web sites and WCM systems both have databases to process content. Boiko (2001) argues that there are compelling reasons to distinguish between the two: "Because you can have a dynamic site that really is not doing CM. In addition, a CM system can just as easily build a static site." He further explains that a static site is faster and much less prone to crashing than a dynamic one, so "you are in a better situation to build a static site from your WCM system." A site does not have to be 100% static or 100% dynamic.

- Full WCM systems function throughout the process from content collection to publication, and manage content contributors and workflow. A full WCM system contains a relational database serving as a repository of all types of content, from text, HTML files, graphics, to style sheets; a live data source generated by the WCM system for the dynamic parts of a Web site; and many HTML files managed by the WCM system for the static parts of a site.

- Enterprise CM systems encompass the entire content creation and management for the organization, not just the Web site.

A full picture of a Web content management system contains a complex mix of technologies, repositories, processes, and quality control, all of which need to work together. Technically, integration across these areas is a key for a successful implementation of Web content management. The management segment of a WCMS can include management tools for content quality control, workflow control, data on the system users, data on contributors, and so forth. The publishing component contains the process of appropriately arranging content, designing navigation, applying Web design standards, and ensuring useful and practical functionalities.

Workflow management and quality control are two major reasons why many libraries started utilizing Web content management systems or applications. Workflow represents a set of sequential and parallel tasks from project inception, through commission, content creation, review, editing, integration, to publication, and including further revisions or updating. In simple terms, workflow is a cycle or a series of tasks that must be done in order to move the project forward. However, workflow is not created by the system; the people who manage the project define the process of tasks and the technical mechanisms. Many WCM systems offer advanced content management features such as version control, editorial sign-offs, and live date or time control. A WCM system can also set up controls to determine who approves certain pages before they are published live.

Successful Web content management should contribute to a user-centered Web site for the user and streamlined workflow for internal Web developers.

# Needs and Benefits of Implementing WCM Solutions

Libraries are seeking to manage their Web content for a number of reasons, some of which reflect standard business practices and some of which are unique. WCM is used to get a handle on the increasing local content, the number of sources of information, and the variety of documents produced. The sheer volume and complexity of information provided by library staff is increasing. As a result, more staff are included as contributors, many with non-technical backgrounds. Administrators also have expectations that more library services be Web enabled, resulting in more access and information services going online. Some of these services are handled by library automation software, but increasingly Web sites are designed to integrate these services into a one-stop portal-like environment.

Library users are becoming more demanding in their information needs and demanding higher levels of personalization based on their experiences with commercial sites such as those hosted by online booksellers. Expectations are that all library services should be represented on the Web site. Content often requires re-purposing for different audiences or different uses such as handhelds. Additionally, libraries are beginning to focus on content that is unique to the online environment including online news, digital collections, live interaction, and tutorial delivery. Processes and tools must therefore be developed to publish library events, happenings, policies, and other activities to the library Web site (Clay, 2003).

A Web site grows in size and complexity. Web administrators find it often grows "beyond the ability to manage it as a collection of static HTML pages" (Guenther, 2001a). Other aspects surrounding Web development also come into play. In addition to involvement of more library staff in Web content creation, Guenther summarizes the factors that contribute to the rising demand for a WCM solution. More functionality is required to serve Web users and internal Web developers, and standards need to be implemented for a more consistent look and feel (Guenther, 2001a). Some of the pressing needs that are consistently emerging are as follows:

- The ability to personalize or customize content for different user groups
- The ability to streamline internal workflow and reduce workload stemming from tedious and repetitive tasks
- The ability to achieve quality control
- The ability to reduce cost of managing the organization's Web
- The ability to re-purpose, or reuse, content in multiple information sets, to deliver the content to both library Internet and intranet, and for other publications

Hackos (2002) indicates that "content management is no longer an option, given the complexity of information access and retrieval." To meet the above-stated needs, content must be organized in a content management system or application to ensure that it is managed effectively, retrieved easily, and delivered in different formats.

## Content Creation, Updating, Delivery, and Reuse

In many libraries, the need for WCM, lies in the areas of subject guides or pathfinders, lists of electronic resources, library news, library personnel rosters, and more. For example, the process of creating or updating subject guides or pathfinders can be tedious, repetitive, and labor intensive, and it requires subject librarians to be familiar, or even proficient, with HTML coding. A well-designed WCM system can resolve this issue by providing non-technical library staff with an online form or template for content input and update. The content only needs to be input or updated once, and it can be propagated to as many subject lists as needed. Content is stored in a database, where each piece of information is described and tagged with appropriate metadata. Once the content resides in a well-organized database, it can be efficiently retrieved and delivered to either a static Web display or a dynamic display through live searches or pre-defined lists such as subject guides.

The differences between a static Web site and a database-driven or dynamic Web site lie in how the data is stored and written. On a static Web site, content on each individual page has to be entered manually. The content on the page does not change unless the page is edited or updated. Therefore, content and presentation on a static Web site forms an inseparable unit. There are both benefits and drawbacks to static Web sites. Undoubtedly, static Web sites load quickly and are also inexpensive to run. However, there is a prominent drawback: all pages are written in HTML, so that only staff with HTML skills can create, modify, or update pages, which is often a labor-intensive task.

By contrast, content on a database-driven or dynamic site is stored in a database (e.g., Access, SQL, Oracle, MySQL, or home-grown). When the content in the database is modified or updated, the content on the Web pages is changed accordingly. This feature empowers library subject experts without HTML skills to create and update the Web content. As Brown and Candreva (2002) point out: "This puts the power of content generation into the hands of the experts, the librarians, while the burden of Web page layout, design, and coding lies with technology specialists." Guenther (2001a) considers that the heart of most content management systems is the ease with which participants can add content to a Web site. Features found in WCM systems or applications "take the technical burden off the contributors and allow them to participate without having to know HTML."

Using a WCM system or similar application can simplify the content creation and updating process and reduce the number of people involved in HTML coding, thereby dramatically reducing the number of files to maintain, and allow library staff to concentrate on content delivery and instruction. For academic libraries, these changes will inevitably enhance the library's ability to delivery on its major strategic goal-delivering positive learning outcomes to customers and stakeholders (Lakos & Gray, 2000). More importantly, perhaps, it provides library users with the most updated and accurate information.

In static HTML format, content cannot be reused or repurposed for other uses, such as for wireless handhelds. With a properly implemented WCM solution, it can be ensured that the information content is written once, and can be published and updated everywhere, and re-purposed for different user groups and different electronic devices.

## Webmaster Model No Longer Viable

The traditional Webmaster approach has proven inefficient because this model lacks the flexibility and scalability needed to effectively manage the complexity and volume of library Web content. This factor has been clear, as many libraries conceptualize or re-conceptualize and move to WCM solutions. In many libraries today, the publishing of content to the library Web site follows the same model as in early days: Web authors submit pages to the Webmaster who publishes them to the live site. In that model the Webmaster then "became responsible for soliciting content, ensuring stylistic conformity, and handling other coordination tasks" (Antelman, 1999). In most cases, library Webmasters are working overtime and taking on extra responsibilities. While they are dreaming about instant updates and simultaneous changes for all pages, in reality they have no extra time to educate themselves or investigate new technologies. Such a situation clearly hinders the development of new and advanced functionalities as users have expected. In the implementation of WCM solutions, new workflows are created, often relieving the Webmaster or Web editor of having to manually check new and updated pages.

## Look and Feel

Implementing a database-driven solution allows the separation of content from presentation and provides more display flexibility. The strength of the Web is its ability to display data and engage the user, while the main characteristic of the database is to store data. The benefit of a database solution then is to let each do the job they are best at. The main benefit of this arrangement for a contributing librarian is that, in simple terms, "it allows one to focus on inputting rather than formatting" (Westman, 2002). Managing content allows for greater control of the site, resulting in greater consistency in look and feel. The look of the site can be changed more easily without requiring overall reformatting of the content. For example, one change to the calendar updates all instances of the calendar in schedules and posted hours. The organization of the Web site and the navigation structure can be designed to accurately reflect user needs.

## Workflow Management and Quality Control

The demands from external users for more features, and from staff for reducing workload, lead many libraries to consider streamlining the Web development process. In many libraries, content for the Web site is contributed by a variety of library staff, ranging from professionals and paraprofessionals, to student assistants and interns. With so many participants involved, the process of content creation, editing, reviewing approval, and publishing can be disorganized or chaotic. To encourage non-technical members to actively contribute content, easy-to-use tools should be developed or adapted to remove the bottlenecks that prevent them from participating.

As discussed earlier, "content workflow" is the process of breaking down a task into a series of orderly steps. According to CMSWatch.com (2004), workflow answers the questions of what needs to be done, who needs to do it, who needs to approve it, and when it must be completed.

Workflow can be streamlined and roles can be assigned to appropriate contributors in a WCM system or Web content management application through the use of templates. Templates allow non-technical contributors to participate "within a pre-defined role," but they are required to follow a series of steps. Guenther (2001a) states that "a content management system with workflows based on roles, rules, and routes make developing and managing the Web site analogous to workers on an assembly line. Each person has his or her role and, within that, specific responsibilities to carry out before passing it on to the next person within the workflow."

The quality control component in the process of the workflow determines when the content is changed and published and who does it. Quality control is a much-needed process in many libraries. It can prevent errors due to dated content, broken links, and typos on production sites.

## Cost Reduction

The need to reduce the cost of maintaining a library's Web site has also been an important factor. Questions we need to ask ourselves in trying to cut down costs are:

- How many library staff members and librarians within the library develop content?

- How much of the content that they develop is the same or similar?

- How many computer workstations or places (e-mail folders, individual hard drives, or Web servers) are used to store these contents?

- How many different tools are used to produce these contents?

- How much time is spent by each individual to produce the content that is stored in someone else's machine?

Answers to these questions will result in savings in personnel and ultimately in cost. With all library content separated and stored in one well-structured database, the content produced once can be used everywhere by everyone; updated content can be propagated to all pages without updating it on each page. "By reducing the number of steps required to create and deliver information, individuals and even entire organizations save time. Time saving[s] translate, of course, into cost savings" (Hackos, 2002).

Although the needs and benefits of WCM are apparent, it remains difficult nonetheless to move from the realization of its importance to the establishment of Web content management practices in the library.

## Challenges in Web Content Management

As library Web sites continue evolving into a gateway for nearly all library resources and services, the underlying technical structure of most library Web sites also needs to grow in parallel. Many library Web managers are "struggling to control their sites using only the primitive tool of HTML" (Antelman, 1999), which generates obstacles to delivering information. As discussed above, the need for Web content management solutions arise and is identified when Web managers can no longer maintain Web sites with continuously growing content and user demands. The current lack of turn-key library WCM packages present a great challenge for libraries in selecting a viable one. At the same time, many libraries lack the needed technical expertise to attempt to build in-house WCM systems or applications. Funding constraints also prevent many libraries from purchasing commercially available Web content management systems. Recent developments like meta-searching or federated searching for library databases also impact how libraries manage their electronic content. Organizational and cultural obstacles add another layer of challenges to the implementation of WCM solutions.

From the management perspective, challenges are being faced during the entire process of WCM implementation-from the initial strategic planning, when to use a WCMS, through the selection of applications or tools, the implementation of workflow management, quality control, and finally to ongoing updates, site modifications, and technology upgrades.

## Strategic Planning: Key to Success

Establishing key objectives tied to library goals and objectives is key to successfully implementing new Web procedures. It has been shown that formal business strategies will assist libraries in providing structure to the Web site management. Libraries, it also has been demonstrated, are especially good at sharing the technical details and processes attached to project outcomes.

What strategies are employed by libraries to develop the structures and the processes to serve their user groups? Susan M. Ryan (2003) has noted that libraries are replacing or scaling down their lists of subject-oriented links as being unfeasible and a waste of effort considering the increasing availability and quality of third-party sources. They are instead beginning to focus on the creation and delivery of local content that in many cases is more useful to libraries' user groups. Locally provided content can include lists of subscription databases, research guides, reference aids, tutorials, help sheets, tips and other documentation, virtual reference services, and other interactive real-time offerings.

The key strategy then is to streamline processes and create a standard look and feel along with increased functionality to better serve users, library staff, contributors, and system developers. Ensuring that the technology does not get in the way of delivering content is a major hurdle for many companies and by extension libraries. Throwing a high-end sophisticated tool at a low-key problem is never a good strategy. Redefining workflows may become a significant hurdle for librarians who are used to being in control of the whole process. WCM systems take the locus of control from the designer or editor and situate it in the system. Once the design elements are established, content is delivered consistently across the board based on the rules chosen once by the Web team or Web administrators.

McGovern, who has written extensively on the subject since before it was termed 'content management', warns organizations about the peril of putting technology before content. "Content is not a technology problem. Content is about people. People who understand content are enthused by the content itself, not the technology that is used to deliver that content" (McGovern, 2002). As more and more libraries realize that content is the key to their Web site, the next step is to align the determination of content with the organization's key goals. If one of the goals of the library is to communicate the hours of opening, creating a single Web page to reflect that should be easy enough. More difficult, as Ryan articulates, is the goal of teaching information literacy to undergraduates. This goal must be broken into several objectives likely requiring extensive research and resulting in significant numbers of pages, purposeful design, and structure (Ryan, 2003).

*Strategic planning, when followed from start to finish, provides a useful structure for creating, implementing, and maintaining library Web sites. Crafting Web site policies and procedures that systematically address Web site administration, design elements, structure and organization, content, external links, maintenance and updates, and evaluation and assessment provides a strategic context for Web site decision making. (Ryan, 2003)*

Guenther (2001b) also recognizes the necessity of mapping Web strategies based on the organization's goals and objectives, and also designing workflows that respect the authoring environment and result in the production and publication of content to match the objectives decided upon. Guenther's recommendation is for libraries to create a Web strategy for the library that clearly defines what the goals of the library are in establishing and maintaining a Web. Goals should be defined as clearly as possible. Example goals might be:

- creating searchable, up-to-date pages describing the library's databases;
- integrating within parent portal or enterprise;
- maintaining catalog of links; or
- creating personalized or dynamically created subject guides—on the fly.

Web strategic planning takes the essential goals of the central business strategy of the library and applies another level of detail to it—namely Web details. In choosing a WCM system, administrators should be prepared to answer a number of questions. What is required to realize the organization's goals vis-à-vis the Web? What are the goals and objectives of the library? Does the library's Web strategy reflect its own and the parent organization's overall goals? How does the library plan to reach its different user groups and serve them, and how does the Web strategy serve these goals?

## Challenges in Workflow Management and Quality Control

An issue directly related to quality control is the rising number of content contributors. Studies have shown that librarians have long been accustomed to working independently and their Web authoring skills are largely self-taught. They are not used to working with a defined set of rules, or to following workflows or using pre-designed templates. Therefore, redefining workflows and setting up quality control may be an obstacle for many to overcome, both psychologically and in terms of the institution's culture.

In many libraries, controlling quality of Web sites has been uneven due to having multiple content contributors. Thus, streamlining workflow and quality control have become critical issues. While having many contributors can save the Web administrator or team a tremendous amount of Web content generation time, there is a downside: errors can creep in, many pages go unseen or unedited prior to publishing, and contributors occasionally overwrite files or publish content with missing links. In the WCM environment, there are questions that need to be considered: Who approves or denies a suggestion? How should quality control be set up? Who can actually make changes to the workflow system?

One of the key advantages of a WCM solution is to distribute content maintenance responsibilities with well-thought-out and well-managed internal access and privileges. Contributors can be assigned privileges based on the role they play, typically the content areas they can create and edit. For example, subject librarians can create and update content on subject guides and the descriptions of databases; graphic designers can create and modify image files and place them in HTML templates; and system librarians can write, trouble-shoot, update scripts and change file permissions, and add metadata to site content. The basic principle here is that workflow and quality control should be "justified as enhancing the value of the content to the user, and not as a way of 'controlling' content in some authoritarian way" (White, 2003).

## Whether and When to Use a WCMS

As discussed earlier, WCM solutions may contain either a total WCM system approach or perhaps more simply a WCM application approach. Which approach should be used is a decision largely based on the scope of the user's needs. For example, a need to manage online databases and their access may only require a database-driven application that delivers the content through querying a database. Depending on the size of the data and the number of estimated simultaneous 'hits', the database can be hosted using Microsoft Access, SQL database, or MySQL. For this type of need, a full-scale WCM system that manages the entire operation of content management and delivery would be overkill. There are an increasing number of commercial applications, which perform just this function.

Whether or when to use a content management system is also defined by several factors, including the overall organizational strategy for Web development, specific requirements for functionality, and the content management environment-staff skill levels and Web publishing process. McGovern (2003) argues that when you publish at least 10 new documents a week with a minimum of five authors/editors involved, it is time for you to use a WCM system. This assertion is only partially true because it only addresses the need for a WCM system from the perspective of the scope or size of a Web site.

Understanding the strategies of Web content management most suited to the needs of libraries will directly impact the type of WCM applications you choose. While many libraries utilize either a distributed or centralized Web management method, more and more libraries are using a mix of the two. There are advantages and disadvantages associated with these methods. It is fair to say that the distributed model allows people who know the content best to contribute and to post content. This process is often achieved by using form-based content submission. It ensures that "the content follows standards such as look and feel and metadata integration" (Guenther, 2001b). However, the distributed approach may sacrifice content quality due to a lack of editorial control. While the centralized approach can ensure quality and consistency, it often creates barriers for prioritizing tasks and has the definite potential for slowing down the process of publishing.

# Selection of a WCMS

Guenther's considerations for choosing a WCM solution focus on three main areas:

- overall goals and strategy of the library and parent organization,
- the specific requirements for functionality, and
- the content management environment including people and processes.

Criteria to be considered in each area should follow directly from the library's policies and objectives (Guenther, 2001b).

Unclear about what the overall needs of the library really are important may create confusion in selecting the appropriate content management solution. Implementing a content management solution, whether it is a WCMS or an application, is a commitment in terms of cost and work required. Among many factors, content management strategies, functionality requirements, existing resources including funding, in-house technical skills, and staffing are major considerations in the implementation of a content management solution. The decision will be made easier if you really know the strengths and weaknesses in your current process and tools. Whether these weaknesses can be fixed by a content management application or whether it needs a full WCMS will be better understood. The functionality of a WCMS is another issue that comes into play. What functionalities you hope to gain in a WCMS are largely based on your understanding of the product matched against your needs.

Selecting the right technologies to meet these demands has proven to be a challenging process for many libraries. There are a number of factors that need to be considered when selecting appropriate development tools for the library. In addition to cost factors, there are hardware and database platform issues (e.g., how to be sure if it is suitable for your library). Are the new hardware and database you plan to purchase or develop interoperable with the existing library system? Is the software based on open source standards "so that systems integration isn't a total nightmare" (Friedlein, 2001)? How do content contributors and administrators access the system or application? The focus should be on the areas of particular importance to the library. A failed implementation in the largest library organization recently indicated that organizational requirements had not been firmly established before the contractor went to work. Another issue relates to the fact that some Web content management systems or applications are poorly designed to meet current acceptable standards of usability and accessibility.

Although the rapid proliferation of commercially available content management systems makes it easier to find a vendor that might have the right solution, many available content management products do not provide the functionality aimed at library functions and services. The cost to purchase a commercial WCMS is beyond the reach of the majority of libraries. Building an in-house system or application using open source technology is becoming a trend. There are benefits and risks associated with home-grown products. The products may be developed based only on the skill level of the in-house expertise and may only be understood by these individuals. A sudden departure of the developer may post serious challenges for other staff who continue to manage and maintain the product. However, the cost of developing an in-house solution is minimal. Many libraries have recently had success with open source solutions. Again, even with the open source solutions, if implementing is done in-house, time is required to develop the technical background and program skills needed to install and manipulate the system.

The key point to keep in mind when selecting a content management solution is that the ultimate goal is to deliver accurate information and ever-changing resources to satisfy user needs, and that they are low cost and within the scope of the technology, technical expertise, and tools available at the given time.

## Organizational Culture and Acceptance

Many issues are associated with the move to WCM solutions. These include acceptance of changes, decisions on the allocation of personnel, equipment, assignments and tasks. Boiko (2002) suggests asking the following questions when making strategic changes to the Web using a WCM solution:

- Does your staff accept the idea of very organized and constrained processes with known tasks and times?
- How can you maintain people's sense of independence and creativity within these defined cycles?
- How do you recognize that someone doesn't accept the basic premise of workflow?

In his chapter of this book, Whang notes the case that a major challenge in the library where he works was to get librarians to agree on what information should be consistently presented to the user. In this library, librarians created different names for the same categories of materials, and it was a tremendous effort to get librarians to negotiate on the terms used for metadata. "The way the old HTML subject guides were organized and presented, to some extent, reflected the library's organizational culture-people acted along" (Whang, 2004). Mach echoes this situation and indicates that these technical solutions demand a fair amount of compromise in terms of creativity. In many libraries where individuals, not teams, drive the content development process and creativities are most highly rewarded, these technical solutions do not seem feasible (Mach, 2004).

Library staff buy-in and administrative support are key elements in project success. Either database-driven applications or a WCM system can "consume significant staff resources, may require a substantial financial investment in the short run, and involve ongoing support in the long run" (Westman, 2002). In his article, Westman suggests a number of questions about implementing a WCM solution:

- What will be the benefit of the project? Answers can include saving time, providing better access to information, or allowing for more efficient workflow.
- What will be costs in terms of money and staff time?
- Can it be done with the existing infrastructure, hardware, and software?
- What is the timeframe for its implementation?
- How much time and effort will it take to maintain this application?
- How much data inputting and updating will be involved?

Answers to these questions should help raise staff awareness and obtain the understanding and support.

## Cost and Budgetary Constraints

In February 2003, Jupitermedia released a report entitled, "Web Content Management: Covering the Essentials, Avoiding Overspending." It stated that, "over-complicated, end-to-end packages can as much as quintuple Web site operational costs over human alternatives. In fact, 61% of companies who have already deployed Web content management software still rely on manual processes to update their sites" (McGovern, 2003).

Budgetary constraints have prevented many libraries from purchasing a commercially available WCMS or outsourcing projects. According to CMSWatch (www.cmswatch.com), there are more than 200 content management products purporting to manage Web content. Among the most significant 40 products selected by CMSWatch, base licensing for upper tier products can cost up to $125,000 to $175,000 for most implementations. The price varies from $1,000 to $10,000 for low-end products targeting relatively straightforward WCM requirements. There are also ongoing software licensing costs in addition to the cost for extra staff time and effort in programming and tweaking the product. Outsourcing not only can be expensive, but the usability of the outsourced Web site could be sacrificed. We all experienced the frustration (long URLs, '404 not found' messages, and failed search functions, to name a few) recently when a national library association outsourced its content management system to a vendor. In-house solutions on the other hand have largely been viewed as favorable in libraries where technical expertise is available.

## Impacts of New Search Features

Meta-searching, sometimes called federated or consolidated searching, provides another dimension to Web content management in terms of the user's expectations and online experience, coverage of the subject matter, and time/cost factors. One of the major advantages of meta-search is that users can obtain search results from multiple databases, library catalogs, and Web search engines with a single search. Some, especially academic library administrators, deem meta-searching as a way to "meet the expectations and needs of 'the google generation'" (Luther, 2003). One vice president of academic affairs asserted that 85% of their students only wanted a passing grade, therefore library resources should be organized to meet the basic needs of the casual information user (Luther, 2003).

Meta-searching does not necessarily serve the best interests of library users, and it cannot replace subject pathfinders. How locally developed subject bibliographies, pathfinders, and/or subject guides can be integrated with meta-search functions creates many challenges along strategical, technical, and intellectual fronts. Librarians make judgments about the appropriateness for their intended audience and format, but "rarely on such a large-scale, systematic basis" (Morgan, 2003). Many exceptions in the types of databases require a different search protocol to perform the needed searches, such as non-Z39.50 databases cannot be meta-searched at present.

Incorporating meta-searching capabilities into the WCM system is a complex undertaking. As we deal with the new technology and maintain the knowledge base, we manage aggregated databases, e-journal access, changing URLs, IP addresses, licensing, registration, authentication, embargoes, linking, and more. In the foreseeable future, the workload of maintaining meta-search capabilities is going to increase, because the highly complex endeavor adds an ever-changing set of obstacles to day-to-day maintenance tasks and demands for keeping up with the technology.

# Conclusions

A fully functional WCM system with rich and specialized features geared toward library functions and services has yet to come. To move in that direction, librarians must stop thinking of their Web sites as collections of HTML pages. Librarians should view the content of the Web site as dynamic resources for information and services that patrons will use in highly individualized ways. The trend is that content production and presentation will be increasingly separated aspects of the library Web site. Tools that libraries can afford and use quickly to create useful content management applications are now available, but the tools are only part of the picture. The hardest part of transforming Web sites into dynamic systems is the conceptualization of the library Web site strategically. Doing it right is becoming much more crucial than just doing it.

# References

Antelman, K. (Ed.). (2002). *Database-driven Web sites.* New York: Haworth Information Press.

Antelman, K. (1999). Getting out of the HTML business: The database-driven Web site solution. *Information Technology and Libraries, 18*(4).

Boiko, B. (2001). Understanding content management. *Bulletin of the American Society for Information Science and Technology, 28*(1).

Boiko, B. (2002). *Content management bible*. New York: Hungry Minds.

Brown, K.L., & Candreva, A.M. (2002). Managing database-driven Web content. *Library Journal netConnect,* (Fall).

Clay III, E. (2003). Content management and library Web site. *Public Libraries, 42*(5).

Friedlein, A. (2001). *Web project management: Delivering successful commercial Web sites*. San Francisco: Morgan Kaufmann.

Glossary Term. *CMSWatch*. Retrieved February 10, 2004, from *www.cmswatch.com/GlossaryTerm/*

Guenther, K. (2001a). What is a Web content management solution? *Online, 25*(4).

Guenther, K. (2001b). Choosing Web content management solution. *Online, 25*(5).

Hackos, J.T. (2002). *Content management for dynamic Web delivery*. New York: Wiley Computer Publishing.

Kartchner, C. (2001). Fulfilling the promise of content management. *Bulletin of the American Society for Information Science and Technology, 28*(1).

Lakos, A., & Gray, C. (2000). Personalized library portals as an organizational culture change agent. *Information Technology and Libraries, 19*(4).

Luther, J. (2003). Trumping Google? Meta-searching's promise. *Library Journal, 128*(16).

Mach, M. (2004). Web site maintenance workflow at a medium-sized university library. In H. Yu (Ed.), *Content and workflow management for library Web sites: Case studies*. Hershey, PA: Idea Group Publishing.

McGovern, G. (2001). Content is not a technology issue. Retrieved December 12, 2003, from *www.gerrymcgovern.com*

McGovern, G. (2002). The benefits of a content management system. Retrieved December 12, 2003, from *www.gerrymcgovern.com*

McGovern, G. (2003). Why content management software hasn't worked. Retrieved December 12, 2003, from *www.gerrymcgovern.com*

Miller, R., & Manafy, M. (2003). Content management case studies. *EContent, 26*(5).

Morgan, E.L. (2003). Putting the "my" in MyLibrary. *Library Journal netConnect,* (Fall).

Ryan, S.M. (2003). Library Web site administration: A strategic planning model for the smaller academic library. *Journal of Academic Librarianship, 29*(4).

Shropshire, S. (2003). Beyond the design and evaluation of library Web site: An analysis and four case studies. *Journal of Academic Librarianship, 29*(2).

Warren, R. (2001). Information architects and their central role in content management. *Bulletin of the American Society for Information Science and Technology, 28*(1).

Westman, S. (2002). Building database-backed Web applications: Process and issues. *Information Technology and Libraries, 21*(2).

Whang, M. (2004). PHP and PostgreSQL Web content management system at Western Michigan university libraries. In H. Yu (Ed.), *Content and workflow management for library Web sites: Case studies.* Hershey, PA: Idea Group Publishing.

Chapter II

# Methods and Tools for Managing Library Web Content

Johan Ragetli

Kawartha Pine Ridge District School Board, Ontario, Canada

## Abstract

*In this chapter key methods and tools available to libraries to manage their Web content are identified. Content in libraries may include subject guides, calendars, hours of operation, and digital collections. Solutions to manage a wide variety of materials and contributors range from enterprise-wide content management systems to homegrown, open source solutions.*

## Introduction

*"The networked information revolution has arrived but is still in its infancy. I believe that we will spend the next decade or two refining the technology and building up an ever-growing mass of content."* (Lynch, 2000, p. 67)

Digital content continues to grow at huge rates. As most organizations move from paper to electronic documents, it will become redundant even to say digital content in the context of document creation. Clifford Lynch, Director of the Coalition for Networked Information (CNI), is well known nationally and internationally, and speaks and writes widely on issues of technology and libraries. In describing the current state of libraries, he remarks that libraries find themselves today in a state of transformation. They are moving forward from the automation of existing library services and the provision of online access to internal print collections into a new phase of content creation and delivery. They have embraced information technology and are finding ways to innovate and experiment to deliver content that is in many cases external to the library, such as full-text databases. Information technology has profoundly affected the way that libraries conceive of and deliver services.

In the business world, *content management* (CM) likewise has become a juggernaut, applying to all applications and systems dealing with the organization of data, which is reflected in the number of companies and strategies and varying technologies competing in the content arena. *EContent* magazine creates an annual short list of 100 "excellent companies tackling the content space" and perhaps more significantly had difficulty in "defining what categories would prove most useful in attempting to define the space itself" (Manafy, 2002, p. 18).

Bob Boiko (2001), author of the *Content Management Bible,* states that CM is an overall process for collecting, organizing, managing, and publishing content to any outlet. Currently Web content management, or WCM, is mainly reflected in organizations where large-scale Web development projects have been initiated to combat the need to organize large numbers of disparate Web objects and to publish content to one significant outlet—namely the Web.

In contrast to large commercial sites, libraries typically are not dealing with large-scale Web sites, critical updates, huge amounts of content, or frequently updated information. Likewise they are not driven by commercial necessity to provide the latest in Web services. However they are dealing with a changing work environment, and there are increasing pressures to provide personalized services to their users. Libraries as a result are finding ways to reuse content and to repackage data in meaningful and personalized ways. Many organizations are struggling to deal with the challenge of selecting the right technology to address the diversity of tasks required by increasing client demands and changing workflows. Library Web managers too are increasingly faced with growing numbers of contributors and the demands of new functionality and increasingly sophisticated Web applications. A rise in staff and user demands to allow increased participation in and customization of library Web sites leads to a need for better processes and tools. At the same time library users are looking for all of the e-resources available to them under one roof, so to speak.

Ultimately, library Web managers are seeking methods and tools that will enable both experts and "non-technical" staff to easily and actively publish Web content that reflects the needs and concerns of the user, the parent organization, and library staff.

In examining the role of WCM in libraries to identify essential and proven methods and tools, it is hoped that several key questions can be answered:

- What does a Web content management system for libraries look like?
- What does it attempt to manage?
- What structures, tools, methods, and approaches have worked success-fully in libraries?
- What does the future bring?

## What Does a Web Content Management System Look like?

Generally speaking, Web content management as a term is used primarily to describe full-scale systems. Because libraries tend not to employ system-wide solutions, there is a need first of all to distinguish between WCM tools and WCM systems. In the "Methods and Tools" section below, both tools and systems will be reviewed. In the literature and in white papers, there is a confusing tendency to describe a tool as a system. Where WCM tools are designed to manage a particular aspect of the Web site, a full WCM system is intended to manage the entire operation.

An application that enables subject specialists to produce automated topic pathfinders from a collection of links through the use of templates is an example of a content management tool that may or may not be part of a larger system governing the entire Web site. The Web contributors are able to produce consistent pages and publish them to the library Web site with a minimum of editing. The tool has been developed to tackle a single challenge—in this case the automatic generation of research guides.

A database-driven Web site refers to a system whereby content is delivered to the Web site through querying a database. Queries can be produced through online forms or through scheduled processes resulting in dynamic pages. As such, dynamic Web sites also manage content but again are not complete systems, focusing instead on certain content areas, like a catalog of links for example, where a search of the database results in a list of links.

Similarly, portlets and applets are embedded applications that could be used to manage a collection of digital journals and provide a current awareness service. Other alternatives to full-scale systems include Web logs (blogs), which can provide an easy and inexpensive way for librarians to post and maintain information without a great deal of Web publishing knowledge.

All these examples provide single solutions to content challenges, but do not comprise a complete WCM system. However for many libraries a distributed model of content management is the preferred and more sustainable method. As Michael Angeles (2003) points out, a healthy information ecology is one where various forms of information practices can reflect the diversity of roles and values of the library.

Full-scale WCM systems manage the entire operation of content management and delivery. Content management systems have traditionally taken the form of either portal software to integrate applications, or a document management system to control the creation, storing, and delivery of content on a system-wide basis. Many of the big players fall into the above two categories. Many smaller commercial vendors also provide hybrid systems that deal directly with Web content. Web content management as a category of content management describes the combination of systems and workflows that enable Web administrators to manage potentially large volumes of data from multiple sources and to enable contributors to easily and successfully edit files and publish content to the Web site. Forrester Research defines content management as a "combination of well-defined roles, formal processes, and supporting systems architecture that helps organizations contribute, collaborate on, and control page elements such as text, graphics, multimedia, and applets" (Guenther, 2001a, p.82). One of the main benefits of a CMS is that it allows for the design of a common and consistent information architecture through the application of metadata, classification, navigation, search, layout, and design. Inconsistent and poorly designed information architectures plague many Web sites (McGovern, 2002).

One of the main objectives of a WCM system is to enable a large and potentially disparate group of Web authors to easily publish their content to the Web site and make it look seamless. As more people are involved, the difficulty of managing the flow of data is magnified. So at the very least, well-designed WCM systems need to incorporate automated internal review processes, create navigation trees and indexes, and ensure that the appropriate pages get updated as required and so on. "To make this happen, good Web content management packages separate content (written material, images, streaming audio, and anything else that makes up Web pages) from presentation of content, and they include strong workflow capabilities" (Taschek, 1999, p. 61).

Workflow capabilities are critical to the success of the system and are patterned on the steps required to bring content together on a published page, and to provide the appropriate people with the controls necessary to determine layout and design, all without having to know HTML code. "WCM solutions streamline the front-end process of managing content through well-defined workflows and templates, and allow more effective management of back-end processes to include defining, standardizing, controlling, staging, routing, storing, and delivering content. A core foundation of most content management systems is a database to store all assets of the site, including templates, graphics, content, and code applications" (Guenther, 2001a, p. 81).

Essentially a WCM system will provide both users and content producers in the library with the tools to manage the variety and bulk of content and display it in a consistent manner. The method or approach taken by a library will very much depend on the needs of the institution and what it hopes to achieve both in the short term and in the long run.

# Methods, Tools, and Approaches

In this section of the chapter, details of various WCM systems are explored with a view to providing readers with a comprehensive introduction and enough background information to begin choosing the appropriate WCM for their library. The following three areas are covered:

Approaches
• Structure

- Development environment
- Tools, file types, languages, and standards

WCM Systems

- Document management
- Portals
- Hybrids

WCM-Like Systems

- Dynamic Web sites/database-driven content
- Blogging
- RSS
- Wikis and other online collaborative tools

# Approaches

Following the identification of the organizational Web strategy and specific goals (as outlined in the previous chapter), the next key criteria in choosing Web content management solutions are the specific requirements for functionality, and the content management environment including people and processes. The approaches to development or implementation eventually chosen will be key to the success of the project.

# Structure

## *Centralized vs. Distributed Architecture (or Hybrid)*

Setting up appropriate workflows and selecting the right solution will be affected by the approach to authoring and development most favored in the library. Systems that radically alter the preferred methods of writing content are likely to be rejected. A centralized approach favors those settings where central control and a strong uniform presence are desired. A distributed model usually occurs where several small areas or sub-sites are operating in an independent fashion and have unique authoring characteristics based on the nature of the content. Where a database approach works for one unit, another department may wish to have more control over the design and look of their pages. "Distributed authoring puts tools in the hands of the people who know the content" (Guenther, 2001b, p. 85). Hybrid approaches walk the middle ground and provide a range of supports from do-it-yourself publishing to full-service offerings. What works will depend on the existing workflows, the roles and responsibilities of the contributors, and whether that system will be reflected in the new processes created by the implementation of a new system.

Many libraries have a core group of contributors making up a Web team and often working in close proximity. This situation favors a centralized system where control over templates and design is held by key individuals or the team. In some universities, for example, the library Web site is governed by the main university Web team and has standards and systems already in place. To the extent that the WCM system is already chosen, the main decisions will be made in the implementation of templates, integrating library applications and building content. The main strengths of a centralized approach are a consistent approach to authoring and publishing that results in a more seamless look and feel to the site. Disadvantages are that the services to the internal clients must be responsive and dedicated, often requiring the hiring of a staff member to specifically oversee the delivery of services to the library Web team in addition to the other organizational units. Authors previously used to having more control over the display of their contributions may find the new environment constricting.

There are many instances where distributed authoring is more efficient. In cases where the contributors perform many of the administrative functions—as in a Web site review committee for a collection of links—a more distributed environment may be more efficient in terms of workflow. However, it also means that the process of review has to be carefully planned. Where the department or individual publishes directly to the production site, opportunities for errors start to creep in—through disregard for templates or rules—leaving the Webmaster to check for errors after a page has been posted.

Additionally, if the library plans to implement various content management solutions over an extended period using various tools, flexibility and growth are required, and that solution may be more achievable through a hybrid system. If part of the strategic plan is to explore Web services in an ongoing manner with the goal of innovation, a centralized system will not be achievable or desirable. For libraries that have in-house expertise or the capability to design and develop tools, a more distributed environment is called for. In most cases it is more beneficial for the library to remain flexible, open to innovation, and willing to test new ideas, all of which are better supported by a distributed system both in the structure and the method of authoring pages.

Hybrid systems combine the best, and worst, of both models. Some libraries are forced into using hybrid systems because a specific tool developed earlier requires local control, where the rest of the site is managed centrally. Such a system needs to be simple enough to use with full services so that it allows for multiple contributors with varying Web skill levels. At the same time the WCM must be powerful enough to provide individual authoring capability for those with appropriate interest and ability (Guenther, 2001b).

# Development

## *Outsourced vs. In-House*

The development of custom databases and systems using library or resident IT staff is commonplace in libraries. Often individual solutions are found in response to specific Web challenges such as the creation of a database to provide a searchable collection of links. There are risks attached to in-house development however. Customized work is often best understood by the developer. Their departure from the library may present significant issues for new staff. Documentation may be brief or non-existent. Decisions may be based on personal preferences and not system needs. In-house solutions also rarely come with guarantees. Generally costs are low however, and libraries may feel they can trade off some level of frustration in exchange.

In many cases libraries will not have much say in the choice of a database and scripting language. These aspects are decided by whomever maintains the Web and database servers. The first step in managing the library Web site may very well be to procure access to the Web server and install the appropriate technology.

In choosing to outsource, cost becomes a primary factor of course. For smaller academic or public libraries, choosing a full-scale commercial WCM system is out of the question. Likewise, the talent pool may not be adequate to support in-house development. Outsourcing the process of development alone requires writing very detailed RFPs and specifications. The Web team needs to research the process and feel comfortable with the technical terminology, as well as the marketplace jargon, in order to get delivery of a functional system that meets all the requirements. Getting performance guarantees and ongoing maintenance support are strong advantages to outsourcing.

For libraries with little or no technical expertise or no staffing budget to develop services in-house, choosing an outside host may provide a practical solution. Blogs for example can be maintained as a small-scale CMS and hosted externally. By using a proprietary Web authoring suite such as Dreamweaver in conjunction with some hosted services like blogging, and perhaps purchasing additional content from their library automation vendor, libraries can keep content that is up to date and site specific for relatively low cost.

## Tools, File Types, Languages, and Standards

### *Proprietary vs. Open Source Tools*

The question whether to choose open source or proprietary tools has really been made moot lately, with almost all WCMs supporting a variety of file types and programming languages. Support for open object models and messaging formats is especially critical when dealing with legacy systems. Flexible structures that are open to integration of other applications and development are best served by an open source platform. Developers will find that, in the library world at least, many of the most innovative solutions rely on an open source platform, coupled with a middle tier that can integrate with a variety of databases using programming languages that deal effectively with Web objects.

If the development of the WCM is planned in stages, or if the library plans to build its own homegrown solutions, choosing open source or proprietary tools for the back-end structure is the first step. Proprietary databases like Oracle or SQL Server can cost several thousands of dollars, putting them out of the reach of smaller libraries; however, your institution may already provide access to these systems. If developers wish therefore to exploit the developments made in other libraries, creating a similar development environment with support for a range of file types and languages will be crucial. Many of these tools are low cost or free, but require a specific database structure.

Scripting is usually run on the Web server itself and is often connected to a database. Java server pages (JSPs) tend to be more complicated, requiring higher level programming skills. PHP and ColdFusion (CFM) both are considered more user-friendly scripting languages. PHP is open source and is made available from Apache, while CFM is the product of Macromedia. A lot of the most interesting and innovative development in library Webs is happening with PHP and is often used in conjunction with MySQL—another open source product—even though most scripting languages can connect to all sorts of databases. The PHP/MySQL combination appears quite frequently in library Web applications and should be a consideration when building WCM systems and tools in-house (Klein, 2003).

For libraries, adherence to both current and developing standards means tools will be able to handle bibliographic data in an improved manner, displaying results from queries and providing key bibliographic information. Metadata standards for libraries such as Dublin Core (DC), OAI, ONIX, MARC, Z39.50, and the newly developed OpenURL are vital standards in the Web environment. OpenURL unlike the others is "transportable metadata," providing links to resources in multiple databases and is primarily concerned with bibliographic resources (Hendricks, 2003). Proprietary databases that do not support such library standards will diminish the power of any WCM to deal with library information.

Choosing the right approach for future development and performance will depend upon the blend of these structures and tools.

## WCM Systems

Typically, content on the Web is stored in pages, which are often edited manually and contribute to a static Web, one that is consistent for each viewer and does not change unless replaced or edited. WCM systems automate the various aspects of the life cycle of the content from writing to publishing. Setting up the rules and procedures for the collection, maintenance, and display of information, a traditional aspect of librarianship, is key to the successful redeployment of Web content. One thing a WCM system will not fix is poor writing. Having an automated system does not improve existing content, and good writing should always be paramount to any system of delivery.

Managing the scope and amount of content on library Web sites has determined to a large extent the range of implementations currently being used. Libraries typically are not generating huge amounts of content, and most content does not require daily updates. Most libraries are therefore not seeking large-scale implementations, but rather tailored solutions for a specific content challenge: how to manage a collection of links for example, or how to create personalized research guides on the fly.

Generally WCM systems fall into three categories: document management systems geared to big business, portals that attempt to manage all of the organization's content by integrating various applications and delivering results in a common display or interface, and lastly, hybrid systems geared specifically for Web content which break content down into context chunks that can be tagged for redistribution or display. Automating the publishing of chunks of content to the Web requires a variety of tools capable of creating templates, parsing documents, organizing or tagging, and link checking.

## Document Management Systems

Document management (DM) systems have been developed to handle large-scale operations for organizations with many departments, or a variety of operational units which maintain large repositories of documents or complex information in a variety of formats. Sharing this content and publishing to the Web is often regarded as a feature of the DM system, but not necessarily the first priority. DM systems are modeled on a paper-based records management approach that identifies a single document, and classifies and stores it for easy retrieval and display based on the office of origin and the purpose of the material. As a result they place "a strong emphasis on structuring information, building topic hierarchies, indexing content, facilitating collaborative workflows, and providing document imaging capabilities. Strengths include management of complex documents, version control (including check-in/check-out), document level security integration, and audit trail capabilities" (Guenther, 2001a, p. 82).

Strong DM programs handle content from multiple sources, provide full-text indexing supported by metadata, and are extremely scalable. They also provide support for collaborative and remote content creation from various document types like MS Word and PowerPoint, resulting in documents that are broken down into contents that can be re-packaged and re-purposed for the Web. Sophisticated WCM solutions provide support for the entire content life cycle—from creation, import, editing, and approval through publication and expiration (West, Huff, & Turocy, 2000).

While document management systems are strong in managing large collections of documents, they tend to be slow in incorporating many of today's Web development standards. Many document management systems are just now integrating or acquiring the functionality to support Web programming standards like XML and Java (Guenther, 2001a). Web-based administration is often lacking, and other core functionalities of a complete WCM system would be an add-on or require custom programming.

Documents likely to be published by a library which are updated regularly and as such are prime candidates for automation include: books lists, subject guides, library news, bibliographies, events, and calendars. Libraries whose parent organizations already employ a DM are good candidates for utilizing the benefits of such a system, which would be too costly or too large a system otherwise. The author failed to find any libraries that are using a DM system to deliver library content to the Web.

## Portal Software

Portals provide a solution to libraries in need of an umbrella application to integrate access to various library services and provide some kind of common interface both internally and externally. Portals are not intended to manage content in the traditional sense. Enterprise-wide portals place the library as a department in a larger corporate setting, providing a built-in cost-effective solution. Library-specific portals are often aligned with or provided by the automated library system software. Most of the industry-leading automation software vendors now provide a portal technology of one kind or another.

A portal typically contains a customizable interface and a variety of the following: an intuitive and customizable Web interface; personalized content presentation, which is either user selected or previously selected and arranged by employees; security in the form of user login, or patron identification or authentication; and communication and collaboration tools such as e-mail, chat, or bulletin boards (Boss, 2002).

To date, few libraries have chosen portals as a means to deliver Web services. Those that have chosen to implement portals generally have relied on third-party companies which cater to libraries in order to make the system fit well with the automated library system. A smaller number have selected vendors that provide portal applications designed specifically for libraries (Boss, 2002).

The term "portal" is itself relatively new in the library field, and Web portals did not become an independent entry in library literature until 1999. The first library portal designed by Eric Lease Morgan appeared in January 1998 at the North Carolina State University Libraries. The MyLibrary portal (my.lib.ncsu.edu) is still offered today as an open source application. "It was truly a pioneer among academic library Web sites as it allowed individual users to customize the Web page by category" (Zhou, 2003, p.120).

Zhou (2003) also found evidence that it is unlikely that libraries will develop portals if their affiliated universities do not. In cases where the university decides to adopt a portal approach for the entire organization, the library will likely be integrated into the university portal. The University of Guelph Libraries, for example, have recently embarked on an initiative to integrate the Learning Information Centre within an enterprise-wide portal.

In total then, Zhou found that four basic approaches exist for creating academic library portals: building a stand-alone portal in-house, joining a campus portal, partnering with other academic libraries for portal development, or hiring a portal vendor.

The portal is especially relevant to libraries hoping to aggregate content from many applications within the system. One of library portals' key strengths is the ability to integrate with other vendors' products. They can provide access to a variety of databases, and by inserting a security or patron authentication interface between vendor products and the patron, portals can also manage access to library Web content and provide personalized services. Retrieving results can be cumbersome, so additional relevancy ranking and sorting is often included. Other products—termed "content enhancement"—provide links to additional content like book jackets and reviews that appear in the records of the library catalog. Managing this content is handled by the portal server product and integrated into the portal. Providing the content is simply a matter of subscribing to the service.

Most vendors of automated library systems are now developing portals. These portals are essentially expanded versions of Web catalogs designed to be able to search external databases and allow for patron identification to enable logging into external databases.

A portal can be mounted either on a dedicated server or on a Web server that supports other applications. The software is generally described as a portal server product (see Boss, 2003, or Guenther, 2001a, 2001b, for lists of vendors). MuseGlobal is a portal server product specifically designed for retrieval of information by library users. At least one vendor, Dynix, has an agreement to use WebFeat, a major competitor to MuseGlobal. Dynix has recently changed the name of its flagship Web interface from iPAC to Horizon Information Portal or HIP (Boss, 2002).

Of the 17 libraries using portals contacted by Boss, all are limiting the scope of resources accessed through the portal. In most cases only the library's own catalog and the online reference services to which it subscribes are available. The library that offers the broadest scope also includes selected Web sites— including the URLs of some other libraries' patron access catalogs. To date, none envisions facilitating access to the Web at large (Boss, 2002).

## Specialized WCM Hybrids

WCM hybrids are systems that deal with documents much like document management systems, but with more flexibility in the way the content is marked up and made available across the system. Essentially, the hybrid system relies on an underlying content management structure, including forms and template-making capabilities matched with the power and performance of a database-driven Web site to create Web pages dynamically.

Document management systems deal with the documents themselves and how they are classified and stored. In a hybrid system content is marked up or tagged in more discrete units, achieving more flexibility in presenting or calling the information from the database. This flexibility is often achieved using XML that enables the developer to separate the actual content from how it is displayed, allowing content to be easily re-purposed for different audiences with different needs (Guenther, 2001a). In many cases these systems are developed for open source platforms, though the databases themselves may or may not be.

Whereas document management systems handle external multiple sources and file types, hybrids tend to concentrate on providing an integrated environment for content creation through the use of templates or forms so that the database objects are created internally. Many systems come with built-in HTML editors or work with third-party editors to facilitate the creation of Web pages. Also, libraries that already have created ODBC-compliant, MySQL, or other standard databases will be able to quickly create forms and templates to publish and re-purpose existing content in a consistent fashion with the flexibility to easily change views or styles. Output is generated on the fly, tagged, and output in one or more readable formats.

Several open source solutions built on this same model have been introduced in libraries over the past two or three years: Zope—a leading edge development platform, MyLibrary—a portal application, phpWebsite, Xaraya, and most recently, LibData are full WCM systems that are all based on PHP. Because so many libraries are choosing this path to development, a brief technical summary of each of these systems is given below.

## *Zope*

The Zope engine and its layered applications are written in Python, and the whole system is built on top of a Python-based object database called ZODB in a powerful and productive arrangement, according to Jon Udell a Zope user and lead analyst at InfoWorld Test Center. The Zope platform is open source and free. It is often used in conjunction with an existing external database such as Oracle, Sybase, MySQL, PostgreSQL, many ODBC-compliant databases, and others (Udell, 2003). Zope Corp. (previously Digital Creations) relies financially on training and consulting, and sells various commercial products based on its own leading-edge platform which include Zope4Media, a content management system for print and broadcast media, and Z4I (Zope for Intranets), an advanced intranet portal. While developers enjoy its capabilities, organizations have been reluctant to choose Zope for their systems, but some notable organizations are still opting for it. NATO's worldwide intranet is based on Zope, and Boston.com uses Zope4Media. Z4I relies on an underlying content management framework and a page-templating system to support the creation of custom content types with automatically generated editing forms and displays. Using Z4I, as with most portal systems, the library can create portlets, or sub-sites if you will, which can be rearranged on their homepages and the views varied.

Zope's ability to directly utilize SQL, without resorting to additional CGI or Java scripting and its deeply object-oriented system, allow Web librarians to create forms and displays of content quite easily. The integration of common commercial and open source databases and a Zope Web server allows a library Web site to deliver dynamic content based on database queries and to collect information in a structure that lends itself to extensive manipulation (Bennett, 2002). Coding can be quite tricky, and most users agree the learning curve is quite steep at first (Udell, 2003)—all of which makes this tool suitable for organizations with programmers on staff or readily accessible.

At Appalachian State University, staff migrated their Ask-A-Librarian service to a Zope environment. The service offers patrons an opportunity to receive guidance from reference staff while at a remote location from the university. Ask-a-Librarian evolved from simply using an e-mail link on the Web page, through using Web forms that relied on Python scripting, and finally to using Zope. The service also employs a PostgreSQL database, e-mail, and the Web (Bennett, 2002).

*PHP*

---

Both phpWebSite and Xaraya provide complete CMS systems written in PHP and both are publicly licensed. Developed by the Web Technology Group at Appalachian State University, phpWebSite is geared towards developers and system administrators. All client output is XHTML 1.0 and meets the W3C's Web Accessibility Initiative requirements. It will run on a variety of operating systems including Windows, MacOS X, and Linux, and provides a very cost-effective solution for those libraries with in-house capabilities or strong relationships with an IT department. As with most open source packages, a great deal of customization is required.

Xaraya is another example of extensible, open source software written in PHP. It can be run on most platforms. It is written to work with other third-party software applications, and its modular design separates function from form, the content from the design. Authors work in a structured environment, providing relatively simple means to deliver dynamic content. Xaraya provides for a fully database-driven Web site that easily hosts a variety of Web applications like RSS feeds and Web logs. While this system would not integrate well with the library automation system, it could easily provide a full CMS for the remainder of the library's Web content needs. Content areas could include: news articles from RSS sources; articles or columns using Weblogs, personalized subject guides, electronic journal directory, or a Frequently Asked Questions list.

In December 2003, The University of Minnesota Libraries announced the open source software release of LibData: Library Web Management System. LibData is a library-oriented, Web-based application consisting of an integrated database architecture and authoring environment for the publication of subject pathfinders, course-related pages, and all-purpose Web pages. This application was designed for, but is not limited to, academic and public libraries. LibData was built with open source components (Apache, MySQL, and PHP) and is being offered as open source to the library community under the GNU Public License.

LibData's master database—which offers a framework for containing records for resources, services, library locations, staff, and more—was designed to allow for easier management of these resources and their rapid retrieval and incorporation into the variety of Web presentations that librarians create for users. LibData currently offers three distinct page-authoring tools useful to both novice and expert librarian users:

- Research QuickStart Subject Builder (for subject pathfinders)
- CourseLib (for customized course-related pages)
- PageScribe (for free-form, all purpose pages)

These tools are tightly integrated with the main database, making resource management easier to control and ensuring that library users receive well-managed, current information. LibData also features a robust staff management system, user and page statistics, and complete customizability and extensibility (University of Minnesota Libraries, 2003).

MyLibrary is freeware and open source software designed by Eric Lease Morgan, a librarian at North Carolina now at Notre Dame. It allows librarians to collect links to Web sites and other resources and maintain them in a database. Users can customize the display to see only those resources that fit their profile. Librarians can also use the portal to communicate news and items of interest to users. MyLibrary could also be used to implement an Ask-a-Librarian service.

## WCM-Like Systems

Implementing full-scale WCM systems can be costly and time consuming. They follow publishing or document management models that "may not reflect the workflow and information needs of a library Web site" (Klein, 2003). Also, the ways in which librarians would wish to re-use content on the Web site may not work in the document-centric models of the larger WCM systems. Given these factors, Klein suggests a more piecemeal approach. It makes sense to concentrate on the areas with the most activity, and use scarce resources to automate the repetitive large volume areas of the Web site. "The higher the complexity of information, the greater the need to automate. Uniformity of content is important" (Klein, 2003, p. 29). There is a number of options available to libraries wishing to take an evolved approach that features manual and automated components. Features of WCM-like systems include reduced costs, increased customization, and use of open source tools.

## Dynamic Web Sites

Dynamic Web sites or database-driven Web sites, while not employing WCM systems per se, do manage content and produce Web pages on the fly by posting results based on a query of a particular database by a patron or through a scripted program (Boiko, 2001). The data sources for a dynamic Web site are often the same that would be used in a WCM system. Results are posted using page layouts or templates created with Java Server Pages (JSP) or Active Server Pages (ASPs).

In a dynamic site, each time a user requests a page with dynamic content, the page is built from the contents of a database (Brown & Candreva, 2002). The Web OPAC is a prime example of a database-driven system. Requests can also be generated automatically. In other words, a scheduled task may update calendars on a daily basis. In this case the request is made of the database by the program itself.

According to Antelman (2002), creating database-driven Web pages is a widespread practice in libraries today. Applications range from do-it-yourself projects using open source software to using commercial tools to solve sophisticated content problems. In all cases the use of databases and the Web can organize content and extend the reach of libraries to a broader audience by providing new services beyond the online public access catalog. Database-driven Web sites manage content by storing records in a database residing on an application server and serve it to the Web using a Web server. In much the same way that vendors have designed library systems to store and maintain bibliographic records, librarians are also managing other content using the same approach.

Database-driven content offers one of the easiest ways to keep Web content current, providing the option to reuse and customize the information for different parts of the Web site. Information is pulled from a database and displayed on a Web page, without intervention by "the Web group." Dynamically created pages provide content ranging from simple lists that can be searched and displayed in different ways to more complex arrangements of information and displays.

A good example of this type of application is the Research Wizard or RW. This Web application, created by UNO's University Library, was developed as an attempt to solve the problems resulting from changing information sources and changing patron behaviors and expectations. Accessed through keywords or subject hierarchies, a single page provides links to selected electronic indexes and databases, pre-configured library catalog searches, library resources, selected Web sites, and assistance information for nearly 1,300 topics (Hein & Davis, 2002). Keyword topics are easily customized for classes, assignments, current topics, or individual patrons by non-technical staff through the use of Web forms. Constructed under open source philosophy, the database framework for RW was created using a combination of PHP scripts and a MySQL database to transform links and information. Web forms are used to query and organize the records. Customized content is accessible through a single keyword, term, or phrase and doesn't rely on personalization accounts or profiles (Hein & Davis, 2002).

A common feature of library Web sites is the publishing of library Web guides or bibliographies. Using relational databases is a database-driven approach to streamline the creation and management of active, Web-based subject bibliographies. Wesleyan University and the Tri-College Consortium each, independently, sought to solve this problem by creating a database of resource information and a process for mapping guide pages. Before the database approach, library staff expended considerable time and effort compiling subject Web resource pages to guide users to high-quality resources. The process of producing subject guides was tedious, repetitive, and labor intensive, requiring librarians to become proficient at the intricate task of Web page creation. Since identical resources, descriptions, and links frequently appeared on several different pages, there was considerable duplication of information. Different approaches were used contrasting in-house versus outsourcing approaches, an independent database versus one built from OPAC, and open source versus proprietary software.

Library staff at both institutions are now able to create structured subject Web guides without the use of complicated, time-consuming Web-authoring software; resource annotations can now quickly be posted, and pages can be updated, corrected, or deleted easily from a single file. Equally important, any addition or modification to commonly used commercial databases can be updated simultaneously across many subject bibliographies (Bills, Cheng, & Nathanson, 2003).

## Web Authoring Suites

Microsoft's FrontPage and Macromedia's Dreamweaver are packages designed to manage the operation of your entire Web site. In addition to feature-rich Web page editors, the suites also come with tools to organize the structure and to design navigation systems for the site, as well as control the publication of pages to the production site. Both Dreamweaver and FrontPage support the creation of forms that can link to third-party databases as long as they are ODBC compliant. Dreamweaver MX also comes with its own limited database capabilities and can handle a variety of scripting languages, which is enough to provide basic schedules or lists. Both systems include standard templates and also allow template creation. The use of site-specific templates allows the user to create a consistent look and feel by employing themes and common images. Both tools include link checkers. Web authoring tools tend to be smaller scale and are still focused on the generation and management of single pages rather than content components (Boiko, 2001). The central administrative structure and lack of strong versioning control assumes a central Web editor or Web administrator role and does not easily support a distributed authoring environment. Though not designed as portal application software, additional portal server products could easily be hosted on the same server. By using appropriate Server Side scripting, certain processes and tasks, such as counters, date stamping, and more high-end functions like query handlers can be run from the server, ensuring consistent functionality across the Web site.

(At the time this article was being written, Macromedia was releasing the Contribute a Web publishing tool that works with Dreamweaver to enable multiple contributors to publish to the same Web site. This tool promises to make Dreamweaver more capable of providing a reliable, low-cost WCM solution for libraries.)

## RSS

"RSS is a low-overhead way to provide current awareness services within a digital library environment and is a good example of a WCM tool" (Tennant, 2003, p.1). It could form part of the overall Web strategy for the library or sit as a single solution. Roy Tennant writes extensively on wired solutions for libraries and is the list owner of WEB4LIB, a discussion listserv for Web librarians. Tennant further describes RSS in the following excerpt:

*"RSS is variously described as 'RDF Site Summary' (referring to the Resource Description Framework), 'Rich Site Summary,' and 'Really Simple Syndication.' But RSS, as used on most sites, has nothing to do with RDF. It is a very simple XML syntax for describing a 'channel' or 'feed' of information that consists of 'items' (e.g., news items) with titles and URLs. Each channel is required to have a 'title,' a 'link' (URL), and a 'description.' Other tags are optional. Each channel has one or more items, of which only a title or description is mandatory, although most items typically have a title, link, and description (often commentary*

*rather than true description). There are optional fields for each item, but simplicity in production and use is one of its strong points.* (Tennant, 2003, p.1)

Feeds can be read individually or several at a time through an "aggregator" that allows the information to be presented in a variety of ways. Various news readers are now available on the Web. They can also be read using software installed at the client level. Some software is specifically designed to read news feeds, while others like Radio by Userland—a blogging tool—has a built-in aggregator.

Jon Legree at Yorba Linda Library uses an open source Content Management System called phpWebsite (http://phpWebsite.appstate.edu) to manage various information sources in the form of RSS feeds for their site. phpWebsite includes an RSS parser module to include external RSS feeds, as well as an RSS generator to create an RSS feed of the site's content. Because each section of the site uses a separate installation of phpWebsite, each section can create its own RSS feed, which is then included on the main page. These appear in the "What's New" window on the main page. This makes it easy to keep the main page of the site current. As individual librarians update their sections, a link to the new content is added to the main page without any help from the system administrator, and without the librarian knowing any HTML. Upcoming projects include adding a feed based on queries to the catalog to quickly create booklists and bibliographies (Legree, 2003).

According to Cohen (2002), using RSS as a means of providing a current awareness service is now being used quite extensively. Librarians who strive to keep current with the latest news and trends in the field have started using feeds and readers to save time and organize materials. Others who have more knowledge of the inner workings of RSS can use feeds to deliver content to their constituencies, either via portals or collaborative Web logs.

## Blogs

Web logging as a commercial enterprise is only now beginning to enter the market. Previously Web logging, known as blogging, was the domain of Web geeks who specialized in personal diaries providing information about a shared passion. Information blogs have within the past few years grown exponentially and generally tackle subjects from a particular point of view, making them suitable for columnists and news-oriented lists. The capability of blogs to provide persistent links to articles and categorize them for easy retrieval is coupled with a straightforward method of creating pages and articles enabling librarians to use the system to manage online content with little or no intervention beyond establishing the categories.

Blogs in the academic world are used in a variety of ways by researchers, faculty, and students. According to Michael Angeles (2003), blogs may support research development, share industry information, capture and disperse project information among a team, or annotate relevant literature for colleagues. Web logging has proven that it can be a useful way to capture and share knowledge, but the tools that librarians and faculty may use are diverse. XML-formatted data feeds may be the glue that pulls these disparate forms together.

Angeles goes on to envision a new role for librarians as administrators of a library's or company's CM system. The future role of the librarian may well be as content manager, creating a knowledge system using a variety of content management tools including blogs. A resulting bridge between the applications of choice would rely on an underlying standard such as XML. Creating the conditions that would allow contributors—such as staff or researchers—to manage their own information sources, but feed into a larger portal-like application maintained by the librarian, would result in a distributed hybrid model. Local activities networked through various appliances, resulting in a decentralized Web of information, more closely resemble the idea of a distributed network envisioned by early Web developers. Single solutions often result in a forced adherence to style which risks alienating the very contributors managers would wish to lead the charge in information sharing. A healthy multiplicity of content sources and views could be managed by one librarian using such an umbrella application. To ensure future integration among various databases and content sources, system librarians are advocating the use of open source platforms and architecture, while employing standard databases such as SQL, Sybase, or Oracle. Library automation software has also seen the wisdom of this approach, and the leading commercial vendors are using the same development model.

Blogs are also replacing intranet software even in environments where portal software and enterprise document management systems are already employed. The arcane mechanics of publishing in many intranet systems, plus the aggravation of having one editor and many contributors had led many to embrace the ease of use of blogs. Lasnick and Weber, library administrators in a large law firm, turned to blogs as a quicker and easier way to publish a variety of documents to a variety of staff users. They found that sharing documents across different servers was unwieldy and slow, which made the documents rarely used. All in all, it was not a great solution for sharing information. Their law firm had jumped on the intranet bandwagon, and created a template-driven Intranet that allowed different groups and departments in the firm to create and maintain their own internal Web pages; however, due to navigation problems and innate flaws, the intranet was not being used to its full potential, meaning people did not go to it as a source of information. Therefore the pages weren't updated often enough, and information became buried. Since the introduction of blogging, distinct advantages have been realized. For one, information on the page can be archived and searched, something that was not easily achieved on their intranet. Also, they can include a wider variety of information, research tips, and new links, and provide an alert service for staff and other librarians at the firm (Lasnick & Weber, 2003).

Greg Notess (2002) writes that part of the popularity of Weblogging is due to the simplicity of creating one. Blog software is easy to use and may even come bundled with free hosting of the blog. No HTML, scripting, direct Web editing, XML, RSS, or CSS knowledge is required. Simply run through the setup, and then start creating entries. One or more people can be given posting privileges. They just log into a special Web page, and then type in (or copy and paste) their content. Posting it is as simple as clicking a 'submit' button. The software automatically formats and posts the entry. It also automatically archives older ones on separate pages. If categories are used in the creation of entries, the software can also create subject-specific archives based on the keywords used. The site design can be edited within the blog software using pre-defined settings or more sophisticated redesigns.

And while the intent of the blogging software is to create a Weblog, it can be used for many other content management needs. Especially for those without a full content management system, the blog software can be an opportunity to get more people involved in posting content on a Web site. Use it for maintaining a news page, a What's New section, a librarian's favorite books, incoming titles, or any other periodically updated page. It can even be used for more static sections on a site (Notess, 2002).

Darlene Fichter (2003) recommends blogging for libraries where there is a need to keep a wired and engaged user group up to date on the latest books, news, or events. To determine whether a blog is useful for a library, she advises administrators to consider a number of issues. Determining the target audience, key messages, and purpose of the blog is the first step. What blogging tools to choose and how to host the service will depend on the circumstances of the library and its ability to host or maintain a new service.

## Wikis

Wikis and their clones are dynamic online collaborative tools that allow participants to post and author pages online with no HTML or Web-authoring knowledge. Pages are maintained by the software, and most implementations provide some search capabilities. Wikis differ from blogs in that no software is required for guests or readers to add to the online pages. They are similar to hybrid WCMs in their reliance on scripting to deliver pages stored on an external database.

Wiki pages are controlled—created, linked, edited, deleted, moved, renamed, and so on—by a programming or scripting language, and stored either as plain ASCII text files or in an external relational database, such as MySQL, Oracle, or PostgreSQL. Wiki pages are only rendered or displayed as HTML through templates by the wiki Web server. In *The Wiki Way,* Bo Leuf and Ward Cunningham define wiki as "a freely expandable collection of interlinked Web 'pages,' a *hypertext system* for storing and modifying information—a *database*, where each page is easily editable by any user with a forms-capable Web browser client" (Mattison, 2003). Cunningham released the original software as open source in 1995.

Wikis have paved the way for other, more sophisticated tools that have embraced the central idea of online dynamic pages, but utilize more robust platforms and sophisticated programming to approximate a WCM system. Course delivery programs and dynamic bulletin boards often incorporate wiki-like environments. Implementations range from bare bones, highly customizable, open source systems to more developed commercial applications that incorporate multimedia and other data sources. PostNuke, as an open source example, bills itself as a collaborative content management system, and its developers maintain their own interactive site to assist and support developers.

Wikis and blogs are both examples of groupware; each contains design elements for collaborative work. Though the original wiki has proven to be less sustainable and has shown slower growth than blogs, recent developments in social software show a promising future for collaborative WCMs, as shown by some of the recent developments around the world. *Squeak Wiki* or *Swiki* has incorporated a more robust search engine to improve the classification storage and retrieval of wiki pages. Eric Lease Morgan, for example, also recently initiated *mylibrarywiki* using *phpwiki* to discuss and record issues surrounding the creation and maintenance of library-related portal applications, specifically MyLibrary.

# Conclusions

Content continues to grow and develop as libraries create, define, and provide access to a growing number of information sources. There are a number of factors fueling the transformation of static Web sites offering links to common sources. Within the library walls, staff are increasingly expected to provide more personalized services. We are also seeing that the automation of repetitive and time-consuming tasks has become a primary goal at many libraries. External forces are also effecting changes. As libraries transform their ways of providing information services, pushing libraries into the broader context of the publishing marketplace, library Web sites will need to become more professional looking and offer current, relevant, and personalized content in direct competition with commercial information sources such as online booksellers.

The choices in the WCM field are extremely varied, and determining the best course of action needs to be supportable and sustainable. Fortunately, the tools that we are using are getting better and easier to use. Open source applications are enabling even small institutions with high ambitions to build dynamic sites featuring strong local content. Building the library Web content management system that works will depend on a variety of factors as illustrated here.

Few libraries are opting for a complete WCM system, but rather a collection of tools to automate specific components of the library Web, whether it is a collection of links or a current awareness service. Full-scale WCMs are costly and time consuming to implement, and there are very few currently that focus on library needs. Large and small academic libraries often reject complete systems—even where the parent organization is already running an enterprise-wide system—in favor of a hybrid system or distributed model. Rather than tying into a specific portal application for example, many libraries are building their own portals that can incorporate a variety of databases and applications including the automated library system. Additionally, recent advances in the classifying and storage of Web objects using metadata and a standard markup language such as XML means that integrating various applications with standard outputs will become easier. The proliferation of library blogs and hybrid systems using open source platforms suggests that perhaps the market is not responding adequately to library needs, thereby forcing librarians to create solutions based on their own needs and budgets. It may also be the case that system librarians with their do-it-yourself attitude are capable of and confident in developing tools in-house. Accordingly, what is emerging is a variety of custom tools and systems that tackle content challenges on a case-by-case basis, often featuring a distributed architecture that favors flexibility and supports a group of contributors with varying technical skills. This kind of development also allows for a greater sharing of resources, allowing more libraries to capitalize on efforts and gains made by other libraries. This trend is already taking hold in many libraries as system librarians try their hand at programming and database creation, whether it is a blog, a wiki, or a searchable collection of classified links in a relational database.

# References

Angeles, M. (2003). K-logging: Support KM with Web logs. *Library Journal netConnect, 128*(7), 20-22.

Antelman, K. (Ed.). (2002). *Database-driven Websites*. New York: Haworth Press.

Bennett, T.M.G. (2002). Appalachian State University Libraries 'Ask A Librarian: A reference service for ASU students, faculty, staff, and alumni.' In K. Antelman (Ed.), *Database-driven Websites*. New York: Haworth Press.

Bills, L., Cheng, R.J., & Nathanson, A.J. (2003). Subject Web page management without HTML coding: Two approaches. *Information Technology and Libraries, 22*(1).

Boiko, B. (2001). Understanding content management. *Bulletin of the American Society for Information Science and Technology, 28*(1).

Boss, R.W. (2003). Tech notes: Library Web portals. Retrieved November 14, 2003, from *www.ala.org/Content/NavigationMenu/PLA/Publications_and_Reports/Tech_Notes/Library_Web_Portals.htm*

Brown, K.L. & Candreva, A.M. (2002). Managing database-driven Web content. *Library Journal netConnect, 48*(11), 24.

Cohen, S.M. (2002). RSS for non-techie librarians. Retrieved November 13, 2003, from *www.llrx.com/features/rssforlibrarians.htm*

Fichter, D. (2003). Why and how to use blogs to promote your library's services. *Information Today, 17*(6).

Guenther, K. (2001a). What is a Web content management solution? *Online, 25*(4), 81.

Guenther, K. (2001b). Choosing Web content management solutions. *Online, 25*(5), 84.

Hein, K.K., & Davis, M.W. (2002). The research wizard: An innovative Web application for patron service. In K. Antelman (Ed.), *Database-driven Websites*. New York: Haworth Press.

Hendricks, A. (2003). The development of the NISO Committee AX's OpenURL standard. *Information Technology and Libraries, 22*(3), 129-133.

Klein, L.R. (2003). Mixing up Web site management. *Library Journal netConnect, 128*(7), 28-30.

Lasnick, K., & Weber, J. (2003). Blogging: One firm's experience. Retrieved November 29, 2003, from *www.llrx.com/features/blogsatlawfirm.htm*

Legree, J. (2003). Re: RSS feeds on WEB4LIB electronic discussion, May 21, 2003. Retrieved on November 29, 2003 from *http://sunsite.berkeley.edu/Web4Lib/archive/0305/0228.html*

Lynch, C. (2000). From automation to transformation: Forty years of libraries and information technology in higher education. *EDUCAUSE Review*.

Manafy, M. (Ed.). (2002). 2002 EContent 100. *EContent, 25*(12), 18.

Mattison, D. (2003). Quickiwiki, Swiki, Twiki, Zwiki and the Plone wars: Wiki as a PIM and collaborative content tool. *Searcher: The Magazine for Database Professionals*. Retrieved December 12, 2003, from *www.infotoday.com/searcher/apr03/mattison.shtml*

McGovern, G. (2001). Content is not a technology issue. Retrieved December 12, 2003, from *www.gerrymcgovern.com*

McGovern, G. (2002). The benefits of a content management system. Retrieved December 12, 2003, from *www.gerrymcgovern.com*

McGovern, G. (2003). Why content management software hasn't worked. Retrieved December 12, 2003, from *www.gerrymcgovern.com*

Notess, G.R. (2002). The Blog realm: News sources, searching with Daypop, and content management. *Online, 26*(5). Retrieved January 7, 2004, from *www.onlinemag.net/sep02/OnTheNet.htm*

Ryan, S.M. (2003). Library Web site administration: A strategic planning model for the smaller academic library. *Journal of Academic Librarianship, 29*(4).

Shropshire, S. (2003). Beyond the design and evaluation of a library Web site: An analysis and four case studies. *Journal of Academic Librarianship, 29*(2).

Taschek, J. (1999). The scoop on Web content management. *PC Week, 16*(37).

Tennant, R. (2003). Feed your head: Keeping up by using RSS. *Library Journal netConnect, 128*(13).

Udell, J. (2003). Revisiting Zope: An unorthodox open-source approach holds promise for enterprise content management. Retrieved December 4, 2003, from *www.infoworld.com*

University of Minnesota Libraries. (2003). Lib data software release. Retrieved December 3, 2003, from *www.lib.umn.edu/*

West, K., Huff, R., & Turocy, P. (2000). Managing content on the Web. *Network Computing, 11*(21).

Yuhfen, D.W., & Mengxiong, L. (2001). Content management and the future of academic libraries. *The Electronic Library, 19*(6).

Zhou, J. (2003). A history of Web portals and their development in libraries. *Information Technology and Libraries, 22*(3), 119-128.

# Section II

# Case
# Studies

Chapter III

# Developing a Distributed Web Publishing System at CSU Sacramento Library:

## A Case Study of Coordinated Decentralization

Juan Carlos Rodriguez
California State University, Sacramento, USA

Andy Osburn
California State University, Sacramento, USA

## Abstract

*This chapter introduces the steps that were undertaken at the California State University, Sacramento Library in moving from a centrally managed, static, and disjointed Web site to a efficient, collaboratively managed, database-driven Web site utilizing an easy-to-use customized Web content management system developed by the library. It discusses the decisions and actions taken during the various stages throughout the design and implementation of this Web publishing system. The authors introduce the methods and some of the Web-based technologies used, and present the issues encountered and how they were addressed during the development and implementation of the locally created Web publishing system.*

# Introduction

Just after 3:00 p.m., a member from the Reference Department called the Systems Department complaining that she was unable to get her Web page to look right. After the Web developer looked at the HTML code, he realized that the problem was that there was a missing ">" in one of the HTML tags. At that moment, another reference librarian walked into the Systems Department looking for someone to help him create several Web pages. The librarian was familiar with MS Word, but the process of creating Web pages seemed daunting. Shortly thereafter, he received another call came from the Circulation Department Head, informing him that the hours on the Web site were incorrect and that one of her newly hired staff members was not listed on the staff directory. Once the hours had been updated and the staff member was added to the online directory, he remembered that he had several dozen e-mail messages and phone calls reminding him of tasks that needed to be completed by the end of the day. It was almost time for him to go home for the day, and there appeared to be no end in sight.

The Web developer had only been working for the library for several weeks and he had quickly realized that the current model of Web site maintenance would not work in the long run, especially if he wanted to keep his sanity. Something had to be done. Wouldn't it be great if those involved in the creation of the content could also develop and maintain their own Web pages without the need to know HTML, thought the Web developer. He had remembered discussing this issue with some of his colleagues on several online discussion lists. Many had shared their experiences on using databases to manage the creation and maintenance of Web pages. The process didn't seem too difficult. He already possessed the experience in developing databases, and extending this to the Web seemed fairly straightforward. He also realized that there had been several librarians who had been involved with the library Web site from the beginning and many may be reluctant to change their way of doing things. He would need to get the support from the library administration and gradually introduce the new process if this were to be successful. The process began fairly slowly, yet grew to dramatically change the way Web publishing is handled at the library. This case will describe how this process evolved, the issues involved, and the results of the development of a Web content management system at the California State University, Sacramento Library.

# Background

California State University, Sacramento (CSUS) is part of the 23-campus California State University System. Located in the state capital, the campus of approximately 29,000 students is ethnically, socially, and economically diverse. The library employees consist of 32 FTE librarians, 53 FTE library assistants and technical staff, and 37 FTE student assistants. The library has a print collection of about 1.3 million volumes, subscribes to more than 120 electronic databases, and provides access to more than 12,000 electronic journals through direct subscriptions and serial aggregators. The library has a Library Information Systems (LIS) Department consisting of nine members (the director of the department, a digital information services librarian, a Web developer, three full-time technology staff, and three student assistants). The LIS Department maintains the library staff and public networks, the integrated library system (Innovative), as well as the e-mail, Web, and digital collection servers.

The library's first Web site was developed in 1996 and was maintained by the head of the LIS Department. At that time, the LIS Department consisted of two members, an Innovative Coordinator and the head of the department. Others in the library were involved in the content and design of the Web site, but all Web page creation was handled by the department head. The Web site resided on the department head's desktop computer using Xitami for Windows 3.11 Web Server Software. When the department head resigned in 1997, a recently hired staff member in the LIS Department assumed responsibility for the Web site as an additional responsibility. The Web site was also moved from the former department head's desktop computer to the campus Web server. Most of the Web page creators possessed minimal skills and most were self-taught. In addition, the majority of the Web page developers created Web pages in isolation, with little or no interaction with others creating Web pages. As a result, the library Web site was more a loose collection of pages than a unified site.

From 1997 through the summer of 2000, the Campus Computing and Communications Division provided access and space on the campus Web server. The library had a directory on the Web server and had FTP access to this directory. All pages were created locally and then uploaded to the Web server. Access to the campus Web server was also provided to several librarians who created Web pages that were linked from the library's Web site.

# Setting the Stage

The CSUS Library Web site began as a very modest and basic site that provided general information about the library. The site was maintained by the LIS department head, and the content was created in consultation with other library content creators. During the first few years, the growth of the Web site was minimal, and it was fairly easy for one person to maintain the site. The library's Web site resided on the campus Web server, and all HTML pages had to be 'FTP'd' to the campus Web server. For security reasons, FTP access to the campus server was limited to only a select few in the library. This provided an obstacle for future content creators in that they were required to submit their requests to the library Web manager, who in turn uploaded the HTML file(s) to the campus Web server.

During the next several years, others in the library began to create additional Web pages for the library. As with most librarians, librarians at CSUS realized the potential in utilizing the Web as an effective information medium, but were faced with limited resources and could not really take advantage of the Web's potential. As a result, there were a few in the library that assumed responsibility for not only developing the content and marking it up, but also for the interface design and structure. This approach served the CSUS Library well, until the library Web site grew in size and scope. With the proliferation of easy-to-use graphical HTML editors, many librarians began to create their own Web pages. This was an added relief to the library Web manager, but this brought problems as well, namely, an increased amount of requests for pages to be uploaded to the campus Web server, the lack of a uniform design and structure among the Web pages, and the varied skill level among the content creators.

To address this problem, HTML style templates were created, but this also posed a problem as the HTML templates could also be accidentally modified, resulting in pages that varied in design. By mid-1998 there were about 40 Web pages created pretty much in isolation, and many lacked any style or uniformity. Each library department created its own page. The Web site lacked an overall structure that was followed by the departments. It soon became evident that there was a growing need to facilitate the creation of Web pages, provide uniformity across all pages, allow the content creators to have control of the respective pages, and assume library control of the Web server.

In the fall of 1999, the LIS staff member responsible for the Web site left for another position. The LIS department head realized that there was a growing need to have a dedicated and experienced Web developer on staff instead of having Web responsibilities as an additional responsibility. In the spring of 2000, the library hired its first Web developer. Once on board, he quickly began to work on ways to improve the efficiency of the Web page creation process.

An important and widely used section of the Web site was the page that included links to all of the library's electronic indexes and abstracts. This static page was maintained by the Web developer. It was decided that this section would be redesigned and database driven. Several issues needed to be resolved. Authorization and authentication, as well as an intuitive interface that would be used to create and edit the pages, would need to be developed.

# Case Description

## Library Administration's Involvement and Support of the Web

Up until 1998, the library Web site was not considered critical to the mission of the library and was not given adequate attention and support. Although the campus was generally responsive to the needs of the library in terms of continued access and storage on the Web server, there was a growing frustration and a feeling of lack of control over the ability to create new and innovative Web pages. In addition, the freedom to experiment and develop Web pages locally without the need for intervention from campus computing was also desired. In the fall of 1999, the head of LIS recommended to the library administration that a new position be created that would replace a vacant LIS position. This new position's primary responsibility would be to manage and develop the library's Web site. In addition, a Web Advisory Committee was created by the library administration to guide the development of the Web site, as well as to recommend policies and procedures for management and use of the library's Web site. Library administration approved the creation of the new position and that position was filled in the spring of 2000. A request for a dedicated Web server was approved by library administration in the summer of 2000.

## Library Employees' Web Publishing Experience

Up until the hiring of a trained Web developer, most Web page creators were either self-taught or had taken a few basic courses on Web creation offered by campus computing. The skill levels among library employees varied greatly, and most lacked basic Web design principles. As a result most pages were very basic in nature in regards to layout and design. Most participants were involved with the library's Web site primarily because they were interested in the Web and not because it was part of their position description. In fact, only the Web site manager had Web-related responsibilities as part of his position description. Many were motivated by their own personal interest and by the potential they saw in the Web as a new publishing medium.

## Assuming Local Control of the Web Site and Server

The newly hired Web developer and the head of LIS realized the importance of assuming complete control of all aspects of the library's Web presence. This control would provide the necessary foundation for any future growth of the library Web site in terms of publishing and increased functionality. Having a Web server located within the library's network and under library control was the first step of the plan. Without the server, it would be very difficult to enhance Web services in the library. Secondly, a move away from static content was needed to improve the efficiency of content creation and enhance the accuracy of the content as well.

The obvious direction was to make a move away from a static site and to centralize the content into a database. The site was also growing too large for one person to be responsible for every new development and update. Although a database centralized the content, a decentralized approach to content creation and maintenance was needed to empower content providers to create and maintain large portions of the site instead of just a single person. In short, the goal was to create a Web site hosted on a local server that could be administered directly by library staff; utilize a database for dynamic, flexible content; and distribute the workload of Web page creation and maintenance from one person to many.

Selecting and acquiring a server class computer to host the site was the first important change that would have to be realized before an enhanced library Web site could be built. Installing the server on the library's LAN would bring the Web service under the direct control of the library instead of the university's central computing services. It was deemed necessary to be in control of the entire computer, the installation of the operating system, and the configuration of the Web server software in order to design and implement a useful content management system. Web server software such as Microsoft's Internet Information Server (IIS) and the venerable Apache HTTP server has numerous configuration options that directly correlate with the creation of Web/database applications.

It would be difficult to develop the system without administrator privileges to the server. The machine would also have to be joined to the library's existing domain in order to grant domain users directory-level access without using file transfer software. All Web content providers would be given a special Web folder on their desktop (a shortcut to a Web server directory) in which to store Web-accessible documents. Even though it is preferred to use two identical computers to provide a network service, due to budget constraints, one Dell 2400 server was chosen and used to host the site. During the summer of 2000, all of the pages that resided on the campus Web server were transferred to the new library server.

In a normal production environment, one computer is used to actively host the site, the production machine, and one is used for development and disaster recovery. After about one year of service, the budget climate improved and the new LIS department head agreed with the importance of a two-machine production environment. As a result in fall of 2001, we upgraded our investment in hardware from the one Dell 2400 to two Dell 4400s, with Microsoft Windows 2000 as the operating system. Unix/Linux and Apache were becoming the industry standard in terms of operating systems and Web server software. However, due to the lack of expertise with Unix/Linux OS in the LIS Department, and for ease of joining the Web server to library's domain,

Windows 2000 was chosen as the platform for the Web server. Although we realized Windows 2000 may not be the best choice for a Web platform, it was best at the time because of the aforementioned reasons. We moved ahead but still followed the ongoing development of Linux and increased our knowledge of it while keeping an eye on a possible future switch to that platform. With the entire site now transferred to the new machines housed in the library, we were ready to begin phase two of our plan, moving from a site composed of static HTML files to a more dynamic, database-driven site.

## Getting the Library on the "Same Page"

At the time, it was becoming increasingly important to develop some Web guidelines and procedures. Thus, in the spring of 2000, a Web Advisory Committee was established to bring some order to the Web page creation process, and provide some policies and procedures for developing Web pages. The Web Advisory Committee consisted of members from the Reference Department, Bibliographic Control Department, and the LIS Department.

In August 2000, the CSUS Library Web Guidelines were approved by library administration. The guidelines provided information about the types of pages that were allowed on the Web server, discussed the various roles of the library developer and content providers, and provided design and accessibility guidelines. The Web site was redesigned following the new guidelines. However, not all of the pages were redesigned, partly because there was a lack of expertise at the department level or they lacked the time. However, the decision of how these pages were to be created and maintained was still left to the content providers.

A Web page template (see Figure 1) was created, but the use of it was not strictly enforced and resulted in a Web site that was not completely uniform in layout and design. One important section that was also omitted from the guidelines was establishing a framework or organizational structure for the Web site. Although there were guidelines on how pages should look, no structure was provided as to where that Web page would fit in the overall Web site architecture. In addition, it was not clear who was responsible for enforcing the guidelines. As a result, they were not always followed.

*Figure 1. Original Web page template*

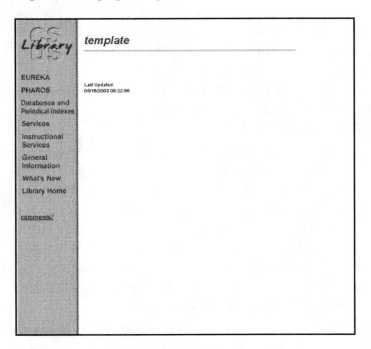

## The First Steps in Decentralizing Content Creation

Consolidation of content into a database (i.e., making the site 'database driven' or 'dynamic') results in manifold benefits. Ease of content creation, standardization of display, efficiency of maintenance, and timeliness of information were among the main points under our consideration. Auxiliary benefits may include the flexibility of being able to export information into other formats and uses, but that is an advanced topic that deserves its own discourse.

Historically, all of the Web pages in the library were created with HTML editors such as FrontPage and Dreamweaver or simple text editors such as Notepad or Wordpad. Two problems arise from using this paradigm of site creation. Using these programs required a certain degree of skill and knowledge that made it difficult for many people to use. Also, with multiple people authoring pages and creating individual graphical design and navigation schemes, the library's Web site was disjointed and lacked a consistent look and feel. A simple alternative was needed to post content and maintain a consistent look over a number of pages. To begin the process of consolidating content into databases, we chose to convert just one section of the site first.

Initially, there were no pages on the library Web site that contained information that was pulled from a database. An important, useful page with frequently updated content would be a good candidate to turn into a database-driven page and begin the process of conquering the learning curve. The page that lists the library's electronic resources, which we call the Databases and Periodical Indexes page or DPI page (see Figure 2), was a reasonable choice because it was an important, high-traffic page that contained very useful content that needed updating often.

In the spring of 2001, an MS Access database was created and populated with the information surrounding the library's electronic resources. Examples of the types of fields that were used include database names, URLs, proxy URLs, category types, full text indication, database descriptions, librarian guides, and so forth. The Web developer was responsible for adding new electronic resources as they became available. This was done by adding new records in the Microsoft Access table. Microsoft's Active Server Pages (ASP) scripting engine and the Jscript scripting language were chosen for the development environment used to the build dynamic pages.

Instead of merely one page, as had existed on the DPI page, the new, dynamic DPI page was crafted to consist of many different "views" of the same data pulled from the database. In effect, each different view was to be a separate

*Figure 2. Original DPI page*

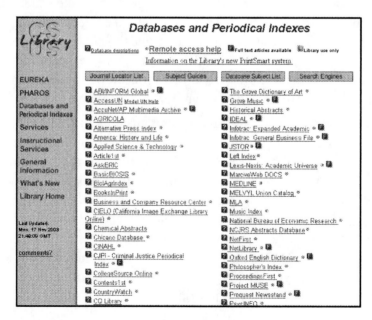

Web page that listed electronic resources and links to librarians' guides that were pertinent to a particular discipline. The librarians' subject guides were static HTML pages that followed a basic design template. An edit button would appear for the librarians on their subject page, and this edit button would only appear on the computer in their office. The edit button would take the librarian to an editing section that had a simple interface where the content of the page could be managed (see Figure 3).

Individual online resources could be chosen to appear on just that subject page from a drop-down menu of all of the library's electronic resources. For example, the psychology librarian could choose Social Sciences Abstracts, PsychINFO, Science Direct, and so forth for their psychology page. The same resource could appear on a number of different pages, however, and when the URL to that resource is updated, it is automatically updated on every page that it appears. Links to librarian's subject guides could also be maintained from the DPI editing page. When a librarian completes a subject guide, he or she could place it into a Web folder and easily link it to the DPI subject page. The published DPI page (see Figure 4) is both easy to maintain and provides the subject librarians with an easy-to-use form for editing content. One-on-one instruction sessions on the use of the DPI edit pages were provided for all librarians responsible for maintaining the DPI page.

*Figure 3. DPI edit page*

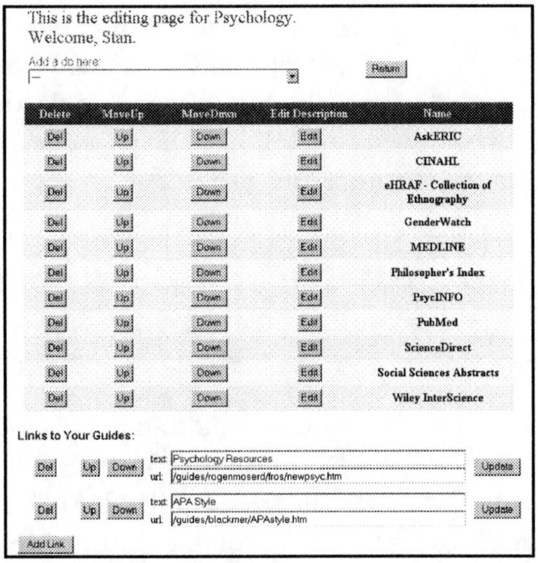

*Figure 4. New DPI page*

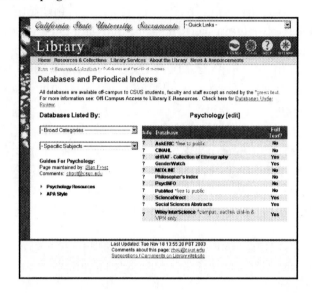

Unfortunately, an authentication system was not in place at the time, so an IP address detection script was used to identify the librarians who were the content providers. Using an IP authentication method restricted the content providers to using only their office computer to do any work to their pages, and that clearly was not ideal. Nevertheless, the new dynamic DPI page proved to be a tremendous improvement and whet our appetites to continue the drive towards consolidation of content. With the release of the new DPI page, our librarians were suddenly endowed with new publishing powers that they heartily took advantage of. There was very little resistance to the new method of maintaining the DPI page. In fact, many welcomed the new approach and enjoyed having the ability to easily manage the list of electronic resources and subject guides. As of November 2003, the DPI page consisted of 62 different pages and links to 164 librarian subject guides.

# Developing and Implementing the Web Content Management System (WCMS)

With the success of the DPI pages, we would attempt to convert the entire site to a database-driven WCMS. During the fall of 2001, we began to look at the possibility of moving the Web site from a collection of static Web pages to a completely database-driven site. We continued to use MS Access because of its ease of use and acceptable performance. But two main issues would have to be resolved to implement a fully functional WCMS. We needed true user authentication instead of IP authentication and a replacement for HTML editors.

Even though the DPI page implemented decentralized content management, with multiple people updating the content in the database that drives the page, they could only do the updating from their office computer. For proper user authentication, all of the content providers should log in with a username and password to verify their identity. The system should then check for the pages that the user is allowed to edit and present only those pages to them for editing, a process known as authorization. A goal was to have the users present the same username and password that they use to log into the domain to log into our WCMS. In fact, we would like our users to only need that one username and password combination to access all data, services, and applications provided by the library.

With this in mind we chose to use an authentication method known as Windows Integrated Authentication, because it allows users to log in via a browser into the Web server using their domain username and password, and hashes the credentials as they travel the wires. One caveat to using Windows Integrated Authentication was that the only browser that could take advantage of it at the time was, unsurprisingly, Microsoft Internet Explorer, but the advent of the open source browser Mozilla Firefox recently provided that functionality also. Now the content providers could create new pages and update existing pages from any computer that has a browser and is connected to the Internet. Authentication and authorization became the cornerstones of our WCMS, and we moved on to the challenge of integrating an in-line editor.

In lieu of using an HTML editor to create pages, a process known as "in-line editing" was employed to ease the difficulty of creating content and standardize the site's look. In-line editing is a process of calling up the content of any particular page and editing the content in WYSIWYG fashion using only a browser. The user is only concerned with the content portion of the page and doesn't worry about the overall layout of the page, style, or navigation to any great degree. Quick, simple, and to the point, a word processor-like interface is loaded into the browser, where the content of the page is worked on and saved without the use of a confusing HTML editor. A free, ready-made in-line editor was available for ASP, which worked with our system, with a fair degree of tweaking of course, so there was no need to create it in-house from scratch.

*Figure 5. Create and edit page*

The edit pages were designed to mirror the look of the actual published page. Figure 5 shows an example of what the "Create and Edit" page with the in-line editor looks like. From the pull-down menu, other items or sections of the page could be included, such as a one-column paragraph, a two-column paragraph, or a divide line (i.e., <hr> tag). One problem with the in-line editor we chose, and many others we tested, is that it uses a browser feature known as I-Frames to operate, an MS Internet Explorer-only feature! A future improvement would be to eliminate any and all of these proprietary lock-ins in favor of open standards.

When using in-line editing, all aspects of a page's appearance, headers, footers, navigational elements, images, and so forth are kept in one place and applied to every page that is controlled by that style, thus standardizing the look and feel over many pages. Since the elements that are found on many pages reside in one spot, a change made to an element in the place where it is housed results in that change being propagated to every instance where it is displayed. Efficiency of maintenance is achieved this way. With a properly implemented database-driven site, the entire site can be converted from one look to another far easier and much more rapidly than can be achieved with a static site. Along with ease of content creation, standardization of display, and efficiency of maintenance, a database-driven approach can also be leveraged to bring about decentralized content management that keeps the information on the site fresh and timely while reducing errors.

The content editor and management interface was coded by hand in Visual InterDev, an integrated development environment from Microsoft. Four different languages were employed to complete the job: ASP (Microsoft Active Server Pages), SQL (Structured Query Language), HTML (Hypertext Markup Language), and JavaScript. Small snippets of each of these languages were used to create each interface page. All HTML code was written by hand without a WYSIWYG HTML editor. Besides Visual InterDev, the only other development software used was MS Access, which was used to create the database tables.

When creating a decentralized content management system, the design of a solid and flexible authorization schema is fundamental. We chose to use the familiar technique of placing users into groups, then assigning privileges to the groups, not the users. One top-level administrative group has unbridled access to all pages and sections of the WCMS. Any member of the top administrative group can create groups and grant or revoke authorizations to all other users by including them or removing them from other groups. Certain pages of the site required the creation of custom, sophisticated editing interfaces that were unique to editing that page, somewhat like the DPI page. A special interface was needed because those pages drew upon many unique fields that all had to be simultaneously updated in a holistic fashion. An example of one of these

*Figure 6. Schedule of hours page  (Fall 2003)*

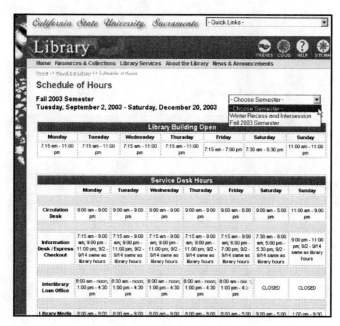

unique pages would be library's schedule of hours page (see Figure 6) that keeps lists of hours for semester and intercessions for the various service desks and departments, as well as general building hours. Simple in-line editing would not be effective in these instances.

Groups were created to grant access to the editors of these pages. The department that determines hours of operation, and published the traditional printed hours listing, is the department most naturally fitted to be in the 'Hours Editor' group, which in the case of our library is our Administrative Department. Illustrated in Figure 7, the hours edit page's design mirrors the actual published schedule of hours page. From the schedule of hours management page (Figure 8), you are able to determine the default hours page that is displayed from the library Web site, as well other hours pages accessible from

*Figure 7. Hours edit page*

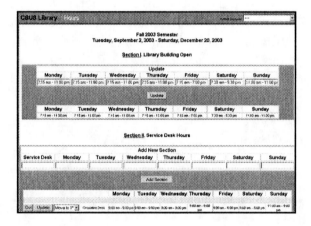

*Figure 8. Hours administration page*

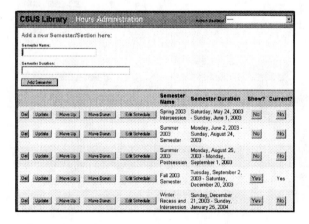

*Figure 9. Library faculty and staff directory*

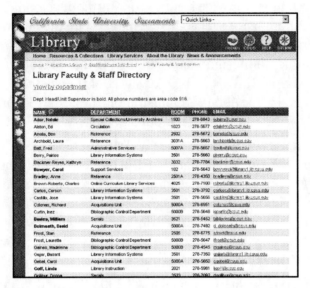

the drop-down menu. In general, we determined most all of our access levels based on who was most naturally fitted to perform the editing. In most cases, they were already performing the same function on paper, and we just developed an electronic version of the process and created a group for those same people to do the editing.

Other special editing sections built into our WCMS include a staff directory editing section. The staff directory editing section allows faculty and staff to be added, deleted, and updated, along with all of their personal information (phone number, room number, department, title, and so forth). Publicly viewable directory pages can be sorted by first name, last name, room number, and department (see Figure 9).

## Separating Design from Content

With the development of a complete WCMS solution underway, the Web Advisory Committee was charged with the development of a new design and layout that would take advantage of the dynamic nature of the WCMS. The goal of redesign was to separate the design from the content. During the design process, issues such as structure, navigation, and functionality all contributed to the design of the WCMS. By the spring of 2002, we had developed a design document that included content elements, interface design elements, organization structure, as well as functional requirements. All library employees were given an opportunity to provide feedback during the development of the design document. Although not everyone was happy with the new design, almost everyone agreed that this was a significant improvement over the current design. Also, since the design was separate from the content, future modifications to the design and layout of the Web site could be easily and quickly done. With the approval of the library administration, the design document served as the blueprint for the continued development of the WCMS.

The move to a library-wide usage of the WCMS was to be made simultaneously with the library's Web site redesign. Much of the content from the Web site was outdated and/or inconsistent in design and structure. The LIS Department staff assisted with the initial migration of content to the new WCMS. This was also an opportunity for departments to both update the content and give them tools necessary to maintain their respective pages without a lot of intervention from the Web developer.

The library Web site went live in January of 2003. The new Web site coexisted with the old Web site. However, all new content was to be added only to the new site using the WCMS. This proved helpful in two aspects. First it encouraged the use of the WCMS among library employees, and second it helped ease the library employees' resistance to moving to a new Web site since the old site was quickly becoming outdated. The old site was removed in mid-April of 2003.

## Adding and Managing Content

In order to add a new page to the site, the user logs into the system and chooses "Create and Edit Web Pages" from the WCMS Administration Management Menu. Most content providers will only have the ability to create and edit pages. Other functions available from the Administration Management Menu will be discussed later in the WCMS Administration section. The Create and Edit Web Pages portion of the WCMS is divided into two sub-sections: the "Pages Not in the Tree" section and the "Pages in the Tree" section (see Figure 10). We chose to use a tree structure to represent the hierarchy of pages in the site, and having these two sections shows which pages have been placed into the hierarchy, or published, and those which are still works-in-progress and hence "not in the tree" or not published. If it is the first time that the content provider has created a page in which both sections will be empty unless the site administrator has already assigned them a page. Clicking the button "Add New

*Figure 10. Create and edit management page*

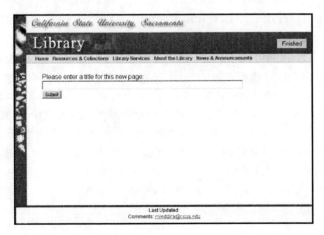

Page" creates a new page entry in the "Pages Not in the Tree" section and presents the user with a blank library template page (see Figure 11). From here the user can add a title to the page and choose a paragraph type to begin adding content.

Types of paragraphs include single-column, plain-text paragraphs; double-column, plain-text paragraphs; and rich-text paragraphs. Rich-text paragraphs utilize the HTML in-line editor. At this point, the content provider is using the process of in-line editing to author a Web page. An unlimited number of paragraphs of different types can be added to the page, one after the other, and

*Figure 11. Blank create page*

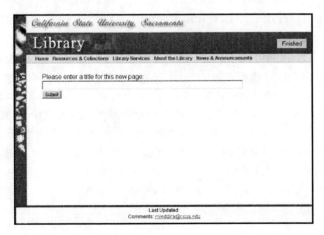

*Figure 12. Example of content edit page*

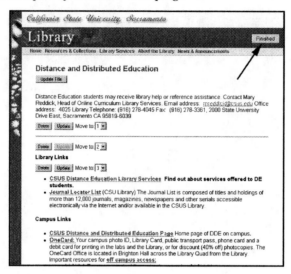

they can be re-arranged at any time. Once the user is happy with the new page, he or she can click the "Finished" button to save the page (see Figure 12). The newly created page now appears in the "Pages Not in the Tree" section, along with three buttons—Del, Update, and Add. The Del button will delete the page, Update will open the page back up into in-line editing mode, and Add will add the page to "Pages in the Tree" section. At least one page must already exist in the "Pages in the Tree" section in order to add a page to the tree.

The site administrator adds the first page for the user, which is linked into the site at the appropriate place, to give them a starting point in developing their own tree hierarchy from that point forward. There is no limit on the number of pages that the content provider can make from then on, and there is no approval process to go through when adding new pages. It is solely the content provider's responsibility to publish material that is relevant to the library, appropriate, and accurate. Also, from this point forward, when the user adds a new page to the tree, her or she will have the choice of placing it under any of his or her existing published pages, much like the familiar directory structures in modern operating systems. The placement of pages into the tree structure is significant in that it directly creates the "breadcrumb" links on the page when the public views it (see Figure 13). Once added to the tree, the page can be deleted, updated and, moved at any time. The page creation process proved to be very easy and was well received by the content creators. As with all new procedures, there was an initial learning curve. However, once this was

*Figure 13. Example of published content page*

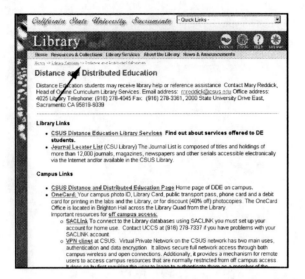

overcome, the content creators became comfortable with the new approach. In fact, the biggest users of the WCMS were the ones who had never created a Web page.

## WCMS Administration

As mentioned earlier, there is a top-level administrative group of users, Site Administrators, who have control of every aspect of the site. Administration of the site is divided into just a few sections: Users, Users & Groups, Departments, Home Page & Second Level Pages, and Links. These sections are available from the WCMS Administration Menu (see Figure 14). All users (i.e., content creators) of the WCMS, those who can log in and are listed in the

*Figure 14. WCMS administration management page*

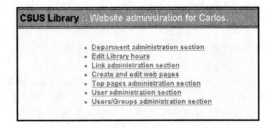

*Figure 15. User administration page*

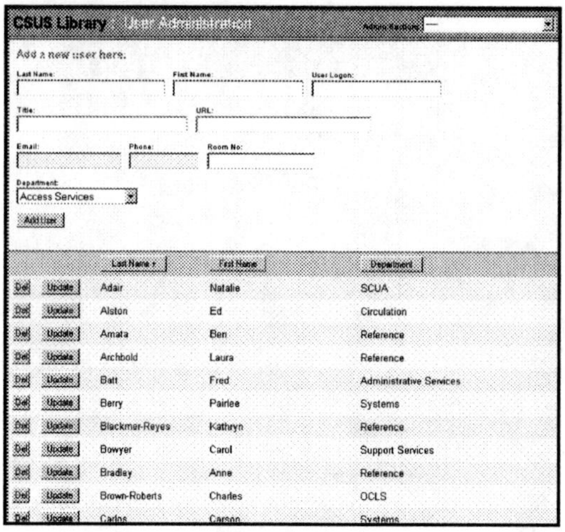

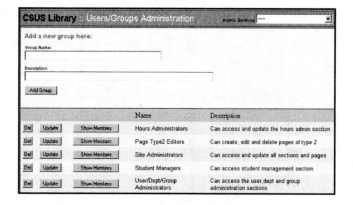

directory, are managed in the "Users Administration" section. A simple form is used by a WCMS Administrator to add a user, along with some basic information about the user such as first name, last name, login, title, department, and so forth (see Figure 15).

Closely associated with the "Users Administrations" section is the "Users/ Groups Administration" section, where the WCMS Administrators control access to the various restricted editing sections of the WCMS by creating a group and granting it the ability to access that section. Users are simply added and removed from the group to grant and deny them group permissions (see Figure 16). The "Department Administration" section is where all of the departments in the library are entered and updated. Just like the "User

*Figure 16. User/groups administration page*

*Figure 17. Department administration page*

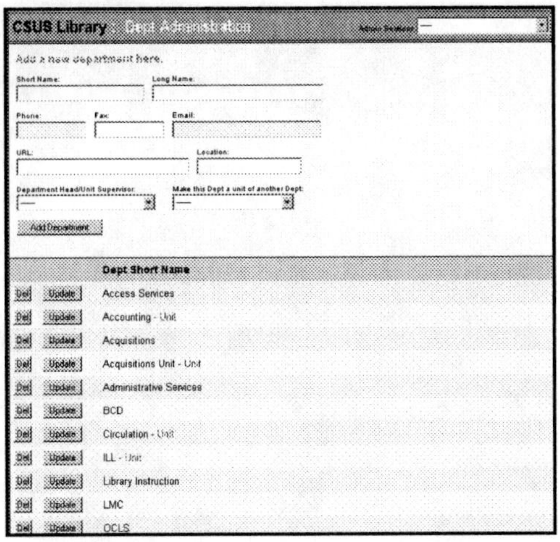

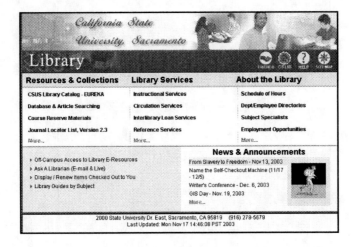

Administration" section, the "Department Administration" section is just a simple form that takes in basic information about the library's departments (see Figure 17). Users and departments are properly associated together to produce the library faculty and staff directory section of the Web site.

The last two administration sections are the "Top Pages" and the "Link Administration" sections. The homepage and all second-level pages are considered "Top Pages." Both sections are managed in conjunction with each other and can be thought of as one and the same. Every link on the homepage (see Figure 18) and second-level pages (Resources & Collections, Library Services, About the Library, News and Announcements) are pulled from a set

*Figure 18. New homepage*

*Figure 19. Second-level page (Library Services)*

of links that is managed in the "Link Administration" section. Figure 19 shows the "Library Services" second-level page.

The "Link Administration" section is, again, just a simple form that takes in a name, URL, and short description of a link and stores it in a master set of links (see Figure 20). Once a link is created, it must be associated with one of the second-level pages in order for it to be displayed. The homepage consists of several components or sections that can include links. In addition to the

*Figure 20. Link administration page*

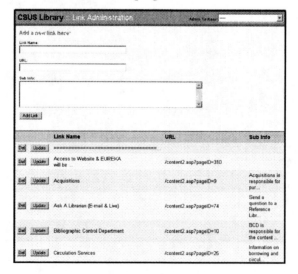

*Figure 21. Top pages administration page*

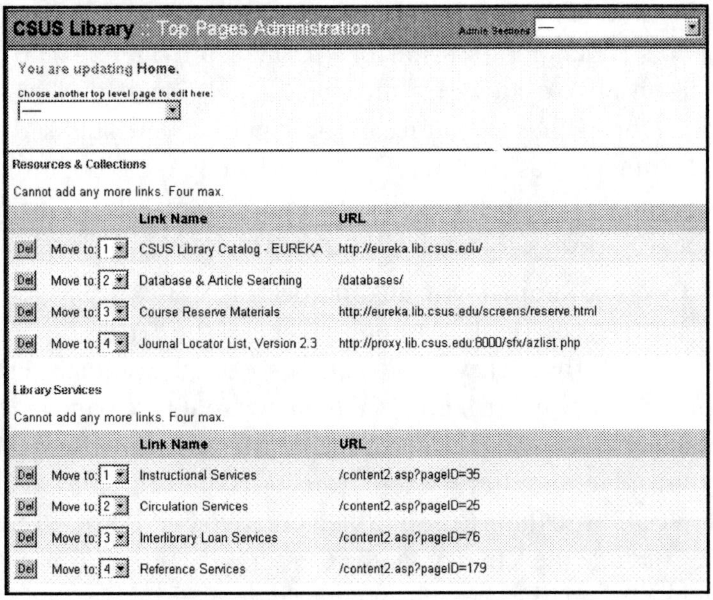

second-level pages mentioned previously, there are two other sections that can contain links. These are "Top Links" and "Quick Links." Top links are ones that are displayed from the homepage. Quick links are accessible via a drop-down menu from all pages in the library Web site.

On the homepage, each section draws from the set of links that was chosen for the corresponding second-level page. For example, if the second-level page, Library Services, has 15 links that were associated from the master set of links, the "Library Services" section on the homepage can draw upon the same 15 links that were chosen for that second-level page (i.e., Library Services). The homepage is restricted to listing only four of those links, however. From the "Top Pages Administration" section (see Figure 21), you are able to add links, remove links, as well as change the display order. With these few administration sections of the WCMS, the Site Administrator is easily able to quickly handle most of the daily routine tasks needed to maintain the CSUS Library's Web site.

## Promoting the WCMS and Encouraging Use

We anticipated that there would be some resistance to the use of the WCMS, particularly since it would change the way Web pages were created. We still provided the ability to create HTML pages using an editor, and then copying and pasting the HTML code into the WCMS editor pages. We had an instruction and orientation session for all content providers. There was also in-depth one-on-one sessions for all content providers taught by the Web developer. During these sessions, the advantages were stressed. One of the major advantages was that no HTML knowledge was required to create uniform pages, and it only took several minutes to create basic pages. Also, all navigational links were dynamically created based on the content of the page.

Many had become familiar with this approach using the DPI page and thus the change was not as difficult. Although some of the earlier content creators initially felt limited by the new approach, most of them eventually embraced the new approach since we still allowed them to create the pages in the HTML editor of their choice and then insert the HTML code into the WCMS editor. We also did not require library departments to solely create pages using the WCMS. We allowed them to utilize their creativity and skills to create pages. Examples include the Library Media Center page (http://library.csus.edu/services/lmc/) and the Japanese American Archive Collection (http://library.csus.edu/collections/jaac/). This flexibility provided the freedom and control that the experienced Web page creators requested.

## Inherent Advantages and Benefits of Distributed Web Publishing

Decentralized content management, empowering many content providers to create and maintain the site, was the third goal to be achieved with the WCMS. Instead of library staff and Web site users alerting the Web developer that a certain piece of information is out of date, we considered a better method to keep information accurate that would allow the people who understand the content the best to be directly responsible for its accuracy and upkeep. The idea is that the individual responsible for a set of pages would be the first person to know when something needs to be updated because they know the details surrounding the information the best. Many people constantly reviewing and updating the site's content would keep it fresh, accurate, and timely.

Many of the advantages and benefits of implementing the WCMS were unforeseen. For example, we did not expect the increase in Web publishing to occur so rapidly. During the first year of use, the amount of people involved in the creation of Web pages tripled from seven to 21. Most of the new Web page creators had very little experience with HTML and were the ones who were the most excited about this newfound capability. The amount of Web pages created has also increased three-fold since the introduction of the WCMS in the fall of 2002. This was primarily due to the ability to quickly and easily create new pages. Exposure to the possibilities of the Web was also increased. The LIS Department began to receive a lot of requests for training on the use of the WCMS as well as suggestions for innovative uses of the Web. The Web site no longer was viewed as a secondary publishing tool, but as important as, if not more than, traditional publishing methods. Over the last three years, the library has hired about 10 new employees. Many of the new library employees have embraced the new method and have easily and quickly expanded their departmental pages.

# Current Challenges and Future Directions

Overall the development and implementation of the WCMS has been a huge success. The participation level for content creators has considerably increased since the launch of the WCMS in the fall of 2002. The WCMS has empowered the content creators and has introduced the world of Web publishing to everyone in the library regardless of their experience.

Many of the issues that were not resolved early on due to technical limitations or lack of experience still need to be addressed. Also, there is growing interest among the LIS staff to pursue open source alternatives. Work is underway to migrate from proprietary solutions such as MS Windows, IIS, and MS Access to more open standards such as Linux, Apache, and MySQL. The seamless integration of Directory Services as the authentication scheme to be used across multiple applications including the WCMS is also currently under development. The LIS Department staff is also reviewing and considering the integration of more robust content management systems such a Plone (http://www.plone.org) and Zope (http://www.zope.org). Examples of enhanced functionality that could be integrated would be the ability to "time stamp" items so individual links can come and go on schedule without human intervention. Other areas of future enhancements could be the ability to integrate some sort of automated review process before the content is made available on the Web site—a sort of "staging area" that could be reviewed by the appropriate person before it is published to the Web site.

Although the move from Windows as the desktop's primary operating system to open source alternatives may not occur soon, there remains the need to integrate Windows and Linux environments. Through the use of Samba (http://www.samba.org), it is possible to access Linux-based servers via a Windows Desktop. From a user's perspective, a mapped network drive on their desktop no longer needs to be a Windows server. Also, as access to the WCMS is provided remotely, the issue of improved security becomes of great importance.

The library is in the process of developing and implementing a Web-based intranet that will build on the experiences of the WCMS. The goal of the intranet would be to fully empower all library employees to easily and effortlessly create content on the Web without really thinking about it. The WCMS would be the tool that would facilitate its creation. The intranet would be the library employee's portal to all of his/her information objects (i.e., files, images, etc.), as well as quick access to all campus and library information. As the shift to Web-based applications continues, so does the need to provide a WCMS that will allow library employees to effectively and efficiently use the Web as a publishing, information access, and management tool.

Of growing interest among Web content creators is XML and the great potential it has for interoperability. XML would serve as the digital glue to transfer data from one system to another, and transform the style and layout to different forms. All future developments of the WCMS should take into consideration the integration of XML.

Future plans include abandoning the practice of keeping directory information in our WCMS and instead pull all of this data from a global directory service that houses an authoritative listing of people and departmental information. Every application, including the WCMS, in the library could refer to this global directory service to retrieve user information.

# Conclusion

Several factors contributed to the success of the WCMS. Initial support and the articulation of that support by library administration were and continue to be essential. Although financial support (i.e., funding for equipment and staff) is necessary, the support for continued development by allowing the LIS staff, along with others in the library, to explore new ideas and methods was equally, if not more important. Library administration realized the potential of technology and the Web, and has made it a priority. The gradual introduction to Web publishing through the use of the DPI page set the stage for initial change and allowed for the eventual migration to the WCMS for all Web page creation. The involvement of all library employees in both the Website design phase, as well as including them as potential WCMS participants, provided a feeling of mutual development and created an environment that began to stress the growing importance of the Web as the primary publishing medium.

Within three years, the goal of developing a WCMS that would facilitate the creation of Web pages, provide uniformity across all pages, and allow the content creators to have control of the respective pages for the most part has been achieved. Reaching that goal has become the first step in creating a Web publishing model that will enable Web publishing to become an integral part of the functions carried out by all employees of the library, and a providing a powerful, intuitive, and easy-to-use tool that will be available to everyone.

Chapter IV

# Indiana University Bloomington Libraries Presents Organization to the Users and Power to the People:
## A Solution in Web Content Management

Diane Dallis
Indiana University Bloomington, USA

Doug Ryner
Indiana University Bloomington, USA

## Abstract

*This chapter describes how the Indiana University Bloomington Libraries created a database-driven Web system that enables librarians and staff to publish content to the libraries' public Web site that maintains a consistent design and places the content into a logical and consistent structure. The system comprises the libraries' public Web site interface, the content manager (CM) administrative interface, and an intranet. The new Web system was designed to replace a decentralized process that was previously followed to maintain a large Web site of 8,000-plus static HTML pages. The new system made it possible for their large decentralized organization to present a unified and well-designed public interface on the Web. The authors describe the technical and conceptual development of the content management aspect of the system with the hope of increasing understanding of content management systems.*

# Introduction

The Indiana University Bloomington Libraries created a database-driven Web system that enables librarians and staff to publish content to the libraries' public Web site that maintains a consistent design and places the content into a logical and consistent architecture. The system comprises the libraries' public Web site interface, the content manager (CM) administrative interface, and an intranet. The libraries' public Web site was designed and created to operate with the content manager, which includes all of the input forms for pages and content within the libraries' public Web site, as well as a component called the Resource Manager which, controls and makes available all of the IUB Libraries' online subscription databases and resources. This case study will focus primarily on the creation of the content manager.

# Background

The Indiana University Bloomington (IUB) Libraries consist of 16 libraries holding more than 6.5 million items. The IUB Libraries subscribe to more than 300 electronic databases and provide access to more than 30,000 electronic journals through direct subscriptions and serial aggregators. The libraries serve the research and instructional needs of Bloomington faculty and students— including more than 31,000 undergraduates, more than 8,000 graduate students, and more than 1,700 faculty—as well as the residents of Indiana. The IUB Campus is well known for its broad technology access for students and faculty, and has been rated as one of the "most wired" campuses in the U.S. (Bernstein, 2000). Excellent user service is highly valued and the libraries have long been campus leaders at providing resources and services electronically. The libraries have a tradition of empowering library employees to create publications and Web sites to serve users.

## Setting the Stage

The IUB Libraries electronic presence began with a well-received site on the university's text-based Academic Information Environment in the 1970s, and the libraries were among the first to create a Web site on the Bloomington campus. An HTML template was created to make it easier for staff to develop Web pages that would ensure "site-wide consistency" with "a predictable navigation and orientation framework." The library Web site was envisioned to be "the BEST site for our primary users to find the scholarly information they need for their teaching, research and studies…" (IUB Libraries Web Policy Committee, 1998).

The pages that made up the site were stored on 80-plus separate Web server accounts held on a series of large UNIX Web servers owned and maintained by the University Information Technology Services (UITS) department. Full-time staff and librarians of the IUB Libraries were eligible to apply for and receive access to server accounts to publish Web pages. Anyone working in one of the libraries, library departments, or a member of a library group or committee with the ability and knowledge of creating a Web page was able to participate in the creation of the site. Web pages were published using HTML within the Web server account or any type of Web publishing software, such as Microsoft FrontPage, and uploaded to the server account using Telnet or Secure Shell (SSH). All Web server accounts were separately managed and owned. The management of the site was decentralized, and it grew to an estimated 8,000 pages over a period of five years. Searching of the site was made possible by standardizing the names of the Web server accounts. The guideline for account names used the letters "lib" for the first three characters and the rest of the letters used the beginning of a specific library's name. For example, the account name for the Education Library was "libeduc." The URL for the library homepage would then be www.indiana.edu/~libeduc. However, the naming convention was not consistently applied.

Many of the content providers (librarians, staff, and student staff) used the templates that imposed a minimal level of consistency in appearance and navigation. Although training in HTML using the library template was offered, it was not mandatory, and new staff members were not routinely trained. As a result, the services and resources on the sites varied greatly between each campus library. In some cases the HTML code of the template was maintained by a succession of staff members who implemented variations of the template to meet the needs of their library or department. The libraries' public Web site was in need of a redesign that would make it possible to make site-wide changes and present a unified appearance among all of the pages of the site.

In the spring of 1999, IUB Libraries contracted with two consultants to help review the libraries' Web site. The consultants worked with selected librarians, and conducted usability tests with various user groups to provide a plan for the architecture of the site. The work of the consultants and librarians resulted in reports and plans that guided an interim change to the electronic resources Web page and ultimately guided many architecture decisions for the present IUB Libraries' public Web site.

The consultants recommended that the site be redesigned to improve and increase intuitive user access to the scholarly information and resources needed for teaching, research, and studies. Due to the vast amount of information, the many providers of information, and the resulting potential for duplication, the consultants recommended that the libraries develop a consistent, efficient, and timely process for publishing to the Web by utilizing a database-driven system and to hire a single person charged to manage the system.

In July of 2000, the IUB Libraries posted the Web Administrator position. Key qualifications for the libraries Web Administrator were experience with database-driven Web sites and project management experience. The search was conducted both inside and outside the library community. In July of 2001, the libraries' new Web Administrator was selected from the business community. He was experienced in designing database-driven Web sites with significant amounts of content, and had received awards for his work in the business and nonprofit community.

One of the Web Administrator's first tasks was to appoint a working Web Team to represent and understand the needs of the diverse users of the libraries' Web site and to work with the administrator to create the new site. In the fall of 2001, the Web Team members were selected and included staff from public services, collection development, campus libraries, and information technology. Librarians, professional staff, and support staff were represented. Most of the members' position descriptions did not include the work of the Web Team. In Winter 2002, two half-time programmers were added to the Web Team. Also, the libraries hired a professional graphic designer for the project to design the look and feel of the public site and the content management system.

The first act of the Web Administrator and the Team was to create a plan for developing and implementing a new database-driven Web system. In the fall of 2001, after a review of all materials concerning the state of the previous Web site, a proposal was created to produce the new IUB Libraries' public Web site and content management system. The Team approached the development in two phases, conceptual and practical. Because the Team was developing the public Web site as part of the system, the early steps of the conceptual phase focused heavily on the architecture of the public Web site. A strong yet flexible architecture was the foundation of the development of the content manager. The following is a brief description of the planning and strategy steps taken early in the conceptual phase. The first part of the process was to define the project in detail, with the objective of understanding and communicating the project mission, goals, risks, and requirements. The following steps were taken:

Step 1:      Identify Users of the Libraries' Public Web Site

Step 2:      Determine the Scope of the Project

Step 3:      Write a Project Mission Statement

Step 4:      Develop Communication Tools/Process to Inform Stakehold ers of Progress

Step 5:      Developing the Sitemap

Step 6:      Identify the Technology

Step 7:      Communication, Documentation, and Expectations

While all of these steps were essential to developing the system, the most important for the content manager were steps 2, 5, and 6. The Team had to gain a clear understanding of the types and volume of information available on all of the library server accounts to gauge the scope of the project. There were thousands of Web pages, and most did not have navigation or supporting architecture. The Team surveyed library content providers, and documented all of the server accounts and their owners to learn who would be using the new Web system. In order to develop the sitemap and architecture for the libraries' public Web site, the Web Team spoke with all current Web content providers about their library sites. The Team also asked all stakeholders who would publish content on the new Web site for information about who provided the content, published the content, and how often the site was updated to gain a sense of the users of the content manager. The draft sitemap was then taken to a series of meetings with library staff to learn if the content within the sitemap met staff expectations. Gaining the staff support and confidence about the architecture of the site was important in insuring their satisfaction with the content manager.

As the sitemap was developed, it became clear that the libraries needed a mature and flexible product that combined digital resource management and Web content management. No commercial product available in Fall 2001 could handle the volume, breadth, and depth of the resources and content of the libraries' Web site, and the decision was made to create a system. The training and background of the Web Administrator was in MySQL and PHP scripting language, and the University Information Technology Services were offering a new MySQL database service. In addition, PHP has built-in compatibility with MySQL, and both tools are open source, so the cost to use them was minimal. The Team wanted to leverage the open source nature of the project and release for others to use and contribute. MySQL was chosen because it is fast, powerful, and affordable.

## Content Manager Development Climate

In Fall 2001, when the Web Team presented their development and implementation proposal to the Library Administration, an implementation timeline was established. This structured the development process and defined the administrative expectations. The Team publicized the phases, timeline, and relevant documentation on a Web site that the Team created for the project which was made available to all librarians and staff and began the development.

The Team was assigned a relatively short deadline for launching the new public site. Because of the large-scale and decentralized nature of the previous site, there was no option available for automating the transfer of content from the previous site. The tight schedule for the public Web site launch required the Team to implement an interim content management system in order to populate the libraries' public Web site with content before launch. This required members of the Web Team to input minimal content into the pages of the new site representing libraries, departments, and collections, because it would have been inefficient and potentially very confusing to train staff on a temporary system. The experience with the interim CM served as a preliminary test of using a content management system.

The new Web site, launched in October 2002, was very different from the previous site. The library staff perceived the new architecture as being too strict in contrast with the lack of architecture of the previous site. This, combined with the timing of the release (four weeks into the academic year) of the new public site, yielded an unfavorable response from many librarians and staff. Staff perceptions of the new public Web site posed challenges for the Team in the implementation of the content manager.

# Case Description

The new public Web site was created as a database-driven system and was initially populated with content using a rudimentary content management system administrative interface with a very basic *What You See Is What You Get* (WYSIWYG) HTML editing tool. The IUB Libraries Web Team was charged with the responsibility of creating a stable, user friendly, scalable content management system, and training librarians and staff to use it within a seven-month window (January-July 2003). The new system needed to manage the content of a variety of different pages such as public Web pages for departments, campus libraries, and library collections. The case description will present the development of the CM in two phases.

## Conceptual Planning and Development

The Team's experience with populating the public site with content gave them a strong understanding of the possibilities and challenges that the large scale of the public site might present in creating the content management interface. They made the decision to release the content manager in phases related to the depth of the architecture. The first phase included the ability to manage the homepage for each library, collection, and department, as well as all of the pages and sections of the central libraries' Web site. Later phases would include "deeper" pages such as pathfinders, resource guides, and subject-specific Web resources common to campus library Web sites. The phased development-and-release approach made it possible to meet the implementation deadline, and it presented opportunities to include more library staff input into the development of subsequent phases.

The Team communicated with librarians and staff from various campus libraries and departments to learn the types of information that they needed to present on their public pages. There was consistency among many of their needs, which made it possible to create one flexible template design and adapt it throughout implementation. The template included standard areas for consistent content such as contact information, a link to hours of operation, and links to subscription library resources. Each template also included a flexible, open text area for content specific to that library or department.

The Team worked with the visual designer for the libraries' public Web site to create the interface for the content manager. The designer specialized in interface design, and his involvement with the public site and his familiarity with the sitemap were crucial to the CM interface development. The interface is organized functionally, utilizing templates to manage the input and output of information based on the type of content, how it is input, maintained, and displayed. Figure 1 presents the CM interface relationship to the public Web site content.

*Figure 1. Content Manager Template Relationships*

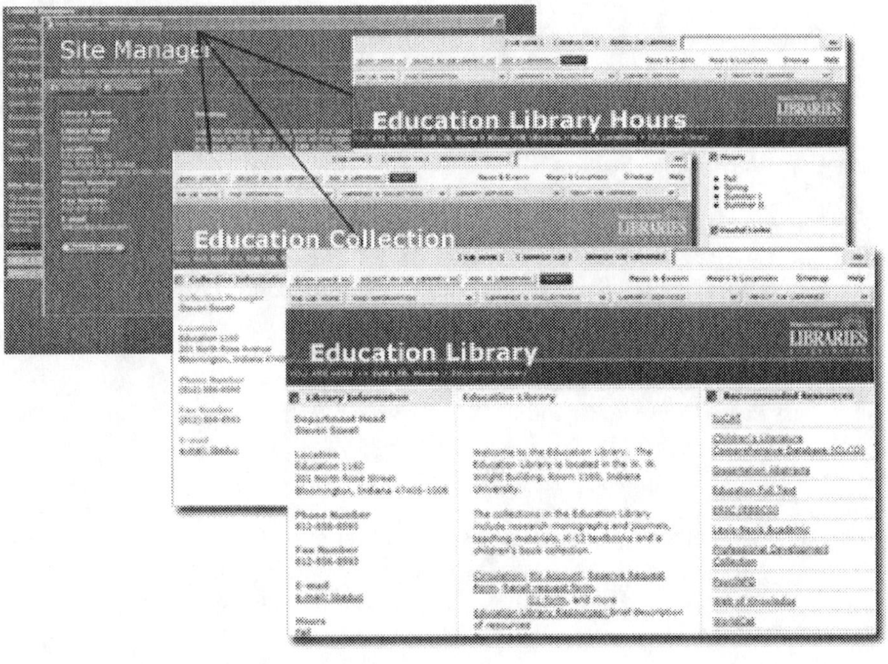

For each template, it was necessary to identify how, where, when, and by whom the content will be provided or maintained and accessed and displayed on the public site. This was essential in designing the database tables to collect and store information to be used by the template. To create the interface for each template, they followed a standard procedure. First, members of the Team created template specification documents that described the type of content that would be stored in the specific template, descriptions of the various fields, notations on which fields would be seen by the public and which would not, and additional descriptive information that would help the designer determine the look and functionality of the template. Metadata was a standard

*Table 1. Templates*

| | |
|---|---|
| Site Homepage | Content Copy Block |
| Library Homepage | Content Copy Block & Picture |
| Library Useful Links Section | Site Search |
| All Collections List | News & Events Homepage |
| Collection Homepage | Library Hours |
| Collections Links Section | Site Sitemap |
| Collection Resources Section | Help |
| List of All Departments List | Departments & Staff Directory |
| Department Links Section | Staff Directory |
| Department Resources Section | Departments Directory |
| Class Pages List (Guides for Specific Courses) | Find Information (All Subscription Resources) |
| Class Page (Guide for Specific Course) | Search Help |
| Libraries at other IU Campuses List | Subscription Resource User Guide |
| All Libraries at IUB List | Subscription Resource Description |
| A-Z List | E-Mail Comments Form |

part of every template. While the metadata fields varied based on the template, common metadata fields for pages included:

| | |
|---|---|
| Page ID | Date Added |
| Page Name | Date Updated |
| Page Title | Parent Relationship |
| Page Description | Page Owner |
| Page Keywords | Page Status (Live or Hidden) |
| Page Author | Page Permissions |

Using the specification document, the designer would create a graphic representation of the interface for the template using Photoshop software. The team would review the PSD (Photoshop Document) and discuss or suggest changes accordingly. When a final PSD was produced, the programmers would take the PSD to create the graphics and program the template. Figure 2 is the template used to submit the hours of operation for a library.

*Figure 2. Library hours template interface*

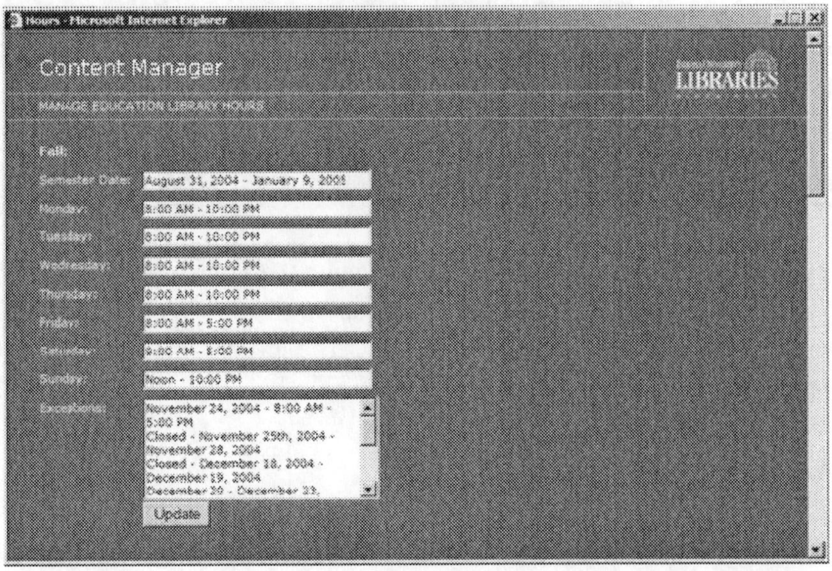

Staff designated as the content provider for each library enters their hours of operation into the hours template. Library hours are accessible from several locations on the public site including the homepage for that library.

Templates were divided into "managers" for different parts of the public site. For example, a Library Site Manager included a template for the text or content for their homepage, the hours of operation template, a template for creating a list of Useful Links section of the page, and a template for creating a Recommended Resources (online subscription resources) section of the page.

In addition to creating a content template for each page of the live public site, the team also had to describe the workflow for publishing. In most cases publishing content was designed to be very direct and immediate. Libraries would be responsible for the content of their hours, collections, and homepage. However, there were some pages of the public site that were designed to undergo review prior to publishing. The diagram in Figure 3 defines the workflow for submitting items to publish on the "News & Events" section of the public Web site.

All Librarians and staff may submit news items to the News & Events Manager to publish on the News & Events Section of the public site. The page owner (The IUB Libraries' External Relations and Development Office) receives e-mail notification that there are news items pending review. The owner has the option to review and edit the item before publishing or to reject it.

The first phase of the content manager allowed staff a minimal level of flexibility in presenting their content. The system allowed content providers to indent, bold, italicize, and underline text and create links, bulleted lists, and anchors. Figure 4 is the input form for editing the content of a library page. The same input form was used for departments and collections pages.

## Practical Development

Prior to the development of the content manager, the libraries' had to purchase new servers for development and operation of the new Web system. Three servers were purchased and housed in one of the server facilities operated by University Information Technology Services. The basic specifications for each of the servers is in the table as follows:

| Server Type | Web | Web | Database |
|---|---|---|---|
| Purpose | Development /Testing | Web Site/Content Manager | Database |
| Operating System | Solaris 9 | Sun | Solaris 9 |
| Environment | UNIX | UNIX | UNIX |
| Software | PHP | PHP | MySQL |
| Processor | 248Mhz (floating point) | 750 MHz (floating point) | * |

*Figure 3. News & Events workflow*

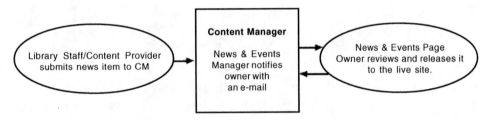

The libraries had a cooperative relationship with UITS and relied on them in providing server maintenance and support for the IU Library Catalog (IUCAT) and other technology-based public services. UITS houses the Web system servers and library staff manage the servers.

## Content Storage and Retrieval

Every public Web page of the site is stored in the database with a unique identifier "pageId." The page table of the database contains information regarding the page metadata, page hierarchy relationship, page ownership and permissions, page status, and most importantly, what template to use. Pages are constructed using a series of Server Side Includes in each template to keep consistency and to create modules for isolating sections for editing.

The pageId requested from the public Web site determines which template and content to deliver. There is a common file included in all templates used to

*Figure 4. Web page content template*

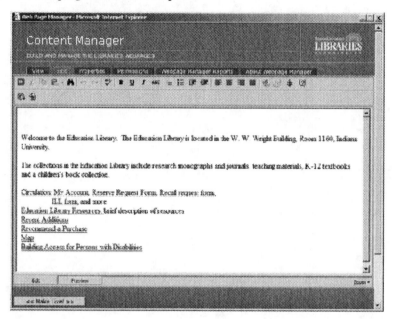

execute all the queries necessary to build the different pieces of the navigation (top navigation, quick list of campus libraries, ticker, main navigation, bread crumb navigation, left sub-navigation). Then the template will execute page- or template-specific MySQL queries such as getting a list of libraries, collections, and departments for the A-Z list. At this point the database connection is closed and the page is delivered. Figure 5 graphically represents the content flow.

In order to develop a fully functional content management system, it was necessary to integrate human resource (HR) information management into the libraries' Web system. Staff records were needed to allow individuals to log into the CM and have access to the Web content in various forms. Also, human resources data defines relationships of staff to departments and libraries, making it possible to create staff directories within each library or department template, as well as making it possible to have a real-time staff directory with current contact and position information available on the public site.

## CM Interface

The CM interface had the potential of being very complex because of the variety and volume of templates. The IUB Library staff workstations are all PCs

*Figure 5. Content flow*

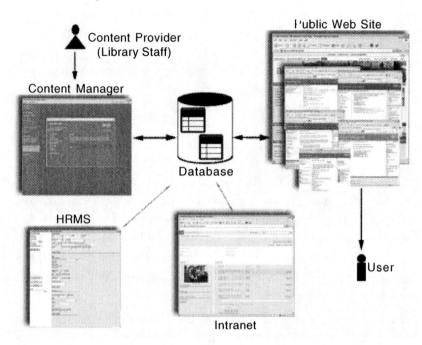

running Microsoft XP, and because the CM audience was internal, it allowed the programmers to leverage tools supported by Microsoft Internet Explorer. To create a system that could display all of the information and still allow for easy management and editing, modeless windows (a feature of IE5 or higher that displays a pop-up window that stays active/visible on the user's screen until it is closed) were implemented for controlling all open windows of the application efficiently. Additionally, Microsoft Internet Explorer afforded the programmers the use of iFrames, enabling processing data without submitting and reloading the Web page. The use of InnerHTML, dynamically generated by JavaScript, was used to make it easier for CM users to interact with the data. InnerHTML allows for many different views of the same page. As users click, HTML content is generated and delivered within the same page, making it possible to use a tab system within each manager window to divide all of the functions that needed to occur (page views, content, properties, permissions, and reports can all appear in one window for a particular Web page). Figure 6 is the content manager interface for managing a library site.

The managers for library, collection, and department pages were built with a series of tabbed "pages" to create access to the following: a view of the current page or content on the public site, a text editor that utilizes a WYSIWYG text editor for word processing features, a properties page for entering metadata about the page, permissions for allowing multiple authorized users to edit the particular page, a reports page that displays logs and other summary information about who has accessed the manager and what changes have occurred over time, and an "About" tab used to describe the purpose of the manager and give initial directions for beginning work.

## Authentication and Access

The HR database allows all library staff to login and view all of the content within the templates, but only page (template) owners can edit and make changes. Library staff log into the CM using their Indiana University Bloomington username and password, then the system verifies the username with the library system HR database records. Access to the system was automatically granted to all IU library staff, but additional access can be requested and issued to other IU students, staff, or faculty.

When a CM user logs into the content management interface, he or she is presented with a list of the pages he or she owns. A CM user can give

*Figure 6. Content manager interface*

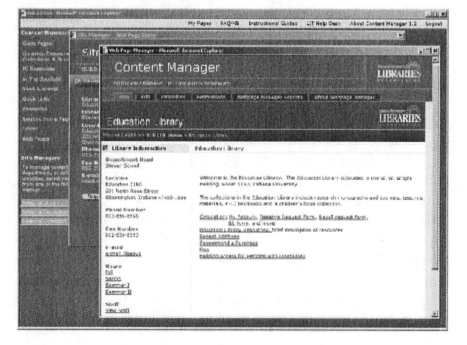

permission to others to edit pages, allowing for collaboration when necessary. While CM users cannot change information contained within the HR database, they can make requests for changes via an automated Request Change form through the content manager if location or contact information is incorrect for a person or a place. Library Human Resources is notified by e-mail from the system that a request for change has occurred. Once that change is accepted or rejected, the system in turn notifies the user, and all pertinent pages on the Web site reflect any changes that have been made.

## Staff Response to the Content Manager

Overall staff response to the content manager was mixed. Some staff expressed frustration that the new system did not allow them to use HTML to change the appearance of their Web pages, while other staff seemed excited at the opportunities the system presented. Some librarians and staff from libraries and departments enthusiastically populated their pages with content, and others simply provided a link to the site on their previous Web site. Most staff responded well because they understood that the system would grow and provide more flexibility over time.

## Training

The phased approach to the development of the CM helped to lessen the impact of learning the new system on library staff. The first release of the CM only included the ability to manage the homepage for each library, collection, and department, as well as all of the pages and sections of the central libraries' Web site. Most staff would only be required to learn how to use and manipulate a maximum of five templates within the CM for the first release.

While the CM interface was being developed, a group of team members worked with the IUB Libraries Training and Staff Development Coordinator to develop the training plan. The plan included three training options to accommodate a variety of learning styles as well as busy schedules. The team members responsible for training provided "Instructional Guides" and created entries for an "FAQ" that are available on a menu bar within the CM. The team members designed a hands-on training session to be offered at various times over a two-month period. The Training and Staff Development Coordinator learned the system and offered on-demand, one-on-one training sessions. For additional support, a CM users' electronic mailing list was established for sending notices about available features as they were released, tips on using the content manager, and announcements dealing with any technical issues.

The team scheduled a series of hands-on training sessions and offered blocks of sessions to groups of staff with similar types of Web pages. Staff members with technology experience attended the training sessions. Permissions were granted at the beginning of every training session to insure that the correct user was designated as the owner of a page. While a user cannot make changes to a page without being assigned as the owner or added to the permissions field, all staff listed in the HR database had the ability to login to the system and browse. However, most of the staff had not seen the CM interface prior to the training session. All library staff could attend training, and librarians were invited to bring their student employee assistants. The team scheduled 90-minute training sessions to allow librarians and staff to populate the new page with content during the session so that they could get help if needed. The scheduled hands-on sessions were offered in July and August, 2003 and received relatively low attendance. Most attendees did not populate their sites at the time of the training session.

## Post Implementation & Content Migration

With the early phases of the content manager and the new Web system complete, it is clear that the UITS Web server accounts previously used will need to remain. There are still significant amounts of content on the previous site housed on the accounts. The pages from the previous site are available through the new site via links on the various library, department, and collections Web pages. Also many libraries, departments, and collections would like to be able to use their server accounts to create specialized and unique Web resources to meet the needs of their users. As the system continues to be developed, it will have the increased ability to meet specialized needs, but the IUB Library system is large and diverse, and staff will have the ability to determine how best to meet their needs.

After the implementation of the intranet and the next phase of the content manager is developed, the team will work with librarians, staff, and administrators to develop a migration plan that will include a system of backing up content from both the old and the new site, and migrating content into the new site and redirecting users from the old pages as they are moved.

# Current Challenges Facing the Organization

The planning and implementation of the Web system was a direct outgrowth of organizational needs identified at the administrative level, and its development continues to respond to changing needs and newly identified organizational goals. As well, this has proved to be a two-way process, as users and administrators reexamine their own needs and goals in light of the possibilities afforded by the system. Following the initial launch of the system, the Web Team interviewed top-level library administrators in order to revisit goals and priorities, and to discuss desirable next steps.

A future priority mentioned by the administrators consulted was the integration of the libraries' Web site with campus-wide Web technologies, specifically Indiana University Bloomington's OneStart portal and OnCourse (course management software). More investigation will need to take place before any action is taken on this priority, but the architecture of the public site and the content manager's flexibility was designed to enhance integration with external resources and new or emerging technologies.

## Web Team

Jon Arnett, Visual Designer, Arnett Communications Media Design

Anne Haines, Library Coordinator for the School of Library and Information Science Library

Diane Dallis, Instructional Services Librarian

Juliet Hardesty, Web Applications Developer

Robert Noel, Head of the Swain Hall Library (Physics, Astronomy, Mathematics, and Computer Science Library)

Tadas Paegle, Lead Analyst/Programmer

Gwendolyn Pershing, Associate Head of the Education Library

Mary Pagliero Popp, Library Information Technology Public Services Librarian

Doug Ryner, Web Administrator

Charles Sweet, LAN Administrator/Technical Support Specialist

The authors acknowledge the many contributions of the Web Team to the case study and throughout the project, as well as the hard work and professionalism of Nancy J. Snyder, Anthony Tedeschi, and W. Dean Thompson, the Web Team graduate assistants.

# References

Bernstein, R., Caplan, J., & Glover, E. (2000, May). America's 100 most wired colleges 2000. *Yahoo! Internet Life, 6,* 114. Retrieved November 9, 2003.

Indiana University Bloomington Libraries Web Policy Committee. (2003). *IUB Libraries Public World Wide Web Site Vision Statement.* Bloomington, Indiana, USA, March.

Indiana University Bloomington Libraries. (2001). *Indiana University Bloomington Libraries Strategic Plan Summary 2001 -2003.* Retrieved November 10, 2003, from *www.indiana.edu/~libadmin/ strategic.html*

# Supporting Materials

## Questions and Answers

Question: What is the overall problem that is being addressed in this case?

Answer: The problem that the IUB Libraries are addressing is the change presented when one technology can no longer meet the needs it was intended to. Control and maintenance of the previous Web became almost impossible and access to the content was compromised by its sprawling growth.

Question: What are the factors affecting the problem related to this case?

Answer: The most significant factor affecting the problem of the previous site was the decentralized management of the site.

Question: Discuss managerial, organizational, and technological issues and resources related to this case.

Answer: Libraries often find themselves with insufficient budget and staff to provide needed services. Only 2.5 of the eight team members have job descriptions that include the development of the Web system and the rest have other responsibilities. There were potential risks to the project by relying on non-dedicated staff.

Question: What role do different players (decision makers) play in the overall planning, implementation, and management of the information technology applications?

Answer: Library administrators impact the deadlines set, the funding available for the project, and the ability to purchase the IT tools and equipment needed to complete the project. Administrators must be kept well informed of all of the issues of the project in order for them to support the development process.

Question: What are the possible alternatives and pros/cons of each alternative facing the organization dealing with problems(s) related to the case study?

Answer: Creating a Web content management system from scratch was an ambitious and at times difficult project that consumed many hours of staff time. A commercial tool would have been less flexible and the cost of ongoing support may have been expensive.

## Epilogue and Lessons Learned

The IUB Libraries Web System includes a database-driven public Web site, a subscription resource management tool, a password-protected staff Web site, and a content management tool. All were integral to the planning process for the content management system and were seen as interrelated. Organizational culture and needs will dictate the type of system needed within an organization. Long-range planning and flexibility are essential to the successful development or implementation of a content management system. The IUB Libraries' Web Team would also like to share the following insights about working on a project of this scale.

## Staffing Model

While the IUB Libraries successfully created a complete Web system, including content management with 2.5 dedicated staff and a team of volunteers, this is not an ideal staffing model for a project of this scale. The team recommends including more people dedicated to educating library staff and more programmers.

## Training/Buy-in/Education

The IUB Libraries' staff use of the system ultimately served as the most effective tool for educating library staff; however, this limited their ability to provide meaningful input into the design and development of the CM. Include time and resources for training and education in the project. Librarians and staff must be well informed of the purpose and benefits of a content management system to insure a smooth transition from an old to a new system. Their understanding of the new system is vital to the development and successful implementation.

## Resource Management

The IUB Libraries include online subscription resources in their definition of Web content. The first part of the content management system that was released was the *resource manager*. This was very well received by librarians and made it possible for those responsible for resources to control the records and ultimately control the way public Web site users accessed them. This solved many problems such as broken links to resources across hundreds of HTML pages, and demonstrated the power and purpose of a database-driven system like no other example could. The Web Team learned that this could have served as an excellent example to promote buy-in.

## Distributed Publishing Scheme

Include content providers in the development of the content management system interface. Outline the process of content creation and migration prior to development. Content providers should define the workflow within their department or unit prior to implementation to enable an efficient transition from the old system to the new.

## Prioritization

Provide training and education sessions as appropriate for library administrators to enable them to make well-informed decisions about project development priorities. Define all major priorities in advance of development to insure that the project addresses the issues that it was intended to solve. Develop a mechanism to respond to library staff and end-user feedback without losing sight of the major priorities.

# List of Additional Sources

Burdman, J.R. (1999). *Collaborative Web development: Strategies and best practices for Web sites.* Reading, MA: Addison-Wesley.

Siegel, D. (1997). *Secrets of successful Web sites: Project management on the World Wide Web.* Indianapolis, IN: Hayden Books.

Chapter V

# ScratchPad:
## A Quality Management Tool for Library Web Sites

Laura B. Cohen
University of Albany, SUNY, USA

Matthew M. Calsada
Atlas Systems, Inc., USA

Frederick J. Jeziorkowski
University of Albany, SUNY, USA

## Abstract

*This chapter describes the planning, development, and implementation of a quality management tool for an academic library Web site. It explains the impetus for the project, presents the rationale for developing the tool, and describes the system components. The tool balances the needs of Web contributors with the assurance of a professional presentation of the organization's Web site by offering a systematic workflow from development to production, with appropriate quality oversight prior to public posting. Implementation outcomes are discussed, especially as they relate to staff engagement and solving post-production issues. The authors hope that technical staff in other libraries will consider implementing a quality control tool to manage their Web sites.*

# Introduction

The Libraries at the University at Albany have developed a quality management system for their public Web site. The system, called ScratchPad, is composed of three components. MockWeb is the development site that the staff uses to create, test, and maintain their pages. WebReview is the application that makes possible the quality review and synchronization of MockWeb and the production site. The third component is the production site viewed by the public. This case study will cover the system implementation from concept through its first two years of operation. ScratchPad is freely available for public use.

The impetus for this project came from the lack of oversight of the work posted to the libraries' Web site by its many staff contributors. Errors in content and design were finding their way onto the site. The process of finding these errors and getting them fixed was time consuming and haphazard. The search for a solution led to the development of ScratchPad using existing servers, software, and staff expertise. The model that evolved split the site into a development and a production site, mediated by an application that generates a list of new and newly modified files for review prior to their transfer to the production site. With this new workflow in place, most issues are resolved on the development site. This has enhanced the quality of materials viewed by the public.

# Background

The University at Albany (UA) is a public institution located in Albany, New York, managed under the auspices of the State University of New York (SUNY). The institution was founded as the New York State Normal School in 1844 and now encompasses three campuses. The University Libraries serve two of these campuses. The main campus, situated at the western border of Albany, was constructed in 1963 and is served by the University Library and the Science Library. The campus of the Nelson A. Rockefeller College of Public Affairs and Policy is served by the Thomas E. Dewey Graduate Library. More than 17,000 students attend the UA in both undergraduate and graduate programs.

The UA Libraries are a member of the Association of Research Libraries and contain more than two million volumes, subscribe to more than 5,400 print periodicals, and house 2.8 million microform items. They employ 48 librarians, 27 professionals, and 73 clerical staff. The libraries provide a learning and working environment within a technological context. Each library offers banks of public workstations that provide access to over 200 research databases and thousands of full-text electronic journals available through both individual subscriptions and aggregator databases. Access to these resources is also available to affiliated users from off campus through the use of a proxy server. In addition, the three libraries offer one or more electronic classrooms for both credit and non-credit bearing instruction. An Interactive Media Center in the University Library provides access to multimedia productivity software and offers classes in media production throughout the year. The libraries also house the M.E. Grenander Department of Special Collections and Archives, which has engaged in digitization projects and produced Web-accessible exhibits. The libraries' management system is highly automated, including its catalog, circulation, and acquisitions modules. Most reserve materials are made available electronically using the Docutek ERes software, while interlibrary loan and document delivery transactions are automated through OCLC ILLiad.

The management structure of the UA Libraries is organized into three divisions: User Services, Collections, and Technical Services and Systems. Each division is overseen by an Assistant Director. These individuals sit on a top-level management body, the Library Policy Group (LPG), along with the heads of the two smaller libraries and the Director of Libraries.

The libraries operate on an annual budget of approximately $12 million, of which approximately half is allocated to salaries. This budget is highly dependent on the health of the SUNY system and, by extension, the State of New York. Budgetary constraints have resulted in significant cutbacks in recent years, especially in acquisitions. Several staff vacancies are being left unfilled. Even in comparatively good years, budgetary constraints have kept the IT staff relatively small and project outsourcing to a minimum. In-house solutions to technical issues are viewed as a positive contribution to library technological development as well as a wise use of limited resources.

The libraries engage in strategic planning within a five-year framework. Objectives are identified annually within the context of campus-wide strategic goals and put forward by each division for inclusion in a library-wide planning document. The plan is reviewed each year by LPG in order to assess progress and refine objectives. More specific strategic planning for the libraries' technological development is carried out by the Digital Library Steering Committee, a group composed of the members of LPG (minus the Director) and staff from the three libraries with primary responsibilities for technology. This group plans within a three-year framework and revisits its goals annually.

Outside of departmental operations, the UA Libraries do much of their work through a complex committee structure. This includes permanent governance committees whose members are elected, administrative committees appointed by the Director, and a myriad of ad hoc groups convened to undertake short-term projects. Technology concerns are usually the purview of administrative committees. These include the Digital Library Steering Committee noted above, the Technology Managers Group that plans hardware and software offerings, the Library Web Site Operational Team that administers the Web site infrastructure, and the Online Public Interface Committee that designs the interface of the online catalog and its subsystems such as SFX. Other committees have a hand in technology planning if only because technology is integral to the UA Libraries environment.

# Setting the Stage

ScratchPad was developed in a library environment in which the Web site was regarded as a crucial component of the institution's provision of resources and services. Moreover, the site had been in existence for many years under stable management that was familiar with the work habits of its contributors and some of the problems these presented. These Web builders (as the UA Libraries staff contributors are called) had direct access to the site and posted new or revised content at will. In essence, there was no supervised workflow. The lack of systematic review of new content was resulting in errors appearing on the public site. As the UA Libraries in-house technical expertise evolved, new opportunities opened up for maintaining the site at a higher professional level.

## The UA Libraries Web Site and its Contributors

The UA Libraries Web site was established in 1994 and now consists of nearly 3,000 pages. A portion of its content is driven by databases, including its lists of research databases, new titles acquired by the libraries, and its subject collection of Internet resources maintained by the bibliographers. The site is typical of an ARL library site in that it features information about the libraries and their services, offers access to academic research and reference materials, provides guides to library research, and serves as a medium for announcing news and events. Many services are available through interactive request forms. Both the Science and Dewey Libraries maintain their own sites, linked from the main screen of the general libraries site. Other sub-sections of the site are maintained by the Interactive Media Center, Special Collections and Archives, Reference, and other departmental units requiring a Web presence. During the 2002-2003 fiscal year, spanning July 1-June 30, the site received approximately 6.3 million page views and 1.8 million visits. The site has a worldwide audience because of the quality of its research materials, tutorials, and archival finding aids and exhibits.

Since its inception, the UA Libraries site has been managed by the Library Web Administrator who is situated within the User Services Division. During its first five years of operation, the site was hosted on a Unix server managed by the campus Academic Computing unit. Web builders were given permission to write to the server on an individual basis. Requests for these permissions were made by the Library Web Administrator to Academic Computing staff. FTP or a Samba server interface were utilized by the Web builders to upload files to the site. The UA Libraries acquired their own servers in 2000 and hosted the site on the Windows operating system. The Library Web Administrator became responsible for assigning write permissions to the Web builders, and file uploads took place within the libraries' internal NT network. Management of the site infrastructure was eventually transferred to the Library Web Site Operational Team convened by the Library Web Administrator.

Management of the UA Libraries Web site is charged to an administrative committee composed of staff from the constituent libraries, with the Library Web Administrator as an *ex officio* member. This group defines the Web site mission and policies, identifies needed new content areas, develops standards for the Web builders, and directs periodic site redesigns. The committee also serves as a conduit for both staff and user feedback. The current group is called the Library Web Site Policy Committee.

Content for the Web site is contributed by a roster of staff from the ranks of librarians and professionals, as well as a number of students who serve as graduate assistants, interns, or temporary employees. These Web builders include bibliographers and archivists from the Collections Division, and reference and instruction librarians from the User Services Division. Currently, close to 40 individuals contribute to the site.

# Web Builder Practices

Web builder culture at the UA Libraries can best be described as independent and hands-on. Knowledge of HTML, for example, has long been considered a virtue. There are two reasons for this. First, the Web site was established before the era of HTML editors. There was little choice but to write code in text editors such as Emacs and Pico on Unix, or WordPad and NotePad on Windows. Hand-coding became an early part of Web builder culture by default. Second, knowledge at the code level is seen as empowering, a skill that gives the Web builders ultimate control over their work. This is especially important, since a wide variety of materials is posted to the site and it is not currently feasible to develop templates to satisfy all needs. Accordingly, hands-on HTML training has been provided to library staff for many years.

Template-based Web page development, backed by an SQL database server, was introduced in 2003 primarily for subject guides. These are listings of Web resources in academic subject areas maintained by the bibliographers in the Collections Division. While this has relieved some of the need to create original pages, much of the UA Libraries site continues to be maintained in independent files.

In recent years, HTML editors have become a part of the Web builders' repertoire. Dreamweaver and HTML Kit have been established as standard tools. Bibliographers have also been using Netscape Composer because of its ease of use. The UA Libraries now require pages to be written in XHTML, and to incorporate the use of Cascading Style Sheets and Server Side Includes. Some knowledge of HTML coding is therefore still required.

To assist the Web builders in their work, tutorial-based training is made available on the UA Libraries' in-house staff intranet site. There are tutorials on writing code in XHTML, using Cascading Style Sheets and Server Side Includes, creating well-formed URLs, constructing interactive forms, uploading files to the site, and others.

Until the implementation of ScratchPad, the supervision of Web site maintenance was minimal. The Web builders uploaded files directly to the site from individual permission accounts configured on the production Web server. The content and design of new pages were reviewed by a subgroup of the Web site administrative committee in force at the time. This activity was limited primarily to the subject pages developed by the bibliographers. Other work usually went unseen prior to production. Revisions of existing pages were rarely reviewed.

This aspect of Web builder practice would prove to be the biggest cultural challenge facing the ScratchPad project.

As a growing number of Web builders produced a greater variety of pages, the system began to reveal its limitations. Errors began appearing on the production site, including broken images, design flaws, dead links, and typos. Out-of-date information was left unchanged. These problems were noticed piecemeal, usually by the Library Web Administrator, who was required to contact each Web builder individually to explain the problem and request a fix. This procedure was proving inadequate for a growing and increasingly important site.

## Technology Development Within the UA Libraries

The UA Libraries technology infrastructure is managed by a Library Systems Department within the Technical Services and Systems Division. This is a small department consisting of a Head and five staff in non-librarian professional positions. The technical infrastructure for the libraries is handled in-house, including Web services and related applications. A majority of these services reside in a Microsoft Windows 2000/SQL Server environment. The one exception is the maintenance of the library management system servers. These reside within the university's Unix cluster, which is administered by a centralized Information Technology Services Department within the university.

In the late 1990s, the UA Libraries' administration recognized that in-house software development was necessary to move the institution forward as it acquired a growing number of digital resources, and its Web site was becoming an essential medium for accessing these resources. This concern led to the hiring of an Electronic Resources Programmer/Analyst. This individual became the source of a number of technology innovations, including the WebReview component of ScratchPad.

The Systems Department utilizes a variety of development tools and programming languages. Based on project needs, the department has developed both Windows and Web applications. Web applications primarily employ Active Server Pages scripted in VBScript with a SQL Server database backend. These technologies integrate with the Windows servers that maintain the libraries' Web presence.

# Case Description

ScratchPad is a quality management system for the UA Libraries Web site comprised of three components: the development site, the production site, and the application that makes possible the quality review and synchronization of the two sites.

The inspiration for ScratchPad came out of an assessment of the overall UA Libraries Web infrastructure by the newly appointed NT Programmer/Analyst. Having come from a position providing content management in the private sector, he identified a need for a structured quality assurance policy and content management system for the libraries' Web environment. This need was reinforced by discussions with the Library Web Administrator, who shared these concerns. As a result of these discussions, they decided to set up a development site so that the Web builders could create their work on a copy of the live site in a real-time server environment. From here, they began to assemble the components of a quality management system that would bridge this test environment to the production site. To achieve this, they formed a team with the Electronic Resources Programmer/Analyst to develop an application that would move content from test to production.

In settling on the ScratchPad system, the project team was aware that there were other models to be weighed as options. In one such model, files are developed off-line, and one or more individuals review all new and revised files and upload them to the site. This was rejected as too cumbersome because of the large number of content providers and the quantity of daily Web development activity. The opposite extreme, in which a complete content management system would be utilized, was also deemed impractical. The UA Libraries employ only one electronic resources programmer, and he could not be expected to develop a system that would encompass the wide range of content, presentation, and design required for the libraries' site. Further, purchasing a complete content management system developed by a third party was beyond the libraries' budget. Another model would allow Web builders to contribute content to the site from their personal Web space provided by the university, which would be linked from the public site. This scenario has never been attractive to the UA Libraries. Although the review process had been limited in scope over the years, the centralized storage of Web site files was an early practice that became embedded in Web development culture and was considered the preferred approach.

Once the project team had defined the ScratchPad system, its development and implementation had to be approved. The team determined that LPG would be the appropriate forum, as this was the highest administrative body in the libraries. The team submitted a proposal to LPG and it was approved.

## The Development and the Production Site

The team set up the development site on a separate machine from the one hosting the public site. There were several reasons for this. Security was a major concern, as so many Web builders had write access to the production environment. This left the site vulnerable to viruses, Trojans, misuse of space, and countless other potential exploits. In addition, the new environment added another layer of redundancy to existing backup systems. Finally, a separate server would provide a place where new ideas could be tested without the risk of bringing down the primary Web server.

The development site, named MockWeb, was configured to be an exact replica of the production site. Write permissions were also duplicated to preserve the Web builders' access to their material.

## The WebReview Application

WebReview is an application that promotes editorial review of Web pages contributed to the UA Libraries Web site. It accomplishes this by generating a list of new and revised files from the MockWeb development site, and transferring them to the production site following their review. The application was created on the premise that the two sites should be synchronized, that is, the development and production sites should mirror one another in structure and content.

It is important to note that WebReview also processes files generated by the UA Libraries' new content management system for the bibliographers' subject pages. This is a database-driven Windows application that provides form-based management of the content of these pages. Static pages are produced by XML-based templates. These pages are sent to MockWeb whenever content is revised. They are therefore picked up by WebReview along with all the others. This strategy has opened up many possibilities for the management of the Web site, since data-driven content can fall under the purview of a central quality review process.

WebReview was developed using Active Server Pages, a SQL Server database, and batch files. It was created as a Web application primarily because the project team was most familiar with this method of development. Moreover, the nature of the project was well suited to this strategy. WebReview's purpose is reviewing Web pages and associated files, so it made sense to develop it as a native Web application.

The following describes the sequence of events executed by WebReview:

## 1. Compilation of a file inventory

SQL Server was employed for this phase of the application because it provided the best option for storing the file metadata of the two sites and allowed for an efficient operation for comparing this metadata. The alternative, which would compare the sites on a file-by-file basis, proved to be extremely inefficient and time intensive.

The basic algorithm uses VBScript to compile an inventory of all files on both sites. The data gathered includes the filename, file path, creation timestamp, and modification timestamp. This information is inserted into two SQL tables, SourceFiles and TargetFiles, using VBScript (see Figure 1) and a stored procedure (see Figure 2). Stored procedures are SQL queries saved on the database server for efficient and repeated use. The efficiency of stored procedures is derived from the fact that the query itself is not sent over the network, but rather only the stored procedure name. As an additional benefit, stored procedures are cached.

The file inventories are scheduled every thirty minutes, and can also be run manually. With this in place, file transfers to the production site can take place any time of the day.

## 2. Web page generation and quality review

After a file inventory is completed, the reviewer launches an Active Server Page that displays data on the new and modified files. This data is derived from the comparison of the file modification dates on the development and production sites. The comparison is performed using a stored procedure (see Figure 3).

The query result is displayed on the Web page in tabular format, with columns for the hyperlinked file name, modification date, and time on both sites, as well

*Figure 1. VBScript for file inventory operation*

```
sub TraverseFolder(objFolder)

 'Only process directories that do NOT start with an underscore or the

 'WebReview directory

 Dim objFile, FileName, FilePath, CreateDate, ModifyDate

        FileName = objFile.Name

        FilePath = objFolder.Path

        CreateDate = objFile.DateCreated

        ModifyDate = objFile.DateLastModified


        'Iterate through each file in the folder

 For Each objFile in objFolder.Files

        cn.Execute "qryUpdateFiles 'MockWeb'," & Filename &_

        & "', '" & & "'," & CreateDate & "'," & ModifyDate &_

        & "'," & Now() & ""

        Next


        'Recurse through the folder's subdirectories if needed

        Dim objSubFolder

        For Each objSubFolder in objFolder.SubFolders

        TraverseFolder(objSubFolder)

        Next

 end sub
```

*Figure 2. Stored procedure for file inventory operation*

```
CREATE PROCEDURE qryUpdateFiles

@server as varchar(255),

@filename as varchar(255),

@folder as varchar(255),

@created as smalldatetime,

@modified as smalldatetime,

@dbload as smalldatetime

AS

declare @count as int

set @count = 0

if ltrim(lower(@server)) = 'production'

begin

        select @count=count(*) from targetfiles where [folder] = @folder

        and [filename] = @filename

if @count > 0

        update TargetFiles set Creationtime = @Created,

        Modifiedtime = @Modified, DatabaseLoaddate = @DBload

        where [filename]= @Filename and folder = @folder

else

        insert into TargetFiles ([Filename], folder, creationtime,

        modifiedtime, databaseloaddate) values (@Filename, @folder,

        @created, @modified, @dbload)

end
```

*Figure 3. Stored procedure for file comparison operation*

```
CREATE PROCEDURE qryFileCompare

as

select s.[filename] as SourceFilename, s.[folder] as SourceFolder, s.[modifiedtime] as

SourceModified, s.creationtime as SourceCreated, t.creationtime as TargetCreated,

t.modifiedtime as TargetModified, s.Status as SourceStatus, s.Comment as

SourceComment, s.StatusDate as SourceStatusDate from sourcefiles s left join targetfiles

t on s.folder = t.folder and s.[filename] = t.[filename] where dateadd(n,1,t.modifiedtime)

< s.modifiedtime or t.modifiedtime is null order by s.folder, s.[filename]
```

as a text box for the reviewer's comments. These comments relate to any problems discovered during the review process and explain the reasons why a particular file was not transferred. There are also columns for "Send" and "No Send," with radio buttons for selecting either option. The form defaults to "Send" (see Figure 4). During the quality review process, the reviewer clicks

*Figure 4. File review Web page produced by the WebReview application*

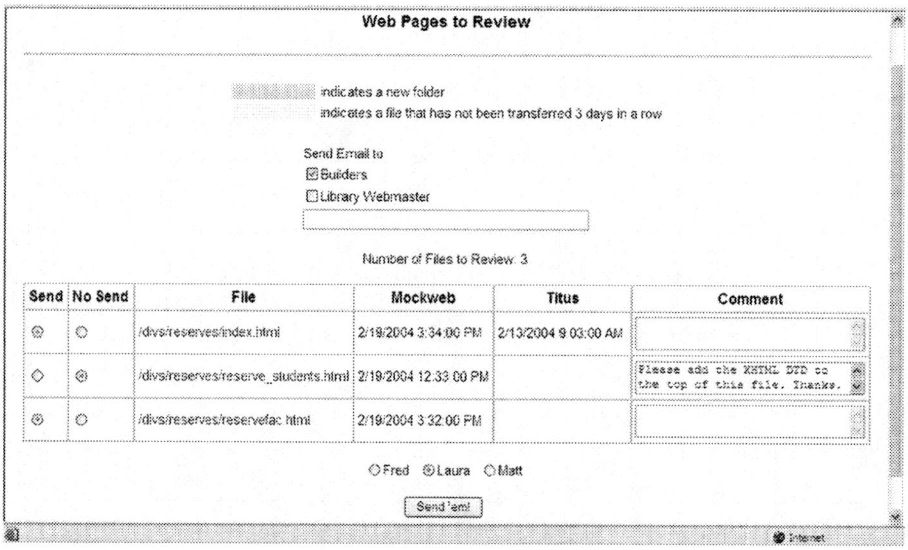

on each hyperlinked file name and scans each Web page. If problems are observed, the radio button in the "No Send" column is selected and comments are entered in the text box. Comments are stored in the database so that problem files appearing on the list in subsequent days will be accompanied by the reviewer's notes.

### 3. File transfer to the production site

When the reviewer has finished checking the pages, a Submit button is clicked and the form is processed. The script creates a batch file to perform the copy operation and also generates an e-mail notification message for the Web builders (see next section). To generate the batch file, the script checks the "Send" or "No Send" designation for each modified file. If "Send" has been selected, a copy command is added to the batch file. If "No Send" has been designated, the file name will added to the e-mail message. The batch file also sends copies of the transferred files to the backup site on another server.

This part of the operation also updates the database in preparation for the next review session. The file status (e.g., sent or not sent), the time of the last review, and any comments are all updated. These are made manifest when the review page is next generated so that, for example, "No Send" becomes the default in rows listing any files not transferred during the previous review session.

### 4. E-mail notification

The WebReview script generates an e-mail message that is sent to the Web builders' listserv to confirm the file transfer. Either one of two messages is sent. If all the modified files were transferred to the production site, the message simply states this. If any files were held back, the message has a different subject line and includes a hyperlinked list of these files along with the reviewer's comments. The hyperlinks allow the Web builders easy access to their files from within the message to confirm the comments noted (see Figure 5).

At this point, Web builders are required to address the reviewer's concerns. Once this has been accomplished, the files in question are copied to the production site during the next review session.

*Figure 5. Message to Web builders about daily file transfer*

---

10/24/2003 7:56:59 AM


A review of recently updated Web site files identified technical problems or files that do

not appear to be complete. If you maintain any of these files, please revise them so they

can be uploaded to the production site.


If you have any questions, feel free to contact Laura.


http://mockWeb.ulib.albany.edu/divs/speccoll/campusbuildings/alden.htm


Comment: I'm sorry, but I couldn't send over the exhibit because the Minerva icon is

incorrectly sized. The width should be "288" and not "228." A search-and-replace should

do the trick.

---

## 5. File and folder deletion

To maintain the synchronization between MockWeb and the production site, a file and folder deletion operation is performed as the final step in WebReview. A separate Active Server Page script executes a stored procedure that identifies files and folders that are on the production site but not on MockWeb. A Web page is generated that displays these items. The reviewer has the option to execute the deletion or copy an item to MockWeb. The latter would be the case if a file or folder on MockWeb has been accidentally deleted. As with the copy operation described above, these deletions are executed from a batch file (see Figure 6).

*Figure 6. Batch job for file and folder deletion*

```
del \\Prod\wwwroot\new\jstor.html

copy \\Prod\wwwroot\new\muse.html \\Development\mockWeb\new\muse.html

del \\Prod\wwwroot\services\newspapers.html

del \\Prod\wwwroot\usered\style\mla.pdf
```

# Current Challenges/Problems Facing the Organization

ScratchPad has been in operation for two years. There is no question that it has succeeded in its goal of establishing a quality review process for the UA Libraries Web site. As with any major change in process that affects a large number of people, this goal was not achieved without difficulties. It is fair to say that ScratchPad provided a learning experience for both the project team and library staff in adjusting to the new system. A number of issues arose following the implementation of ScratchPad which can be divided generally into cultural and technical issues.

## Training

When ScratchPad was launched, documentation was provided to inform the Web builders about the new system and to teach them how to use it. This documentation was mounted on the Libraries' staff intranet site. It included an FAQ as well as a how-to guide with step-by-step instructions, including screen shots, that demonstrated the method of uploading files to the development site. The project team determined that the daily file transfer would take place after 3:30 p.m., and Web builders were advised to complete their work accordingly.

Several months after the implementation of ScratchPad, the Assistant Director for Collections informed the Library Web Administrator that the bibliographers had several questions about using the system. This came as a surprise, as little indication of this had reached her. The Library Web Administrator and Electronic Resources Programmer/Analyst subsequently conducted classes on the use of ScratchPad. These sessions included background on the system and its components, a demonstration of uploading files to MockWeb, and tips about common issues. Approximately a dozen individuals attended each session, including a few who did not even use ScratchPad, but were interested in learning how the system worked. The sessions received positive feedback, and served as a cautionary tale to the project team that instruction sessions should be routine for any newly implemented system.

Another training issue was the endeavor to settle on the optimal method of uploading files to MockWeb. Three different strategies have been taught. Initially, the team recommended that Web builders work from master copies stored in their office computers. Once a file was ready for production, it was copied to MockWeb using a folder shortcut placed on individual desktops. The shortcut was derived by clicking through the libraries' network to an appropriate MockWeb folder. This practice originated in the days before the existence of MockWeb when Web builders posted directly to the production site. It was hoped that staff would review their pages locally prior to posting in order to reduce the number of errors seen by the public.

During the training sessions on ScratchPad, the team introduced an alternative method. Web builders were shown how to create a Network Place to a MockWeb folder. Using the Network Place, they could perform a Save or Save As operation from within an HTML editor.

A final recommendation was based on the proven success of ScratchPad. Since MockWeb was set up as a development environment, and with a daily review process now in place, it was no longer necessary to maintain local copies of files. In addition, the project team was receiving reports that some of the Web builders were having trouble locating their local copies to upload, especially if they had saved multiple versions. The Library Web Administrator released a new set of instructions that recommended maintaining files directly on MockWeb. She held an instruction session to demonstrate the technique, and the use of local copies was discontinued. This strategy has a built-in advantage for a Web site that has common design elements on many of its pages. Since all files are maintained on MockWeb, the Library Web Administrator can make design changes across the site without the concern that these changes will be overwritten by local copies.

# Adjustment to a Quality Control Process

ScratchPad was a major departure from the way in which Web work had been accomplished since the inception of the UA Libraries site. With ScratchPad, Web builders had to get accustomed to a daily review process after a prolonged period during which the freedom to post directly to the public site had become an entrenched aspect of Web development culture. An intermediary now reviewed all files before they could be posted to the production site. This intermediary was most often the Library Web Administrator, and in her absence, the other project team members. A few of the Web builders expressed embarrassment about seeing their files listed in an e-mail message sent to the listserv. The project team made an effort to be tactful in the comments inserted into the message, and over time, the process has been accepted.

The matter of content review was controversial. About a year after ScratchPad was launched, the Library Web Site Policy Committee was convened by the Director. The formulation of a cohesive set of standards for Web development was given top priority. These standards mandated XHTML transitional coding and a number of design requirements. Content on new pages and extensively revised pages was required to be reviewed by the individual Web builder's Assistant Director prior to posting to the production site.

One aspect of the published standard led to widespread misunderstanding. The Library Web Administrator's daily review was mistaken for a review of substantive rather than editorial content. Editorial review performed by the Library Web Administrator concerned only factual accuracy such as contact information or service realities, typos, and the like. The negative response to the new policies led to a revised version that included a careful differentiation between content review performed by the Assistant Directors and editorial review performed by the Library Web Administrator. Once this was spelled out, the controversy abated. Ultimately, the daily review process has reinforced the usefulness of ScratchPad within the institution, since it has helped to insure adherence to the new standards.

# Test Space on the Development Site

MockWeb is a site that does double duty. It mirrors the production site in structure and content, but must also provide test space for the Web builders.

Soon after implementation, the project team identified the need to provide space on MockWeb for Web pages that were still in development. This was, in fact, a key advantage of providing the Web builders with a test environment. Since WebReview identifies all new and modified files, development space was needed outside of the site synchronization scheme. The team decided that any folder named "noupload" would serve as this space. The Library Web Administrator encouraged the Web builders to create these folders wherever they were needed. This has since become a general practice. Once a file is ready for the public, the Web builder moves it out of noupload and into its parent folder, where the WebReview script will identify it.

Noupload folders have presented a few challenges. Files in these folders are not linked to anything on the MockWeb site. Viewing them in a browser requires manual manipulation of the URL in order to make a connection. This has proven to be difficult for some of the Web builders. In addition, the use of relative URLs within noupload folders is also problematic. The Library Web Administrator has long encouraged the use of relative URLs for links to files within the local site. Setting the correct path in noupload URLs can be difficult since files in these folders are at least one level down from their ultimate location. Training the Web builders in these issues has been an ongoing task.

## Format of the Notification E-Mail Message

A number of changes were made to the format of the e-mail message sent to the Web builders' listserv subsequent to each daily review. The project team noted early on that Web builders were having difficulty remembering to complete their work before the 3:30 p.m. deadline each afternoon. The staff frequently complained to the Library Web Administrator that their revisions were not appearing on the production site as expected. To address this problem, the date and time of the file transfer were inserted into the daily e-mail message using a VBScript function. This solution worked well, as questions about the time of the daily transfer eventually ceased.

Another issue with the e-mail message was the repeated appearance of "No Send" files on the list when a Web builder did not make timely revisions. This sometimes made it difficult to locate newly listed files. The problem was solved by using WebReview to compare the file's modification date with the current date and time. If the difference was greater than two days, the repeat file was placed in a secondary reminder list of outstanding issues. This has kept the daily list fresh.

Finally, the name of the project team reviewer was added to the message so that Web builders would know who to contact with questions or concerns. This was accomplished by placing radio buttons on the WebReview page for each member of the team to select as part of the review process. By doing so, the team member took explicit responsibility for decisions made.

## Reviewing Large Groups of Related Files

Large groups of new files present a challenge, especially if they are related pages that link to one another. If problems are identified in one or more of these files, the reviewer must be careful not to transfer all the other related files since this would result in missing content and broken links within the new presentation. Holding back a large number of files can be tedious, as all of the related files listed for review must be individually checked in the "No Send" column on the Active Server Page. The Electronic Resources Programmer/Analyst solved this problem by creating clickable buttons that change the transfer designation across any individual folder.

In a related matter, Web builders have been asked to notify the Library Web Administrator prior to launching large numbers of files simultaneously, for example, a new instructional module or exhibit. This alerts the Library Web Administrator that a cohesive set of files will require imminent review. Web builders have been diligent about providing such notification.

## Special Requests

As noted previously, the WebReview process takes place after 3:30 p.m. on weekdays. Since this deadline imposes a blackout period for posting to the production site, the Library Web Administrator came to the realization that she needed to provide a special request service for manual file transfers. The service could be requested at any time after 3:30 p.m. until the next day's file transfer. The Web builders have gladly taken advantage of this offer. Requests are generally made when staff are anxious about correcting errors or posting important updates. These have not imposed a burden on the Library Web Administrator, and have served the additional purpose of providing flexibility to and "humanizing" the system.

## Issues for the Project Team

While ScratchPad has required adjustments by the Web builders, the project team has faced its own issues. The WebReview application has needed revisions, and support documentation has been frequently updated. The MockWeb site had to be incorporated into daily backup operations.

Any end user technology requires support, and Web builder training has been ongoing. Even many months after ScratchPad was launched, new issues have arisen. For example, a staff member recently informed the Library Web Administrator that she doesn't trust MockWeb to show her pages in their final form. The project team has learned to expect the unexpected and to deal with these issues accordingly.

The WebReview process is a task that had to be added to the Library Web Administrator's daily workload. Since this job is usually completed at the end of the day, it is sometimes an effort to go through the day's files if there is an extensive list. Whenever the Library Web Administrator is away, she needs to arrange for another member of the team to take over this work. In essence, WebReview has become another essential daily task in the maintenance of the libraries' Web site infrastructure.

# Conclusion

In the two years since ScratchPad was implemented, use of this system has become a routine aspect of maintaining the UA Libraries Web site. All Web development activity now passes through the intermediary of WebReview. The daily review process has established a systematic, time-efficient process of quality review and has succeeded in catching problems that could compromise the professional standing of the production site. ScratchPad has also proven its worth in helping to ensure adherence to the libraries' Web development standards.

In recognition of the usefulness of ScratchPad, the project team has made the application freely available at http://library.albany.edu/scratchpad/.

The team recognizes that ScratchPad is not a finished product. As new issues arise and technologies emerge, the system will evolve and be further developed. For example, its ability to incorporate static files fed from databases is providing the team with opportunities to take the UA Libraries Web site to the next level of infrastructure sophistication. Remaining open to improvement is the key.

# Supporting Materials

## Questions and Answers

Question: What is the overall problem in this case?

Answer: The problem was the lack of quality control in the management of an academic library Web site. Web contributors posted their work directly on the production site with little or no review prior to posting. As a result, errors in content and design were finding their way onto the site.

Question: Discuss managerial, organizational, and technological issues and resources related to this case.

Answer: Web management staff needed to come together as a team and determine the appropriate technology to address the quality control problem based on team expertise and technologies available within the organization.

Question: What role do different players (decision makers) play in the overall planning, implementation, and management of the information technology applications?

Answer: The development of the content management tool was a bottom-up project. The team members had to gain approval from top management to develop their in-house solution. Implementation had to be coordinated with the Web contributors' supervisors so that the new system could become an agreed-upon part of the staff Web development obligation. Post-implementation issues were managed cooperatively by the project team.

Question: What are the possible alternatives and pros and cons of each alternative facing the organization in dealing with the problem related to the case?

Answer: A continued lack of quality control oversight would give the Web contributors greater freedom in their work, but also perpetuate the problem of an error-prone site. A complete content management system driven entirely by forms would exert rigorous control, but the organization could not afford such a solution and also preferred to offer latitude in Web development options.

Question: What is the final solution that can be recommended to the management of the organization described in the case?

Answer: The solution is a quality management system that balances the needs of Web contributors with the assurance of a professional presentation of the organization's Web site. The system offers an organized workflow, from development to production, with quality oversight prior to public posting.

# Epilogue

With the implementation of ScratchPad, ongoing quality control of all revisions to the institution's Web site is ensured. All Web site work now takes place on a development site. The WebReview application generates a list of all new and newly revised files for review by project team staff. No files can be transferred to the production site without this review. In the two years since the implementation of ScratchPad, the quality of the production Web site has been noticeably enhanced.

# Lessons Learned

## 1. Problems can be solved when the appropriate staff identify an issue and are willing to expend the effort to act.

In the case described in this chapter, the staff with direct responsibility for the Web site infrastructure agreed that there was an issue they needed to address. The idea for the quality management tool succeeded because the project team sought the appropriate approvals, used existing resources and expertise, and provided post-implementation support. The team was also willing to make the new system a part of their day-to-day Web management operations.

## 2. When limited by tight budgets, in-house solutions can be a good choice, given the requisite staff expertise and appropriate technologies available within the organization.

Creative use can be made of existing technologies when a project is driven by well-defined goals and sound planning.

## 3. Post-implementation issues must be tracked carefully.

The project team must be willing to be flexible about making enhancements to a system once it is in use, and staff feedback inevitably follows. Even the best planning cannot anticipate all the ramifications of a new system.

## 4. Staff engagement and training should be a high priority.

The project team may regard a new tool as so straightforward that it does not need explanation. This is rarely the case. Both written and in-person training is an important way to introduce staff to a new way of doing things, and to engage them in new tasks and responsibilities.

# List of Additional Sources

4GuysFromRolla.com. Retrieved February 23, 2004, from *www.4guysfrom rolla.com/*

Boiko, B. (2001). Understanding content management. *Bulletin of the American Society for Information Science and Technology, 28*(1). Retrieved February 17, 2004, from *www.asis.org/Bulletin/Oct-01/boiko2.html*

Browning, P., & Lowndes, M. (2002). Content management systems: Who needs them? Ariadne, *30*. Retrieved February 17, 2004, from *www. ariadne.ac.uk/issue30/techwatch/*

Good, K., & Ryan, P. (2001). Increasing staff participation in Web content development-the success of the University of Alberta Web site. *PNLA Quarterly, 65*(4), 18-19.

Google Web Directory: Content Management. Retrieved February 17, 2004, from *directory.google.com/Top/Computers/Software/Internet/ Site_Management/ContentManagement/*

McClusky-Moore, N. (2002). Untangling Web content management: Intranet, extranet and otherwise. *Intranet Journal.* Retrieved February 17, 2004, from *www.intranetjournal.com/articles/200004/im_04_18_00a.html*

Nakano, R. (2002). *Web content management: A collaborative approach.* Boston, MA: Addison-Wesley.

ScratchPad. *http://library.albany.edu/scratchpad/*

SQLTeam.com. Retrieved February 23, 2004, from *www.sqlteam.com/*

Windows Script (MSDN). Retrieved February 23, 2004, from *msdn. microsoft.com/library/default.asp?url=/nhp/default.asp?contentid= 28001169*

## Chapter VI

# Website Maintenance Workflow at a Medium-Sized University Library

Michelle Mach
Colorado State University, USA

## Abstract

*Currently, more than half the library staff at a medium-size academic library maintain large numbers of static Web pages using Web editors, rather than content management tools. While not optimal in the technical sense, this process does maximize the individual's creative contributions to the site. Because of this flexibility, feedback about this process has been primarily positive at an individual level. However, a growing number of challenges in the areas of content, priorities, technical skills, and workflow exceptions have cast doubt on this system's long-term prospects. This chapter discusses the balance between individual and group needs, and the true cost of a purely technical solution to the problem of Web maintenance.*

# Introduction

The creation of a Web site is much like the birth of a child. It is a thrilling achievement, one that is certain to change your life forever. New experiences and milestones wait around every corner. Maintenance is decidedly different. "While creating a Web site is exciting, maintaining one often comes to seem a chore" (Cox, Yeadon, & Kerr, 2001, p. 414). There are no pats on the back and hearty congratulations for each diaper change, each broken link fixed. Maintenance can seem dull, routine, and unending. No one seems to appreciate or notice daily maintenance work, unless it is forgotten. No wonder new Webmasters and parents alike suffer from burnout, stress, or fatigue.

As Shropshire (2003) states, "It is essential that there be adequate respect for the dynamic nature of this beast, because maintenance is not part of the problem-it is *the* problem" (p. 99). While site creation is certainly critical, it is those smaller day-to-day decisions that shape and direct the bigger picture. In exploring the topic of site maintenance, one must realize that the concerns of site maintenance differ from those of site creation. A new site may be created by a small team or individual, but a larger group best supports long-term maintenance for several reasons. First, site creation often occurs during a finite compressed timeframe, while maintenance is ongoing. Second, while an individual or smaller group helps keep the site creation process focused, a narrowly focused gatekeeping group that persists into the maintenance phase may inhibit the site's growth, creativity, or flexibility. Finally, creating a basic site structure is simply less work than creating all the details to support it. It is the difference between simply outlining a picture and shading it in beautiful colors.

The special concerns of Web maintenance have only multiplied with the increased size and complexity of many library Web sites. Not only does the single Webmaster model no longer work for most libraries, but the static HTML page is also in jeopardy. Many overworked Web librarians dream about the instant content updates possible with database-driven site or content management software. But while these technical solutions save staff time, they demand a fair amount of compromise. In an academic environment where individual, not team, drive and creativity are most highly rewarded, these technical solutions do not seem feasible.

This case study describes an environment where a large percentage of the library staff maintain one or more static Web pages on the library site without any content management software. A Web librarian provides supervision and oversight of the Web Implementation Team, whose members load the pages and provide technical assistance and advice. While a number of routine maintenance tasks are simplified by the use of special software, this approach is much more labor and time intensive than a completely database-driven site or one that uses content management software. On the positive side, this process maximizes staff creativity and freedom in creating a wide range of highly personalized pages.

# Background

Colorado State University (CSU) is a medium-sized, land grant university with a combined graduate and undergraduate student population of approximately 23,000. The university offers a Web page titled, "Web Site Requirements, Guidelines, and User Responsibilities," which gives minimal information such as placement of the official university logo, and links to equal opportunity and disclaimer statements. However, strict enforcement of these requirements is rare. Many departments, including the libraries, have their own Web servers and maintain their own workflows for their site.

The University Libraries is composed of a main library (Morgan) and two small branch libraries, Atmospheric Sciences and Veterinary Teaching Hospital. A third branch library, Engineering, closed in 1999. The libraries employ approximately 85 classified staff and administrative professionals and 35 library faculty. The faculty are on a tenure-track system parallel to the academic faculty. Creative library faculty or staff are recognized annually by the "Bright Idea or Project" award, given for innovation in any area of work. Since 2001, librarians also offer an annual "CSU Libraries' Faculty Award for Excellence" for outstanding contributions to the libraries, the university, or the library profession.

On Monday, July 28, 1998, a devastating flood hit Fort Collins, Colorado, and the Colorado State University campus. Camila Alire, Dean of CSU Libraries at the time, describes the scene: "On Tuesday morning, we found Morgan Library's newly renovated lower level entirely submerged under water up to one-half foot above the ceiling tiles. A portion of the library's lower-level wall caved in from the pressure of the water beating against it. A flash flood rushed into the entire lower level of the library. The strong force of the water toppled row after row of shelves full of books" (Alire, 2000, p. xix). All bound journals and close to 500,000 volumes of monographs, which made up half the collection in the building, were destroyed (Alire, 2000). A few of the subject areas that were hit the hardest included agriculture, biology, business, chemistry, education, engineering, law, mathematics, music, political science, and sociology.

The library staff did not have much time to dwell on the destruction. The CSU President ordered the library to be up and functioning on August 25 when the students returned to campus. This mandate forced the library to think more creatively about the use of technology to deliver materials and services. The Web site suddenly became a primary, rather than secondary, means of providing research materials, offering instruction, and soliciting and tracking gift donations. The online interlibrary loan system became an integral part of everyday research, rather than an occasional need. As a result, huge strides were made in delivering most requested materials to users in electronic format within a very short (one to three days) time period. The number of electronic databases jumped from 50 to 300 (Cowgill, Beam, & Wess, 2001). This increase contributed to a positive change in more faculty attitudes towards technology. Other technology enhancements during this time included the early adoption of wireless, a laptop checkout program, more services for distance users, exploration of e-reserves, and the development of an information commons area. Ideas for technology innovations flowed both top-down from library administration, as well as bottom-up from library staff. Many ideas originated from individuals at all levels, and then were researched and discussed in small groups at either a department or task force level. Projects typically might then be discussed and approved by either all department heads, or by the library dean and the assistant deans of public services, technical services, and administration. As part of this process, a combination of informal e-mail announcements, "water cooler" discussions, and formal presentations allowed all staff to give feedback throughout the process. While there was a definite hierarchal structure to decision making, the administration's "anything is possible" attitude leveled the playing field. Brainstorming, creative thinking, and innovation were heartily encouraged at all levels. The attitude was always "How can we make this work?" rather than "That's impossible!"

Students and faculty support and influence the increased technology at the libraries. Repeated student requests lead the libraries to offer word processing and other productivity software on library computers in 2000. That same year, 17 faculty on the Provost Task Force of the Library listed numerous technology-related goals in their final report. These goals included augmenting the technology infrastructure, digitizing materials in Archives and Special Collections, increasing the number of links to selected Web sites, and delivering online instruction and virtual reference. While the libraries' Web site was not specifically singled out as an area of focus, it obviously played a central role in achieving many of the stated goals.

## Setting the Stage

The libraries employed several site maintenance models since their first Web page in the mid-1990s. The initial model was an ad hoc system with a single part-time graduate student Webmaster in Library Technology Services (LTS) controlling the site. Unlike other university libraries, there are no librarians in LTS. In 1997 a formal Web Coordination Group was formed that oversaw both design and content of the site for several years, although they did little actual HTML coding themselves. In 1998, a Web Librarian was hired to oversee and maintain the library Web site. With this new position, the oversight and financial responsibility of the Web site shifted to Reference Services. LTS continued to maintain the physical machines and assisted with complicated technical tasks, such as database programming.

By late 2000, the number of pages on the library Web site had tripled from 750 in 1998 to 2,500, but the number of people who maintained the site had not changed (Cullen & Mach, 2002). The combined efforts of the Web Librarian, an undergraduate student, and a staff member equaled two full-time people. The use of the site also increased dramatically, leaping from 215,500 average hits each week in 1998 to more than a million weekly hits in 2000.

## Case Description

In 2001, the libraries experienced a cultural shift as they moved from an essentially one-person Web maintenance model to a more distributed system. There were several reasons for distributing the workload. First, the dramatic increase in pages meant that the Web Librarian could barely maintain the status quo, let alone develop new projects. Second, there was growing dissatisfaction with a Web content approval system that fell outside the normal reporting structure. Printed documents like instruction handouts or guides did not have to go through the same procedure that Web pages did.

The Web Librarian started the discussions with her supervisor, who in turn discussed the idea with her supervisor. Reference Services then discussed the idea as a group, as they would bear most of the burden of ongoing Web maintenance. Initially, the suggestion of distributing the Web maintenance workload received mixed reviews from staff. Some felt concerned about possible increased workload, while others expressed enthusiasm for this new step. With the approval of Reference Services, discussion moved to the Library Department heads and was finally approved by library administrators.

In order to maximize staff participation, the guidelines for official library Web pages were minimal. They were also positively worded, rather than a list of "don'ts." Format guidelines included ideas such as using the official template and checking pages in various browsers. Guidelines for content were closely tied to format, suggesting for example that Web authors "choose meaningful words or phrases for links" and "identify any non-HTML document." Just as with other uses of technology, the idea was to encourage staff creativity and expression, rather than restrict it. Almost everything submitted was published on the site, often with no review of content from anyone except the individual Web author. Author names were placed on the pages, in hopes that this would facilitate feedback and instill some pride of ownership. There was no mention of enforcement, no heavy-handed warnings or scare tactics. It was simply assumed that if a problem arose with a particular individual's site, then his or her immediate supervisor would deal with the issue, just as he or she would with any other employee problem.

The decision about maintenance methodology was influenced by financial and technical considerations. Content management software at the time was prohibitively expensive. WYSIWYG ("what you see is what you get") editors like Microsoft FrontPage, on the other hand, were less expensive and fairly ease to use. In addition, there had been an influx of tech-savvy librarians, with 11 new faculty hired from 1998-2001. The old Web Coordination Group, now dissolved, had a heavy hand in policing the Web site's early development. While the workload would now be distributed, some wanted to maintain at least some control over what was posted on the site. This cultural decision was backed up by a technical one. With the current Unix server, it would be impossible to give directory-level access to the Web server. However, the system administrator felt that a switch to a Windows server that did allow this option would mean additional security risks and other time-consuming problems for LTS.

The main players in the new system were the individual Web authors, a newly formed Web Implementation Team, and the Web Librarian. Originally, it was proposed that one staff person per unit might be assigned to the task of Web maintenance. However, an examination of the site revealed that most pages were affiliated with public services. Consequently, the majority of the 20 volunteer Web authors came from that division. The Web Implantation Team included two staff, two librarians, and two student employees. They were charged with loading Web pages, providing individual and classroom instruction in Web design, and assisting with the more advanced Web components like JavaScript programming or graphic creation. They also completed the majority of routine maintenance tasks. The Web Librarian provided leadership for the new model. Major changes, such as the redesign of the homepage, involved library-wide discussion forums and final approval by all unit heads.

## Maintenance by Web Authors

In order to create a new library Web page, a Web author must first decide page content with his or her supervisor. Web authors have tremendous freedom in creating pages, with only minimal guidelines from the university and library. Next, the author pulls a copy of a read-only template from a networked drive and creates the page. The template uses Server Side Includes to point to a standard header and footer. This allows the Web Implementation Team to make global changes to the header and footer by editing a single file. For existing pages, authors pull copies of the pages from a read-only directory of the site. Since authors are notified monthly about broken links, most authors submit at least one Web request each month.

Almost all authors use a WYSIWYG program such as Macromedia's Dreamweaver or Microsoft's FrontPage to create and edit Web pages. A few also use Adobe Acrobat for long documents or staff-only information like annual reports or desk schedules. The use of multiple editors gives authors maximum flexibility, as most staff express a clear preference based on perceived usability. The choice of Web editors also depends upon cost and training needs. FrontPage is available on all staff desktops as part of Microsoft Office. The university, however, officially supports only Dreamweaver. Campus computing offers free training on Dreamweaver, but individual library units must pay for copies of the software. Another option for Web authors is to use the Web Developer's Station. The Web station includes Dreamweaver, FrontPage, Adobe Photoshop, and other software. A scanner and a digital

*Figure 1. Web author workflow*

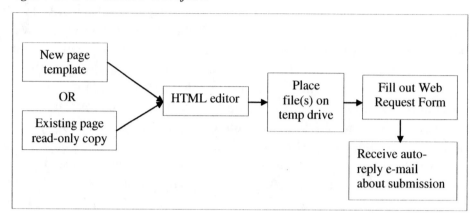

camera are also available. This station is housed in Reference Services and is available to any library staff member on a first-come, first-serve basis.

After the page is created or edited, authors save the file to a networked drive and fill out an online Web Request Form with contact information, file location, and specific directions for the Web Team. He or she receives an automatic e-mail acknowledging the request (see Figure 1). Some staff elect to forward this e-mail to their supervisor or team as proof that the pages have been submitted.

## Maintenance by the Web Implementation Team

Team members use the homegrown Web Request System to monitor requests and load pages onto the server. The student members load the majority of the pages. At the start of each shift, they login to the system and sign out open requests for existing pages one at a time (see Figure 2). The requests are marked with the team member's name and a designation of open, in progress, or closed. The students briefly check the pages for obvious mistakes such as missing titles or author metatags, but they do not check content or test individual links. Pages already on the system are not overwritten, but renamed with a ".old" extension. After the pages are copied to the Web server, the student signs out the request, triggering a second automatic e-mail to the Web author. This e-mail confirms that the request has been completed and lets the author know which team member worked on the request. Occasionally, the author will follow up with another request or correction. These minor fixes are generally completed without going through the Web Request System.

*Figure 2. Web team workflow*

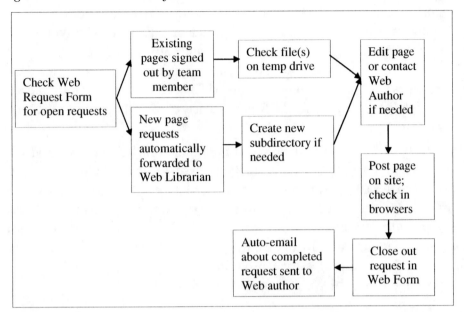

## Maintenance by the Web Librarian

The Web Librarian still bears most of the site maintenance responsibility, although her role has changed to a more supervisory one. She identifies possible new pages or changes to existing pages using a variety of resources, including formal usability testing, Web site usage statistics, e-mail reference questions, and user comments. The Web Librarian also structures larger cleanup projects, such as checking for missing tags (i.e., "alt" tag for images). The Web Librarian also maintains the structure of the site, deleting ".old" or temp files and directories both on the Web server, and the temporary networked directory used for uploading pages. Because new pages often require new subdirectories, the Web Librarian also fields all new page requests.

In addition to monitoring unpredictable maintenance issues, the Web Librarian schedules and completes a number of routine tasks. For example, when staff members leave, the Web Librarian will run a list of pages authored by the person and contact the supervisor to find out if the person's Web pages are to be reassigned or deleted. On the scheduled last day or shortly after, she will direct a Web Team member to make the needed changes. Each week she monitors the Web statistics software to make sure it is generating reports properly. Each month she runs the linkchecking software and notifies authors about their broken links. Annually, she produces lists of pages by Web Author in order to confirm that pages are current and show the correct Web author name. As a result, several hundred out-of-date pages are typically deleted. She also creates periodic backups of the site on CD-ROM for longer range access, as the nightly tape backups by LTS are regularly overwritten and only useful for a limited time.

Both the Web Librarian and the Web Implementation Team use several tools for Web maintenance. By mapping the Web server to a Windows drive, it is possible to use Dreamweaver's search and replace feature to change names, e-mail addresses, and database names and links. In addition to using Sever Side Includes (SSIs) for headers and footers, SSIs are also used for smaller pieces of sites like standard logos and navigation. Because the Web Team does not have a full-time professional programmer, they also depend heavily upon prepackaged code for Web forms and search engines.

## Initial Results and Reactions

Given the increase in new pages after the system was in place, the response by staff seemed to be favorable. From August to December 2001, the first months the Web Request System was running, the Web Implementation Team processed 662 requests from library staff. This number gives a general indication of use and does not directly correspond to the number of pages. (Some authors include multiple pages on one request. Minor fixes by the Web Team may also not be included individually.)

Although average turnaround time for most requests is less than an hour, a couple of staff felt hampered by the inability to place their edited pages on the server themselves. Some have opted to post a few unofficial pages on their personal account. This option is mostly used for temporary instructional pages or staff-only pages. Creating, posting, and maintaining those pages is completely the responsibility of the individual.

In 2001, the majority of official Web pages of the libraries were maintained on a single server. Two exceptions were interlibrary loan and the online catalog. Interaction between those areas and the Web Team about pages on these servers ranged from non-existent to moderate. Other exceptions to normal maintenance workflow included a few database-driven pages such as the LTS problem report form and early digital projects. Staff in various units were responsible for maintenance of those sites, including linkchecking and conformity to university standards.

# Current Challenges Facing the Organization

In 2003, the number of Web authors has gown steadily, with approximately 61 Web authors maintaining one or more Web pages. The number of static Web pages has increased to more than 6,000, although roughly half are automatically generated pages for Web statistics, error reports, and site indexes. The number of Web requests submitted has also continued to grow, from 1,300 in 2002 to more than 1,600 in 2003. Mainstreaming the Web maintenance workflow has resulted in many positive changes for the site and library staff. Staff appreciate the increased opportunities for creativity, service, and technical skill development. Job descriptions for Reference faculty routinely mention Web page maintenance responsibilities. Many faculty proudly include Web pages as part of their vitae, either under "Librarianship" or "Research and Creative Activity." Links to Web pages are sometimes collected and analyzed by a few faculty as proof of the pages' usefulness in the profession. After three years, however, the system is showing signs of wear.

## Content Development, Priorities, and Communication

No matter what kind of technical solution is in place, there are some common issues when distributing Web maintenance responsibilities among numerous staff. One difficulty is monitoring page content. While authors are encouraged to discuss page content with their supervisors, this is not required. Librarians and staff alike are reluctant to offer feedback and suggestions about other people's pages for fear of hurting someone's feelings. Differences in academic status, whether staff/faculty or tenured/untenured, may also play a role in this reluctance.

Unfortunately, as a result, the patron may be offered a confusing array of pages, each explaining how to use the catalog or search the Web in the "right" way. The astute patron may also be puzzled by the unevenness of the site content.

An examination of the Research Guide pages, for example, shows a wide variety and amount of information, from a single link to pages of annotated printed and electronic resources. This is one area where the homogeneity of a database-driven site could enhance site quality. However, this would require a substantial amount of compromise among the subject selectors. In 1999, a task force developed a template for the research pages in order to address the problem of inconsistent content and format. After presentation and discussion of the template in a Reference Services meeting, the majority decided to make use of the template optional. Not surprisingly, few pages follow this model. In 2001, the business research site was restructured as a database-driven site. The impetus for the project was the business faculty who wanted a site that was easier to use and a Web author who wanted something easier and quicker to maintain. Even though response to the site has been very positive on both sides, the other subject specialists have not yet followed suit. A major roadblock is the difficulty (some might say impossibility) of devising a single database-driven set of research guides that would meet every subject selector's preferences and requirements.

Another challenge in this area is that the faculty model encourages and even rewards faculty who pursue narrow or obscure areas of expertise that might not mesh with a library's overall mission or goals. Does a faculty member have the right to translate her library Web pages into Swahili just because she can? Does it matter that few people on campus can speak or read it? What about Web pages that explain how to use databases that the library does not own or access? How much should librarians focus their Web development on the needs of their immediate constituency? What about the "greater good" of the vast Internet community? Questions like these have caused some staff to express a need for additional content gatekeeping. Under the current system, the Web Implementation Team, with its small group of student, staff, and faculty members, does not have the authority, expertise, or time to monitor page content. Web Implementation Team members were selected to a large degree because of their technical skills, not their subject expertise. They have a responsibility for the site (at least its technical aspects), not any authority over it. As a result, format is monitored much more closely than content. It is more than a little ironic that a place that teaches students to value content over format in evaluating sources does such a poor job of content quality control them- selves.

In addition to content quality, there is also an issue with timeliness. For most library staff, maintaining Web pages takes a backseat to their primary job. The peak periods of Web development at CSU Libraries continues to be the winter intersession and summer. Roughly half of the 1,300 Web requests for 2002 came during the months of January, May, and August. This presents a challenge to the Web Team, as those are precisely the times when members, particularly students, are gone. Added to the staffing difficulties, funding for public universities has been cut drastically in the last two years. A recent news report states, "The university has lost more than $34 million in state funding since 2001, leading to the elimination of 70 vacant faculty positions...as well as 280 staff positions" (Kalaaji, 2004). Staff that leave are no longer routinely replaced, making a heavier workload for the survivors. Unfortunately, maintenance is unrelenting, particularly with broken links. Two random linkchecking reports from July and September 2003 show that roughly half of the 800-900 checked links are marked as broken. While some of these links may be only temporarily down, it is still a formidable amount.

Intellectually, staff may agree that pages should be up to date and focused on a unique idea, but emotionally it is sometimes a different story. It is trivial to convince most staff to create a new Web page. It is much more difficult for some of them to delete an outdated page or merge the content of two similar pages. Weeding, whether books or Web pages, is a dreaded process. The amount of freedom staff have in creating Web sites means some may find the process of deleting a Web page even more difficult and painful than weeding books. After all, they only selected the book for the collection; they did not personally research, organize, write, and illustrate it. The issue of ownership in Web site development and maintenance process deserves some attention. If someone simply inserts text into a Web form and pushes a button, does he or she still make a real contribution to the site? Intellectually, yes. Content is king, after all. Emotionally, maybe not. Motivation, attachment, and pride of ownership may be lost for some individuals.

In order to try to address the growing concerns about Web site content, a small subset of the Web Implementation Team drafted a new "Web Page Content Policy" in December 2003. This policy, approved by the department heads in early 2004, guides the placement of new links on the homepage and other top-level pages. It also formalized some procedures already in place, such as the selection of the "Current Highlights" that appear monthly on the homepage. About the secondary pages (anything not linked directly from the homepage), the policy states:

"CSU Libraries supports academic freedom and encourages staff to contribute to the development and maintenance of the Web site. However, given that the

CSU Libraries Web site is a major research tool for patrons, efforts should be made to ensure a clear and efficient path to accurate information. Multiple pages on an identical topic may confuse patrons. Outdated pages, while not linked on the site, may still be available via a search engine. It is the responsibility of the Web authors and their supervisors to monitor library Web pages for duplication and currency."

Lists of Web pages with similar titles or metatag keywords will be used to indicate starting points for determining overlapping content. It will be up to the supervisors to determine how seriously and to what extent they wish to enforce this policy. While the new policy is not a surefire cure to all the content-related issues, it is a good starting point.

## Web Authors and Technical Skills

This do-it-yourself maintenance system is highly dependent upon a certain level of skill. There was an initial spurt of training during the original mainstreaming phase in 2001, but that has tapered off. Most staff are now comfortable creating a simple page with text and links. A few have ventured into more advanced techniques like images, tables, or frames. Most Web authors prefer individual one-on-one training to formal classes. A few have been extremely resistant to any Web responsibilities.

The kinds of questions and requests sent through the Web Request Form give some indication about training needs. In addition, the current linkchecking software, LinkBot, lists author-induced errors such as broken anchors, missing page titles or attributes, and links to local files. The largest number of errors, generally 15-20%, is from missing attributes. This includes items like missing height and width on images, attributes that are linked to accessibility. This is an area where there is an obvious gap between the minimal and ideal skill levels. As the linkchecking report demonstrates, Web pages are usually modified to accommodate accessibility requirements, rather than being designed for accessibility in the first place. The Web Implementation Team and Web Librarian currently bear responsibility for this aspect of maintenance. To date, flaws in accessibility have been taken care of with major site reviews. The challenge is to first make Web authors aware of their responsibility in this area and to train them in basic accessibility design techniques.

# Digital Projects and Other Exceptions to Normal Workflow

In 2001, exceptions to the normal Web maintenance workflow were not a major issue. However, the number of exceptions, including database-driven sites, digital projects, and additional servers, has grown dramatically (see Figure 3). In 2000, there were three database-driven sites, including a problem report form for LTS. In 2003, there are at least 11 such sites. The majority of these are staff-only databases, including the instruction statistics, Web Requests System, building proctor request system, and "sticky wicket" (for difficult Reference questions). The public pages include the databases listing, the staff directory, and purchase request forms. In addition, during the last few years, separate servers have been added to house-specific projects like MetaLib. Separate servers give staff more autonomy in managing their own workflow, but also increase the likelihood of a fractured Web site splintering off in different directions.

## Database-Driven Sites

Several projects either have been converted from static HTML pages to the database-driven model or have been initiated as such. These originally static

*Figure 3. Exceptions to normal Web maintenance workflow*

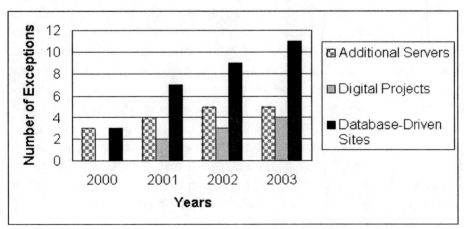

pages included the databases listing, the staff directory, the purchase request form, business resources (a research guide), and the International Poster Collection (a digital project). While initially time consuming, in the end, the ease of maintenance and updates makes the project worthwhile. Text changes are entered into a Web form and made immediately available. Feedback from those who maintain these database-driven pages have been consistently positive.

While these projects have been successful, they are considered exceptions to the Web maintenance workflow, rather than the rule. Occasionally, staff in Library Technology Services or other units have attended demonstrations of database-driven or content-management software packages. These were typically casual events, nothing dictated by policy, library-wide discussions, or administrator mandate. High cost was initially prohibitive. However, now it appears that the barrier is elsewhere. Why is that? One reason is that most authors seem happy with the current system. Roughly a third of the Web authors maintain fewer than 10 pages (see Figure 4). This is not a great burden for them. However, there are six individuals who maintain more than 100 HTML pages. One person is listed as the owner (either individually or jointly) of nearly 1,000 pages! It is a bit of a paradox. Content management software and database-driven sites are often touted as a solution for those who have a low level of technical skills. But at CSU Libraries, it is actually the most technically proficient who might benefit most from another type of workflow. Freed from large amounts of routine HTML, these highly productive elite could assume new challenges on other projects. For the staff as a whole, a stronger technical solution might further underscore the importance of site content.

Another potential barrier to a changed workflow is the staffing issues. There is limited in-house technical expertise at a database-creation level. Few in-house staff have these special skills and typically have a backlog of projects. Staff may not have the patience, time, or energy to wait until assistance is available. Database-driven sites, while they do save time in the end, require careful thought and planning. There is also a strong "do-it-myself" mentality among staff. Web authors, particularly faculty, typically want to be deeply involved in all aspects of achieving their vision. Finally, following the flood, the libraries were able to contract out the technical assistance to complete many database projects. This "special projects" mentality is widespread. While authors may consider a database-driven site for their individual projects, a broader implementation for the site as a whole has never been discussed. Database-driven sites are viewed primarily as a niche solution, not a global one.

*Figure 4. Distribution of Web maintenance workload*

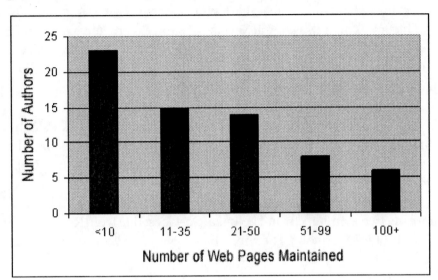

## Digital Projects

Digital projects are also increasing, in part because of a new library dean with an interest in this area. When she arrived in 2003, there were at least four projects completed or underway that used ContentDM software or a home-grown database to display hundreds of images, audio files, and other digital objects. Digital projects have typically not followed the standard library template for several reasons. First, they tend to be jointly administered by other departments or agencies. Second, they often receive special grant funding, and can afford to pay for additional goods and services such as special equipment and staff. They are also on a compressed timeline. Over time, these projects can take longer to maintain, particularly since they are more vulnerable to staff turnover. In the last few years, project leaders have tended to place the technical aspects of a project in the hands of students who, while bright and innovative, do not necessarily have the range or length of experience needed to construct robust, easily maintained sites. Communication among digital project managers and the library as a whole is still an issue. A bi-monthly staff newsletter on Web projects appeared for a year, but was dropped due to time constraints.

During 2002-2003, several groups centered on digital projects either emerged or became more active. First, a revived ContentDM group now meets a couple of times a year to discuss digital project issues. Second, a new model for digital project management, one centered in technical services, was implemented in 2002. Under this model, a Digital Services Team was created with staff from the departments of Bibliographic Control & Electronic Resource Services, Acquisitions, and Preservation. This team is responsible for all activities, including pre-processing of originals prior to digitization, scanning, development, Web site design, rights management, conservation treatment, and archiving. This model marks a new trend away from public services and Library Technology Services, although both departments are mentioned in a list of "others with whom the team will coordinate and consult" (Bastian, 2003, p. 51). Finally, a new Digital Facilitation Group debuted in June 2003. Its charge is to "coordinate and advise on digital efforts in the libraries." This group, comprising two members from Technical Services, one from Reference, and one from Library Technology Services, has not yet been very active beyond its initial meeting.

Whether digital projects, database-driven sites, or Web sites on additional servers, the growing number of exceptions has caused some dissention in the ranks. The basic library template, with its standard header and footer, has come under increased scrutiny by library staff. Some view it as a major barrier to their creative vision. Supervisors have started to approve Web pages, such as those used to advertise exhibits, that do not follow the standard template. Unfortunately, these pages also tend to lack the basic information in the header and footer, such as the name of the library and contact person.

## Conclusion

This distributed maintenance structure gives Web authors the maximum in creativity and flexibility without a complete loss of central control. The use of a Web Team for technical assistance increases the steady workflow and lessens the bottleneck of the single Webmaster model. There are several issues with this system in its current form. First, while this system ensures a similar look and feel to most pages on the libraries Web site, it lacks strong content monitoring. Hopefully, the "Web Content Policy" will be a first step in improving the overall quality of Web site content. Second, the lack of continual training can also lead to a technical staff that is more of a clean up crew than architects of more sophisticated systems. This makes it difficult to retain high-skill technical employees. Third, the increase in exceptions means an increase in the number of separate Web maintenance systems. This splintering seems likely to lead to overlapping content and increased confusion for library patrons. It is also frustrating to staff. For example, the digital projects managers are now used to maintaining their data in the image database software, ContentDM. However, simple HTML pages must still go through the regular process. It used to be an "all or nothing" system-either you used the library maintenance process or you did not. Now there is a confusing mix.

In order for there to be a solution, there has to be agreement that there is a problem. The majority of the Web Authors, especially those maintaining small numbers of pages, are largely satisfied with the current system. Most do not use other servers, nor do they experience the routine maintenance problems on the same scale as the Web Implementation Team. Individual authors may fix one or two missing HTML tags, not hundreds or thousands. While authors may occasionally quibble about guidelines such as use of a standard header or footer, they appreciate the freedom they have in designing their sites. The burden of instigating change will likely fall on those who are maintaining large numbers of pages, primarily the Web Implementation Team. With new leadership in place at the administrative level, it seems the right time to begin recognizing and discussing these problems with a larger audience.

Many others are quick to point out the problems of a largely static site. "As sites grow both in size and the number of people involved, the sheer volume of HTML-coded pages and the links they contain have become unmanageable. Templates, validators, and link-checking utilities can stave off the chaos only so long" (Antelman, 1999, p. 176). Even with its flaws, this can still be a strong Web maintenance model for an intellectual, highly motivated, and technically innovative staff. Faculty can create highly individualized instruction pages for specific classes or follow their own narrow, personal interests in developing pages. Web pages can be quick to create, especially in small numbers. The major strength and weakness of this system is the individual. One person can exercise tremendous influence over the site in both format and content, either positively or negatively. The problems that Colorado State is experiencing are largely those of scale and proportion. For a small site, HTML coding may still be worthwhile, especially in terms of personal satisfaction. However, with increasingly uneven workloads and the decrease in staff and money, the question becomes not *if* we must change, but *how* and *when*. Unlike database-driven sites or content management systems, the current system is cheap in terms of technology, but very expensive in staff time. So the question remains: How much longer can we afford it?

# References

Alire, C. (Ed.). (2000). *Library disaster planning and recovery handbook.* New York: Neal-Schuman Publishers.

Antelman, K. (1999). Getting out of the HTML business: The database-driven Web site solution. *Information Technology and Libraries, 18*(4), 176-181.

Bastian, D.E. (2003). Creating a digital services team at Colorado State University: A collaborative effort among departments. *Colorado Libraries, 29*(3), 50-52.

Cowgill, A., Beam, J., & Wess, L. (2001). Implementing an information commons in a university library. *The Journal of Academic Librarianship, 27*(6), 432-439.

Cox, A., Yeadon, J., & Kerr, M. (2001). Practical content management. *Library Association Record, 103*(7), 414-415.

Cullen, K., & Mach, M. (2002). A task management system to cure your 'Webmaster blues'. *Computers in Libraries, 22*(10), 10-12, 70-12.

Kalaaji, R. (2004, January 25). Budget could force CSU enrollment cap. *The Coloradoan.* Retrieved January 27, 2004, from *www.coloradoan.com*

Shropshire, S. (2003). Beyond the design and evaluation of library Web sites: An analysis and four case studies. *Journal of Academic Librarianship, 29*(2), 95-101.

# Supporting Materials

## Questions and Answers

Question: What is the overall problem(s) in this case?

Answer: While offering individual creativity and flexibility to library staff, a static HTML site cannot be effectively maintained beyond a certain size. As more staff members with varying skills and priorities participate in site maintenance, the more unwieldy the site becomes.

Question: What are the factors affecting the problem(s) related to this case?

Answer: Some major factors include shrinking numbers of staff and funds, increased user demand for online materials and services, differing priorities among staff, increased exceptions to the normal Web maintenance workflow, and a faculty environment in which individual achievement is valued over team effort in the tenure process.

Question: Discuss the major issues of Web maintenance.

Answer: At minimum, Web maintenance requires checking and fixing broken links, as well as monitoring site content for currency, accuracy, and relevance. Maintenance is an ongoing task that typically receives little recognition. A distributed Web maintenance system with many individuals works best when everyone has similar priorities and technical skills.

Question: What are the advantages to having a site that is primarily HTML coded, rather than database driven?

Answer: One advantage is the individual's ability to control Web page format and content. Web pages can be produced quickly and require much less planning than a database-driven site. These factors of flexibility and creativity lead to individual satisfaction, pride of ownership, and increased interest in site development and maintenance.

Question: What changes (organizational, financial, managerial, technical) might be needed to help solve this case?

Answer: The first step would be to recognize and discuss the problems at an organizational level. Some possible changes could include scaling down the site, installing content management software, moving financial responsibility of the site to library administration, or restructuring the current workflow to include enforced content review by managers.

# Epilogue

Like others in higher education, CSU Libraries is at a crossroads. Users are demanding increased access to online resources at the same time that the institution is receiving less state funding. New challenges at CSU include the launching of a new university portal and increased focus on specialized digital projects, including institutional repositories. Fewer resources, including staff, means that labor-intensive activities like Web maintenance need to be reexamined. While a content management system may seem like an obvious solution, it clashes with the personal satisfaction that many get with hands-on Web development. Some library faculty have recently revived discussions of how Web development counts in tenure review. CSU Libraries needs to figure out whether it is still possible, or even desirable, to continue to balance individual needs with those of the group.

## Lessons Learned

1.   Web maintenance solutions must be scalable.

   Static HTML pages may work for smaller institutions or smaller Web sites, but not on a larger scale.

2.   Web maintenance activities follow the 80/20 rule.

   No matter how well maintenance is initially distributed, a minority of staff will maintain the majority of the Web pages.

3.   Never underestimate the influence of an individual on an organization.

   In a static HTML environment, the individual can more noticeably influence site development. This influence may be either negative or positive.

**Chapter VII**

# PHP and PostgreSQL Web Content Management Systems at Western Michigan University Libraries

Michael D. Whang
Western Michigan University, USA

## Abstract

*This chapter introduces the design of a PHP and PostgreSQL content management system as a means of maintaining content within a library's online subject guide collection. It argues that the content management system, combined with distributed authorship, provides an efficient and effective way to manage a large growing body of content that changes frequently. Furthermore, the author hopes that understanding the process of building a content management system, from system and data requirements to database design and content display, will not only inform librarians and technical staff of good system design practices, but also assist in the understanding of a content-driven library Web site.*

# Introduction

The Web has fundamentally shaped how librarians deliver and support library services to a new breed of students and faculty expecting more and more content to be online and accessible to them, suiting their research and lifestyle needs. With the expectation of conducting research on or off campus, librarians are faced with challenging questions of how to manage extremely large, growing collections of online resources and present those resources effectively to target users. As Fountain observes (2000), "With the exponential growth of the Web, we need to change our focus from simply locating information to locating the most relevant information in an efficient and cost-effective manner" (p. 89).

The Web plays a significant role in Western Michigan University Libraries' efforts to support the teaching and research needs of over 29,000 students. Western Michigan University offers 168 bachelor's degrees, 70 master's degrees, and 30 doctoral degrees. There are 903 regular teaching faculty supporting 23,309 undergraduates and 5,869 graduate students. Western Michigan University Libraries employs 27 faculty and 65 staff, and provides access to 8,549 print and electronic subscriptions, 114,101 slides, 211,958 maps, 5,235 CD-ROMs, and 1,995,762 print and non-print titles.

Librarians at Western Michigan University (WMU) use the library Web site extensively for bibliographic instruction, conducting on- and off-campus reference services, publishing how-to guides and self-paced tutorials, and marketing an array of library services, news, and events to target user groups. Much of the site's popularity is its content, linking users to a large collection of information resources ranging from print library holdings and subscription databases to resources found on the Web.

The challenge of hosting a content-driven library Web site is keeping that content current and ensuring that all Web links remain valid and up to date (i.e., no broken links). It also involves finding a convenient, efficient, and effective way to manage and update a large body of content. In addition the overall architecture of the Web site needs to be easily understandable and maintainable by library staff, and most importantly must be intuitive for target user groups to learn and use.

All of this requires a change in the way today's academic libraries build and maintain Web sites, where librarians must maintain hundreds, if not thousands, of Web pages. The question is, how do libraries build a content management system to effectively maintain content that changes frequently?

Today, libraries have several options for creating a content management system, or CMS, where Web page content is stored in and retrieved from a database. This chapter focuses on the use of PHP: Hypertext Preprocessor (PHP) and PostgreSQL, an open source database management system to design a no-cost CMS for the WMU Libraries' online subject guide collection. The Office of Information and Technology (OIT) centrally manages the computing environment at WMU. WMU is primarily a UNIX- and Windows-based computing environment and supports PHP and PostgreSQL, an embedded, server-side scripting language and an open source relational database management system, respectively.

The libraries' CMS project began in June 2003. It took one month to design and develop the two major parts of the CMS: a database and PHP template pages. PHP page templates can be broken down further into two types of pages: PHP administrative interface, or series of Web forms (i.e., Web pages that only content authors have access to) and public PHP Web pages, or pages that users see when accessing the libraries' Web pages. A production version was released in August 2003.

# Setting the Stage

One feature of the library's Web site that is heavily used by WMU librarians, students, and faculty is the online subject guide collection. The collection includes a comprehensive listing of print and online resources such as subscription databases and indexes, books, journals, CD-ROMs, and Web sites. There are 58 subject guides available to users online. Each guide is created and maintained by a library liaison responsible for specific fields of study at WMU. Librarians exercise academic freedom over these subject guides, deciding what resources are listed and how those resources are presented and organized on the page. A problem with this creative latitude over authorship is that every librarian has a different value system as to how resources are named and categorized on his or her Web page. For example, each subject guide contains a listing of resources organized into categories such as Books, Journals, CD-ROMs, and Encyclopedias; however, librarians create different names for the same category of materials. For instance the 'Articles' category exists under a variety of different names such as 'Journal Articles', 'Indexes to Articles', 'Indexes to Journal Articles', or 'Selected Journals'. All together, there are 29 different names used for this category alone. There is an excess of 340 different category names used throughout the entire subject guide collection. Moreover, the order in which these resources are presented on the page varies, depending on the author's discretion. One librarian may wish to list 'Guides to the Field' first on the page, while another librarian might choose 'Indexes to Articles' as its first entry.

In addition, there is considerable variation in how specific information about each resource (i.e., title, coverage, frequency of updates, URL, publisher, call number, and resource description) is presented to the user. Many librarians list a resource (i.e., a subscription database) and provide an in-depth annotation that includes many, if not all, information elements just mentioned. Some librarians simply list resources by name only, without annotation. As a result, subject guides vary in breadth and depth in the type of information accessible to users.

The overall design and development of the WMU Libraries Web site rest primarily on the shoulders of the libraries' Web and Internet Services Department and the Library Web Committee. The Web and Internet Services Department is responsible for the maintenance and development of the library's Web site. Two people staff the Web Department—the faculty Web Librarian/chair of the Library Web Committee and a staff Web Developer. The Web Librarian takes a leadership role in the design, development, and maintenance of a continually evolving Web presence, identifying and implementing new technologies as appropriate. As head of the library Web Department, the Web Librarian sets priorities and manages the work of the Web Developer and student employees. The Web Librarian and Web Developer are mutually responsible for the scripting and programming of Web pages and applications, and are also responsible for the maintenance and administration of several library Web servers. The Web Committee is a body of librarians and staff involved in Web development at various levels, to reach consensus upon site improvements, refining Web policies, setting priorities, establishing ongoing usability testing, and providing a vision for future Web redesign projects. The Web Committee is composed of nine tenured and untenured faculty librarians and one staff member, the Web Developer. The most technically proficient members of the committee are the Web Librarian and Web Developer, and they translate to the committee what is and is not humanly possible to create or develop. Together, the Web Department and Web Committee played key roles in the design and development of the online subjection guide collection CMS. The Web Department was responsible for the technical specifications and the actual building of the system, while the Web Committee played an advisory role in the types of content and how that content would be organized and presented to the end user.

## Maintaining Static HTML Files

Prior to developing a content management system, WMU librarians created and edited individual HTML files using Macromedia Dreamweaver, an HTML Web-editing program. When completed, librarians sent a request to the Web Librarian, who then uploaded the file to the Web server. This system of managing content worked well when the collection was first born and the number of print and online resources minimal. But over time as the collection grew, editing individual HTML files became a time-management nightmare for both subject author and Web Librarian. For instance, database vendors often change their Web addresses. When this happens, the Web Librarian manually searched and replaced all instances of the old Web addresses with the new addresses. The subject author would then help the Web Librarian by reviewing the subject guide, ensuring that all instances of the old Web addresses were updated. At times, some instances were missed and the Web Librarian would have to repeat the process until all instances were updated throughout the Web site.

In the case of the online subject guide collection, content authors needed a better way to track, manage, update, and share both print and online resources throughout the collection. The solution was to design a Web application that would allow content authors the ability to add, delete, or update any information about a particular resource, regardless of where the resource was listed in the collection (i.e., listed under multiple Web pages within the collection). Together, the database that stores subject guide content and the PHP page templates that pull content out of the database form a Web-based content management system. The power of a CMS is its ability to share a resource across many different Web pages without editing those Web pages individually. Instead, information about the resource such as its title, description, coverage, and URL is stored in and retrieved from a database. This allows a resource to be updated only once by editing only the database and not individual Web pages.

# Case Description

## Literature Review

The Web and Internet Services Department conducted a literature review of library content management systems designed specifically for subject guides, or gateways. A particular CMS implementation that caught the attention of the Web Department was designed by the University of Nottingham Library, which utilized PHP and MySQL to build a database-driven subject guide collection (Gardner & Pinfield, 2001). Since the Web and Internet Services Department was familiar with PHP, the University of Nottingham's model quickly helped the Web Librarian and Web Developer to conceptualize the project.

## Definitions

### Resource, Resource Type, and Subject

The power of a CMS is the ability to share a resource across many different Web pages. A resource can be the library's online catalog, a subscription database, book, journal, Web site, or other reference material. A resource type is essentially a category, or grouping, of resources. Examples of resource types include Annual Reviews, Books, Biographies, Company Information, Organizations, and Dictionaries. Resource types and resources are then grouped under a subject category such as Art, Biological Sciences, Communication, and other academic disciplines.

## Information Elements

What makes each subject guide so valuable to students, faculty, and librarians is the amount of information that each guide contains related to a specific subject discipline. The Web Department and the Library Web Committee created a core list of information elements, or fields, that describe a resource.

- Title—Title of the resource
- Subtitle—Books are a good example of resources that may contain subtitles

- Alternate Title—Sometimes databases change in name. This field can be used for cross-referencing, or 'see also'
- Author—Person or corporate body responsible for the intellectual or artistic content of the work
- Publisher—Person or body responsible for issuing the work
- Call Number—Library of Congress and Dewey Decimal Classification numbers
- Location—WMU Branch Library or Collection and floor level
- Web Link—URL (Web address)
- Subjects—Other subject guides this resource is linked to
- Media Type—Identifies the resource's format (i.e., CD-ROM, Slides, DVD, etc.)
- Coverage—Dates covered by the resource
- Frequency—How many times new records are added to a database or index published daily, weekly, or monthly (i.e., newspapers, periodicals, journals, etc.)
- Description—Text description of a resource's contents
- Librarian's Comments—These are comments made by the author of the subject guide, explaining any special instructions, search tips, keywords, or other information that users may find helpful

However, not all information elements are presented to the user at once. It was decided by the Web Committee that only 'Title' and 'Description' be initially presented to the user and then offer a 'Details' link (see Figure 2), connecting users to the full list of information elements, or fields, for that particular resource

*Figure 1. Default view of page display*

> **Title:** WorldCat
> **Description:** Comprehensive database of print and electronic holdings from many libraries around the world. Items located through WorldCat must be requested through InterLibrary Loan unless they are also listed in WestCat. Details

*Figure 2. Default view of 'Details' page listing all available information elements for a resource*

**Title:** Social Sciences Citation Index
**Alternate Title:**
**Author:** (Web of Science)
**Publisher:**
**Publish Date:**
**Call Number:**
**Web Link:** http://isiknowledge.com/wos
**Coverage:**
**Frequency:**
**Description:** The Social Sciences Citation Index is a multidisciplinary database that indexes more than 1,725 journals spanning 50 disciplines, and selected, relevant items from over 3,300 of the world's leading scientific and technical journals. Disciplines include: anthropology, history, industrial relations, information & library science, law, philosophy, political science, psychiatry, psychology, public health, social issues, social work, sociology, urban studies, women's studies. Because the information about each article includes the article's cited reference list (or bibliography), you can also search the databases for articles that cite a known author or work. Coverage is from 1956 to present. Please LOGOFF, so others may use the database.
**Librarian's comments:**

Close Window

(see Figure 1). This would ensure that users received information in easily digestible portions and provide an option for users who want to learn more about the resource if desired.

## Requirements

The Web Department, along with the Library Web Committee and library subject liaisons, identified several important requirements prior to the creation of the database.

1.   The database must contain a number of information elements related to a resource: Title, Subtitle, Alternate Title, Author, Publisher, Call Number, Location, Web Link (URL), Subjects, Media Type, Coverage, Frequency, Description, and Librarian's Comment.

2.   The responsible librarian must be able to select a resource and assign it to one or more subjects and resource types.

3.   The responsible librarian must be able to add, delete, and edit a new resource, resource type, and subject.

4.   The database must provide the ability to order, or rank, resources and resource types on the display page.

5.   The database must allow the responsible librarian to add context-sensitive annotation (Librarian's Comments) to each resource description.

6.   The database must allow the librarian to retrieve resources by resource type.

## Administrative Interface

For content to be dynamic, there needed to be a way to manipulate—add, delete, or update—content in the database, so a series of Web forms were created to allow this interaction between author, content, and database to take place. Librarians can log into an administrative interface, or series of Web forms, via a username and password, to edit their subject guides. No external HTML editor or FTP program for uploading files to a Web server is required (see Figure 3).

How the administrative interface works is simple. An author logs into the administrative interface via a username and password. Authors may then add, delete, or update content by simply typing or copying information into the form fields, and then they submit the form. Each field in the form is associated with what is known as a variable. A variable is simply a name that stands for some value. When the author submits the form, the form passes the data (variables) entered into each form field to the database, where the database then stores this new information. PHP wraps the necessary instructions (e.g., SQL), allowing data to be passed to the database where the data will either be added, deleted, or updated.

Essentially, every content management system needs a way for the user to add to, delete from, or update data in a database. Web forms are the best way to

*Figure 3. Adding a resource to a subject guide via a series of Web forms*

## Resource Type Tool

(compatibile with IE 5.5+, Netscape 7.1+, Mozilla 1.4+)
Search
New Record

**Adding Record**
*Resource Type Name: [                                    ]

**B** *I* U ≡ ≡ ⊚ <> ▤ ✂ ▨ ✓

Subject Specific Intro: [                                    ]

[ Add Record ]  [ Reset ]

do this because they allow content authors to edit content virtually anytime and anywhere. All that is needed is an Internet connection and a Web browser to connect to the administrative interface.

## Ranking Resources and Resource Type

To give librarians the flexibility they wanted in organizing their subject guide Web pages, a ranking system was created, allowing librarians to discriminate which resources and resource types fall first on the page. The way it works is simple. The default display of resources is alphabetical; however, each Resource and Resource Type is assigned a value—the first to be listed receives a value of zero. Any subsequent resource and resource type is then assigned a positive number (i.e., 1, 2, 3, and so forth). Librarians can easily reorganize a subject guide utilizing this simple ranking system via the administrative interface.

## Context-Sensitive Annotations

To add value to each resource description, a 'Librarian's Comment' field was created to accommodate any special instructions, search tips, keywords, or other information librarians wanted to append to the resource description. In addition, the 'Librarian's Comments' allowed librarians to cater specific information to select target user groups regardless of where the resource resided. For example, a resource such as FirstSearch, listed under the Education subject guide, would only contain specific information targeted to education students. The same FirstSearch resource, listed under the Art subject guide, would only contain specific, targeted information for art students.

## Ability to Find Resources by Type

Librarians wanted the ability for users to find resources by type. This feature would allow a student looking for book reviews to select, from a core group of resource types, a 'Book Reviews' category and retrieve all available resources related to book reviews.

## Database Design

The goal of the subject guide CMS is the ability to add, delete, and share both print and online resources on any number of Web pages and edit those resources from one source, the database. Essentially, the subject guide collection contains a number of subject areas. Each subject area contains a number of resources. These resources are then organized into categories of resources. For example, the Art Subject guide (subject) contains Dictionaries & Encyclopedias (resource type). Within Dictionaries & Encyclopedias there are a number of art-related dictionaries and encyclopedias (resources).

The current iteration of the CMS consists of 13 tables (see Figure 4). The best way to interpret the diagram is by starting with the R2S table. The R2S table is a relational table that ties resources to subjects. Within the R2S table is the Librarian's Comments and Rank fields. The Librarian's Comments field contains text specific to resources within a given subject. The Rank field determines the order in which those resources are listed.

The RESOURCE table contains the information elements such as title, alternate title, author, publisher, and so forth. The SUBJECT table contains the subject name and whether the subject guide is live. If the guide is live, then it is viewable by the public. If it is not, the subject guide will not display on the Web page.

*Figure 4. Database tables and relationships*

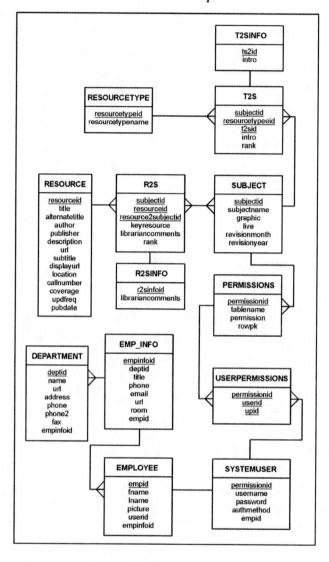

Authors may also add a revision month and year to each subject he or she is responsible for.

Tied to the SUBJECT table are two tables, the PERMISSIONS table and the T2S table. First, each subject is associated with an author and each author is assigned a username and user password. Usernames and passwords are tied to the library staff directory database. This ensures that authors can only edit their own subject guide(s) and no one else's. Second, the SUBJECT table points to the T2S (Type to Subject) table. It connects a subject to subject-specific resource types. In other words, not all subject guides will contain the same resource types or categories of resources. For example, a Geography subject guide contains only geography-specific resource types such as 'Atlases' or 'Maps'. Categories that individual resources are listed under are stored in the RESOURCETYPE table. To speed performance of the database, a separate table containing introductory text for each resource type was created. For example, under the Geography subject guide, the author may want to include some introductory information about the library's atlas collection. The T2SINFO (Type to Subject Information) table stores this introductory information.

# Database Definitions

- RESOURCE—Contains all information elements
- RESOURCTYPE—Categories that individual resources are listed under
- R2S—RESOURCES TO SUBJECT is the relational table that ties resources to subjects
- R2SINFO—RESOURCE TO SUBJECT INFO holds the 'Librarian's Comments' and will help speed up database performance if a separate table like this is created
- T2S—TYPE TO SUBJECT is the relational table that ties a subject to subject-specific resource types
- T2SINFO—TYPE TO SUBJECT INFORMATION is identical in function to R2SINFO, holding introductory text and increasing database performance if a separate table like this is created
- SUBJECT—Actual subject guides
- PERMISSIONS—Defines permissions for individual subject guide authors
- USERPERMISSIONS—This is the relational table that ties permissions for individual subject guide authors to their user name and password
- SYSTEMUSER—Contains subject guide author's user name and password
- EMPLOYEE—Contains the first and last name of library staff
- EMPLOYEE_INFO—Contains information about individual library staff
- DEPARTMENT—Contains more information about individual library staff

## Development Tools

*PHP*

PHP: Hypertext Preprocessor (PHP) is free software and is available for commercial and non-commercial use under the terms of the PHP License, published by the PHP Group (www.php.net). Moreover, PHP enjoys a large community of users and support (www.webmin.com), and many libraries, both in the U.S. and abroad, are using PHP to develop a variety of CMSs (www.oss4lib.org). Already familiar with PHP and its known compatibility with many open source and proprietary databases, the Web and Internet Services Department decided to use PHP (Version 4.3.3) as the HTML-embedded, server-side scripting language to dynamically generate Web pages.

*PostgreSQL*

Since the WMU Office of Information Technology supports PostgreSQL, the Web Department used PostgreSQL (Version 7.3.2), an open source database management system, to create the database. PostgreSQL is free software and is available for use under the BSD License (www.postgresql.org).

*Webmin*

Webmin is a Web-based system administration module for Unix (www.webadmin.com). It uses a Web browser, allowing an administrator to manage Apache, user accounts, and view the PostgreSQL database. Webmin is free, open source software and is available for commercial and non-commercial use under a BSD-like license (www.sourceFORGE.net).

## Dynamic Subject Pages

When a user selects a subject, the 'subjectid' variable is passed to the results page, where an SQL statement queries the T2S table to retrieve the associated RESOURCE TYPES. The page is then dynamically generated on the Web server by PHP and sent to the Web browser as an HTML document (see Figure 5).

*Figure 5. Sample SQL statement what resource types are associated with 'subjectid*

```
<?
$sql="select t2s.rank,t2s.intro,
resourcetype.resourcetypename,resourcetype.resourcetypeid
from t2s,resourcetype where t2s.subjectid=$subjectid and
t2s.resourcetypeid=resourcetype.resourcetypeid
order by t2s.rank, lower(resourcetype.resourcetypename)";
$result=pg_query($sql);
for ($i=0;$i<pg_numrows($result);$i++) {
 $rt=pg_fetch_object($result,$i);
 echo "<li><a
href=rt.php?subjectid=$subjectid&resourcetypeid=$rt->resourcetypeid>
$rt->resourcetypename</a></li>";
}
?>
```

When a user selects a RESOURCE TYPE (e.g., Educational Resources), the 'resourceid' is passed to the results page, where an SQL statement queries the R2S table to retrieve the associated RESOURCES associated with the RESOURCE TYPE and SUBJECT. The page is then dynamically generated on the Web server by PHP and sent to the Web browser as an HTML document (see Figure 7).

# Current Challenges Facing the Organization

A major challenge for the project was getting librarians to agree on what information should be consistently presented to the user. There were several issues that took considerable time to resolve.

- Resource Descriptions—What type of information should be included in the description? What type of information about the resource will users find helpful? Is it possible to create a one- to two-sentence description at all?

- Resource Type Categories—Consolidating the existing 340 Resource Type categories down to a manageable list of 30 involved a great deal of time and negotiation because librarians had to decide collectively the

*Figure 6. Subjectid results page*

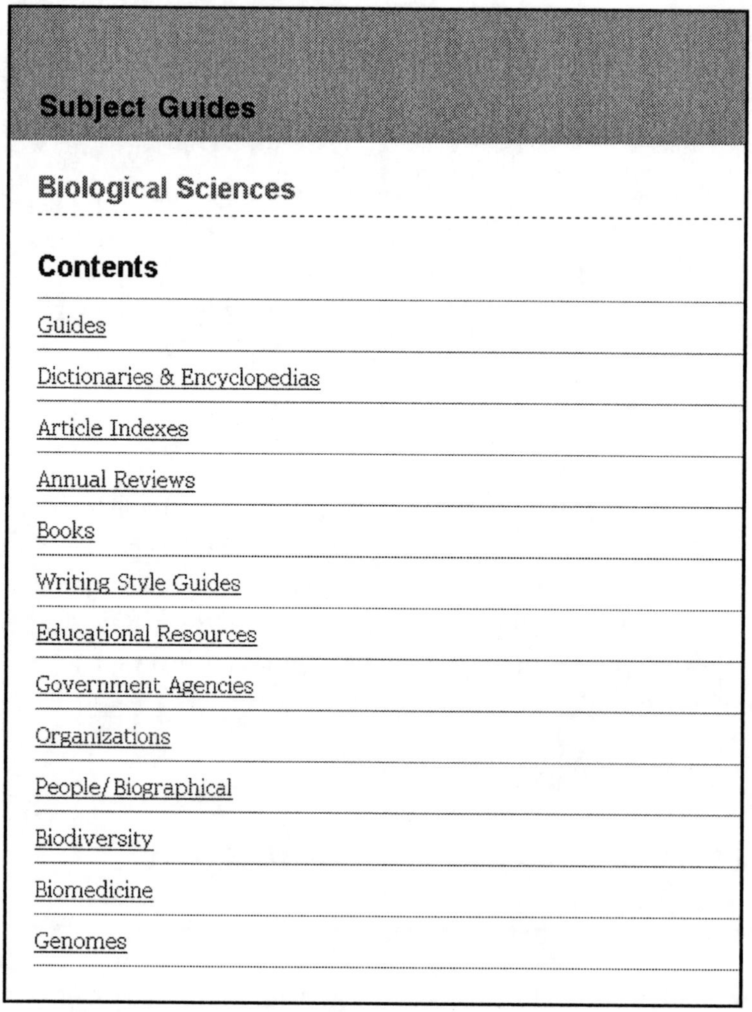

**Subject Guides**

**Biological Sciences**

**Contents**

Guides

Dictionaries & Encyclopedias

Article Indexes

Annual Reviews

Books

Writing Style Guides

Educational Resources

Government Agencies

Organizations

People/Biographical

Biodiversity

Biomedicine

Genomes

names of each category. (i.e., Selected Journals, Indexes to Articles, Journal Articles, or Article Indexes).

- **Display of Information**—How will the page be displayed?

- **Librarian's Comments**—A few librarians did not like the term 'Librarian's Comments' and spent a great deal of time brainstorming other possible terms.

To get librarians involved in a change in their work, the Web Librarian and Web Developer created an inventory, cataloging over 340 resource types. Documenting the different names librarians used for the same category of materials

*Figure 7. Resourceid results page*

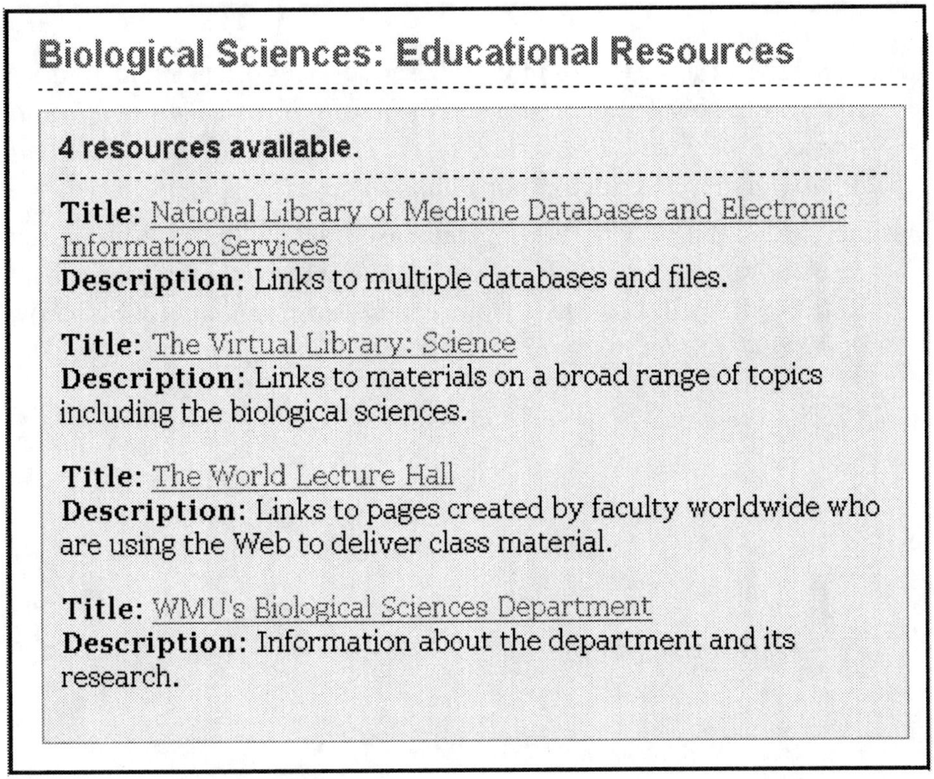

**Biological Sciences: Educational Resources**

----------------------------------------------------------------

**4 resources available.**

----------------------------------------------------------------

**Title:** National Library of Medicine Databases and Electronic Information Services
**Description:** Links to multiple databases and files.

**Title:** The Virtual Library: Science
**Description:** Links to materials on a broad range of topics including the biological sciences.

**Title:** The World Lecture Hall
**Description:** Links to pages created by faculty worldwide who are using the Web to deliver class material.

**Title:** WMU's Biological Sciences Department
**Description:** Information about the department and its research.

helped the Web Librarian and Web Developer build a case for the CMS. The inventory actually helped librarians realize just how disorganized the current subject guide collection had become.

# Conclusion

The library released a production version of the subject guide CMS; it can be seen at www.wmich.edu/library/subject. The next step for the WMU Libraries is to further enhance and customize the CMS based on librarian and user feedback, and through further usability testing and focus groups.

# References

Fountain, L.M. (2000). Trends in Web-based services in academic libraries. In P.D. Fletcher & J.C. Bertot (Eds.), *World libraries on the information superhighway: Preparing for the challenges of the new millennium.* Hershey, PA: Idea Group Publishing.

Gardner, M., & Pinfield, S. (2001). Database-backed library Web sites: A case study of the use of PHP and MySQL at the University of Nottingham. Retrieved April 14, 2003, from *eprints.nottingham.ac.uk/archive/00000004/ 00/database_backed_Web_sites_preprint.pdf*

**Chapter VIII**

# Database-Driven Web Pages Using Only JavaScript:
## Active Client Pages

Stephen Sottong
California State University, Los Angeles, USA

## Abstract

*The California State University, Los Angeles (CSULA) Library decided, as part of an overall redesign of its Web site, to use database-driven Web pages (also called dynamic Web pages). When the servers for the database-driven pages were closed down due to a virus attack, a new method of creating the database-driven pages without the necessity of special servers was devised. The resultant Web pages use JavaScript arrays to simulate a database and embedded JavaScript programs to provide the dynamic content for the pages.*

# Introduction

The John F. Kennedy Memorial Library is the university library for CSULA. The school has approximately 22,000 students in an ethnically diverse, urban setting. The library has nearly one million volumes, but has in recent years concentrated on remotely accessible resources to accommodate its decentralized, commuter clientele. Most students now use the library through its Web site. This has made the Library Web a key mode of communication.

Implementation of the Library Web began around 1994 through the efforts of one librarian. Over time, other librarians and staff added their talents and the site grew to over 400 pages in various styles with redundant content. Several cleanup projects took place over the years, but a full-scale reevaluation of the entire site had not been attempted. In 2002, a team project was initiated to completely rework the Web site. Goals for the project included improved usability and maintainability, consistent interface, increased currency, and reduced redundancy. Part of the implementation strategy called for the use of database-driven Web pages.

# Database-Driven Web Pages

Database-driven pages look like normal HTML Web pages, but are created when requested. They consist of fixed portions made of HTML and variable portions that are filled with information drawn from a database. The information in the database can be used for multiple Web pages as well as other applications. Database-driven Web pages are much easier to keep current since information only needs to be updated in one central database instead of hard coding it into many pages. Database-driven pages can contain logic that sorts the data (e.g., placing a list of personnel in alphabetical order) or chooses data based on criteria (e.g., displaying bibliographic databases that contain full-text articles). Database-driven pages are most useful where information changes frequently or where common information is used in many Web pages. Some examples are personnel pages and pages that list bibliographic databases. Flexibility and ease of updating make database-driven Web pages highly desirable.

Currently there are four main technologies used to create database-driven Web pages:

- Active Server Pages (ASP), a Microsoft product that is the most popular technology, but only works on the Windows® operating system and the Microsoft SQL Server database

- Java Server Pages (JSP), a Sun Microsystems product that works with most operating systems and databases

- ColdFusion, a Macromedia product that works with most operating systems and many database products, and is popular with large organizations because of its versatility and the availability of tools to help create pages

- PHP, a free, open-source product that works on many operating systems with the MySQL database

All four of the technologies work in essentially the same way. When a page is written, the fixed portions of the page are coded in HTML while the variable portions are coded as small, embedded computer programs. Once a page is written, it is placed on a Web server. When a page is requested by a patron's Web browser, the Web server sends the page code to a pre-processor program on the server where the embedded programs are run and the needed information is drawn from the database, processed, and placed on the final page for transmission to the requestor. The necessity to either know how to write code in a computer programming language like Java or Visual Basic Script, or to buy complex software tools that can produce the code automatically makes writing database-driven Web pages difficult.

# Setting the Stage

CSULA had made plans to update the main campus Web site using ASP, so the library decided to also use this technology since the campus would maintain the necessary servers and provide tools and training for creating the pages. Our Web design team had completed a database-driven personnel page and a bibliographic database selection page when the "SQL worm" struck in the Fall of 2002. The SQL worm infected unprotected Microsoft SQL Server databases and spread to computers that were hooked to the database, destroying data on some of the infected computers. Our campus computing department shut down the SQL Server until the problem could be diagnosed and fixed. Six months later, the problems had not been resolved.

# Databases

The breakthrough to our database-driven Web page dilemma came with the realization that a set of JavaScript arrays could simulate a database. JavaScript is a programming language used to add dynamic content to Web pages. JavaScript programs are embedded within Web pages, but are processed by the Web browser on the patron's computer rather than on the Web page server. JavaScript was originally a Netscape technology, but is now supported by all major browsers (e.g., Netscape, IE, Mozilla, Opera, etc.).

To understand how JavaScript could simulate a database, it is necessary to examine what a database is. A database is a set of records that contain related facts. For example, a database of books and authors could look like Table 1.

Items within the database are identified by their Field Name and Record Number. So **Author 3** is Ray Bradbury and **Book 2** is *Foundation*.

A JavaScript array is a set of variables (memory storage locations) that share the same name and are distinguished from each other by a numeric index. An array of days might be:

*Table 1*

| Record Number | Author | Book |
|---|---|---|
| 1 | Adams, Douglas | The Hitchhiker's Guide to the Galaxy |
| 2 | Asimov, Isaac | Foundation |
| 3 | Bradbury, Ray | The Martian Chronicles |
| ... | ... | ... |
| 98 | Zelany, Roger | This Immortal |

```
Day[1]="Sunday";
Day[2]="Monday";
Day[3]="Tuesday";
Day[4]="Wednesday";
Day[5]="Thursday";
Day[6]="Friday";
Day[7]="Saturday";
```

Similarly, the book/author database could be achieved using the following JavaScript code:

```
Author[1]="Adams, Douglas";
Book[1]="The Hitchhiker's Guide to the Galaxy";
Author[2]="Asimov, Isaac";
Book[2]="Foundation";
Author[3]="Bradbury, Ray";
Book[3]="The Martian Chronicles";

   .           .

   .           .

Author[98]="Zelany, Roger";
Book[98]="This Immortal";
```

The indexes of the array are equivalent to the Record Numbers of the database, and the variable names are equivalent to the Field Names. The data in a JavaScript database can be manipulated in much the same way as data in a standard database.

With a database technology in place, all that remained was to create a way to use the information from the database. A test Web page similar to an ASP page was created. The page consisted of segments of HTML code with small embedded JavaScript programs that read and manipulated the data in the JavaScript array. The test pages were successful, and we went on to design our personnel pages (see Figure 1) and a bibliographic online database selection page (see Figure 2) using the technology. All of the processing for the Web page

*Figure 1*

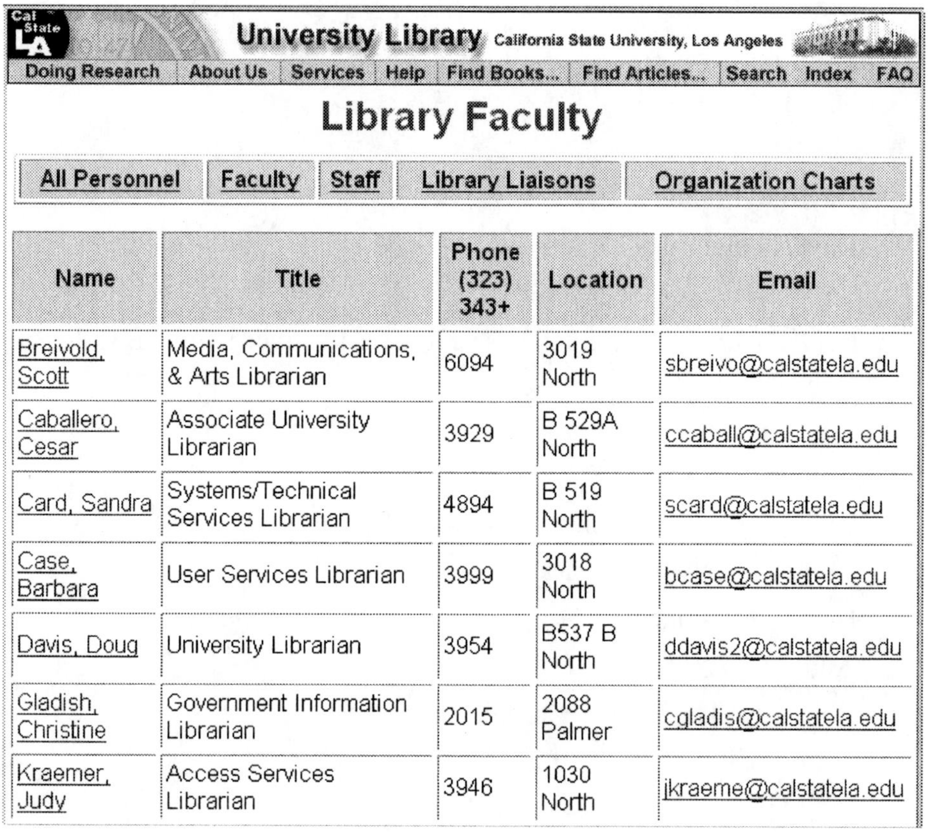
Cal State LA University Library California State University, Los Angeles

Doing Research | About Us | Services | Help | Find Books... | Find Articles... | Search | Index | FAQ

# Library Faculty

All Personnel | Faculty | Staff | Library Liaisons | Organization Charts

| Name | Title | Phone (323) 343+ | Location | Email |
|---|---|---|---|---|
| Breivold, Scott | Media, Communications, & Arts Librarian | 6094 | 3019 North | sbreivo@calstatela.edu |
| Caballero, Cesar | Associate University Librarian | 3929 | B 529A North | ccaball@calstatela.edu |
| Card, Sandra | Systems/Technical Services Librarian | 4894 | B 519 North | scard@calstatela.edu |
| Case, Barbara | User Services Librarian | 3999 | 3018 North | bcase@calstatela.edu |
| Davis, Doug | University Librarian | 3954 | B537 B North | ddavis2@calstatela.edu |
| Gladish, Christine | Government Information Librarian | 2015 | 2088 Palmer | cgladis@calstatela.edu |
| Kraemer, Judy | Access Services Librarian | 3946 | 1030 North | jkraeme@calstatela.edu |

takes place on the client's machine, so this new technology has been dubbed Active Client Pages.

A search of the library literature showed a number of articles on server-based database-driven Web design, but none on client based. Books on the subject also failed to mention this technique; however, a check of the Web showed at least three sites that mention using similar techniques. In all cases, the technology seems to have been discovered independently. This is not surprising since it is conceptually simple. The sites include *AccessObject-Javascript Database* (www.javascriptdatabase.com), the *British Archeological Jobs Resource Web Site* (www.archaeo.freeserve.co.uk/Main.html), and a tutorial *Database Front End: Using DHTML for Client-Side Storage and Display* (www.Webreference.com/dhtml/column4/index.html). All sites were last accessed in late December of 2003.

*Figure 2*

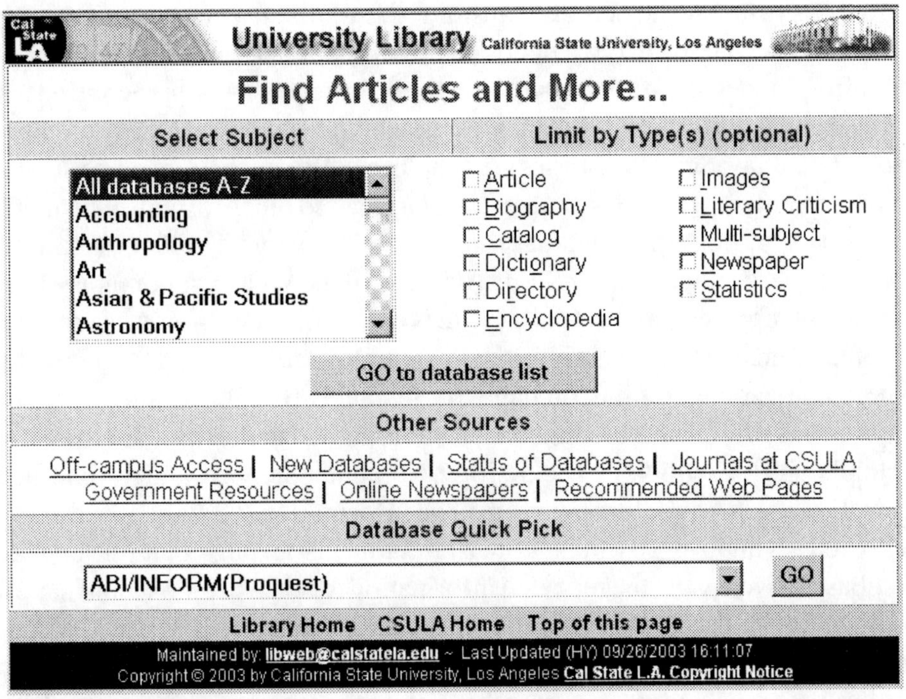

## Advantages and Disadvantages

A primary advantage of Active Client Pages is the relative simplicity of creation of the code. No special tools or software are needed to create a JavaScript database or the associated pages. A text editor such as Notepad® is all that is needed. JavaScript is also a much simpler language to learn than Java or Visual Basic Script, and the commands needed to retrieve and manipulate JavaScript arrays are significantly more straightforward than database query commands. Active Client Pages are also independent of the software on the server where they reside. They will work correctly with any Web server. They do not depend on the Web server's software or operating system as server-side databases do.

The primary disadvantage is download speed. The patron's Web browser performs all processing, so it must download both the Active Client Page and the entire JavaScript database before the page can be displayed. Using a 56k modem, the Active Client personnel page shown in Figure 1 requires 10 seconds to initially download, and the bibliographic databases selection page shown in Figure 2 requires 20 seconds. These times seem short except when actually staring at the screen waiting for it to display. On most systems, however, the database only needs to download once per session, with all remaining accesses being drawn from the browser cache, so a second access to the database selection page takes less than five seconds. Another mitigating factor is that JavaScript databases are simple text files, so they are much smaller than conventional databases. As a test, I uploaded the information from the JavaScript bibliographic databases array into Access®. The Access file was four times larger than the JavaScript file. Also, if the Web page contains a large amount of repeated data, download times can be faster with an Active Client database since the information is only downloaded once and then inserted wherever needed. Our liaison page, for instance, lists 96 organizations for which our 16 librarians are liaisons; I was assigned to the three Engineering Schools, and the schools of Technology, Computer Science, and Psychology, as well as the NASA Stars program. The information for some librarians is repeated as much as 10 times. For a standard HTML page or a server-side, database-driven page, the repeated information for each person would have to be downloaded each time it is used within a page. In an Active Client Page, the information is downloaded once with the database, and the JavaScript program on the user's machine inserts it into the Web page as many times as needed. For the liaison page, the combined downloads of all needed databases and the Web page are 40% smaller than either the original HTML-coded Web page or the ASP page.

The major advantage of server-based database pages is that the database, which can be very large, is not downloaded to the patron's machine. Only the requested information is sent. Additionally, all processing is done on a server, which generally has greater processing power and larger memory capacity. The disadvantages of server-side database pages are the complexity of writing the pages, the cost and complexity of the special programs needed to create the database, and the difficulty in creating and updating the database due to security restrictions on the server.

## Creating the Database

As with any database, care must be taken in planning a JavaScript database. Since the entire database will be downloaded, it must be as small as possible. Evaluating what information to place in each database requires significant preplanning. The library's personnel database is used for two sets of public pages—pages that list personnel by type (faculty or staff) (see Figure 1), and pages that list liaison responsibilities (see Figure 3), as well as several pages on the library's intranet. The listing by type pages did not require information about liaison responsibilities, but the liaison pages needed this information, as well as information about the faculty who serve as departmental contacts. To minimize the size of the files that have to be downloaded, the information was split into two databases. The first database has names, job descriptions, phone numbers, e-mail addresses, office room numbers, library Web page address, and whether they are faculty or staff. For example:

WebPage[40] = "/library/hmpgs/ssotton.htm";

Name[40] = "Sottong, Stephen";

Job[40] = "Engineering, Computer Science, Technology &amp; Psychology Librarian";

Ext[40] = "5168";

Room[40] = "1025 A North";

Mail[40] = "ssotton@calstatela.edu";

Status[40] = "Faculty";

The second database has a list of all organizations with which the library has liaison relationships, the faculty representative from that organization to the library, and the library faculty member who has liaison responsibility to the organization. For example:

School[31] = "Computer Science";

Liaison[31] = "40";

Coordinator[31] = "Lu, Chen";

To relate the organization to the personnel database, the record number for the liaison is used. In the above example, the liaison is number 40 which is Stephen Sottong.

Splitting the files in this way means that unused organization information is not downloaded when viewing lists of personnel. Additionally, since the organization list is independent of the personnel list, the organizations can be arranged

*Figure 3*

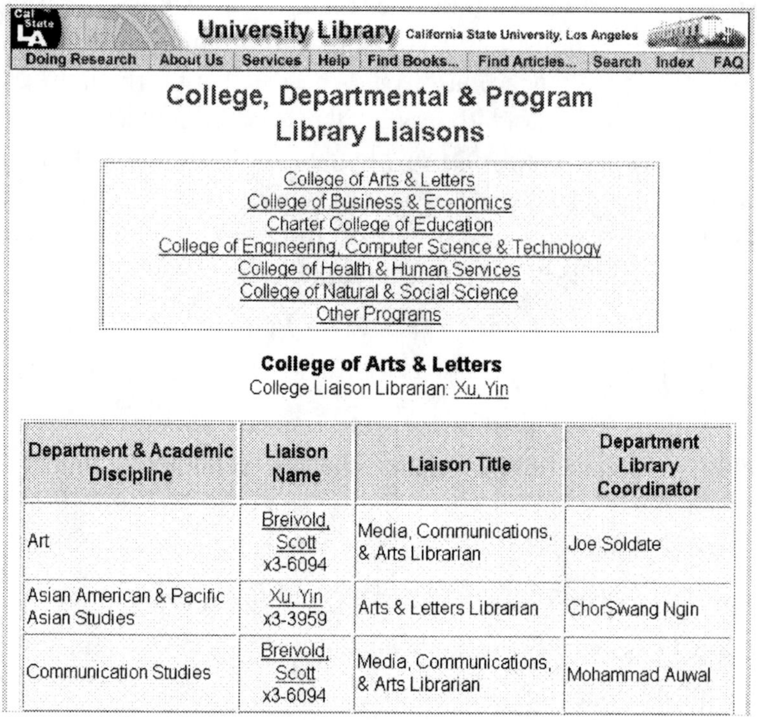

in the order in which they are to be displayed, which eases page formatting.

A balance must be reached between splitting the database into multiple files and co-locating related information. The personnel database, for instance, could be split into seven separate files, but this would make updating information a nightmare.

Using record numbers to relate one database file to another (e.g., Liaison[31] = "40";) has significant advantages. The number can be used as an array index to directly retrieve data from another JavaScript database without the lengthy sorting required if a name was used. Numbers also reduce the amount of redundant data in the database, keeping it optimally small. However, using record numbers can also create problems. In a true relational database such as Access® or SQL Server®, links between records are automatically updated whenever records are added or deleted. In a JavaScript database, this process must be done manually. As such, renumbering a database that contains numeric cross-references is a time-consuming task that should be avoided. To minimize the number of times this must be done, provision was made for blank records in all of the display code. If, for instance, Name[49]=""; and the liaison code is 49, the field in the output can be left blank or the entire record ignored.

Because JavaScript databases are actually small programs, a few additional lines of code are required in each database to complete it. In addition to individual entries in the databases, each array in the database must be declared at the beginning of the database file, as in this example from the library personnel database:

```
var WebPage = new Array();
var Name = new Array();
var Job = new Array();
var Ext = new Array();
var Room = new Array();
var Mail = new Array();
var Status = new Array();
```

Finally, the number of entries in the database must be passed to the display program:

```
NumPersons = 47;
```

The JavaScript database for the bibliographic database selection page posed a different set of needs. The selector page chooses from a set of display pages that have a preset list of bibliographic databases. The information to be displayed is contained in a JavaScript database. A typical results page is shown in Figure 4.

The JavaScript database had to contain considerable information for each bibliographic database. A typical entry in the database looks like this:

```
URL[82] = "http://Web.lexis-nexis.com/universe"
Name[82] = "Lexis-Nexis Academic"
AltName[82] = "~Academic Universe"
Descr[82] = "All subjects; emphasis on business, law, politics."
```

Help[82] = "/library/dbs/~L2.htm"

Index[82] = "full"

Type[82] = "multi-subject|article|newspaper"

Coverage[82] = "varies"

Proxy[82] = "y"

The first line of the entry is the URL for the bibliographic database's search page, followed by an entry for the database Name. The AltName line is used for several purposes depending on the initial character in the name. In the example, the tilde at the beginning of the name indicates that the name that follows is a former name for the bibliographic database. Other possible uses are alternate names and the databases' aggregator (e.g., EBSCOHost). The AltName line and the Type line can contain an indefinite number of pieces of data which are joined using a bar (|) character. These pieces of data are parsed by the JavaScript display program. The Descr line is a brief description of the database. This description is used by default when displaying; however, it can be overridden within each display page. The Help line is the URL for a separate

*Figure 4*

page that contains the help information. Placing actual help text within the database would have made the database too large. The Index line indicates whether the bibliographic database is full-text, partial full-text, or indexing only. The Type line is a string of multiple types (e.g., article, encyclopedia, etc.) which describe the information in the database. The types are taken from a preset list. Coverage is a date range for the bibliographic database and, finally, the Proxy line states whether the URL for the campus EZproxy should be appended to the search URL.

Specifying which files appear on a page is handled by a separate set of JavaScript databases, one for each discipline. The entries in this database have the form:

```
DbNum[1] = 0;
altDescr[1] = "Most Useful";
DbNum[2] = 56; /*database name= "EI Village"*/
altDescr[2] = "Primary database for Engineering research. Use this
database to find articles from all major engineering societies and publish-
ers. Includes conference proceedings.";
DbNum[3] = 0; /*database name= " "*/
altDescr[3] = "Also Useful";
DbNum[4] = 16; /*database name= "ASCE"*/
altDescr[4] = "";
```

This sets of entries corresponds to the display seen in Figure 5. Each entry has two lines. The DbNum line can either be **0**, which indicates that the text in the accompanying altDescr entry is a new heading for the page, or the DbNum can be the number of a listing in the JavaScript database of bibliographic databases mentioned above. So the first entry would create a heading with the text "**Most Useful.**" The next entry would draw information from the database of databases for "EI Village," since EI Village is the 56th entry in the database of bibliographic databases. The altDescr line of this entry is used as the description for the database in the display. In contrast, the fourth entry in this set has no altDescr entry, so the default description from the database of bibliographic databases would be used.

*Figure 5*

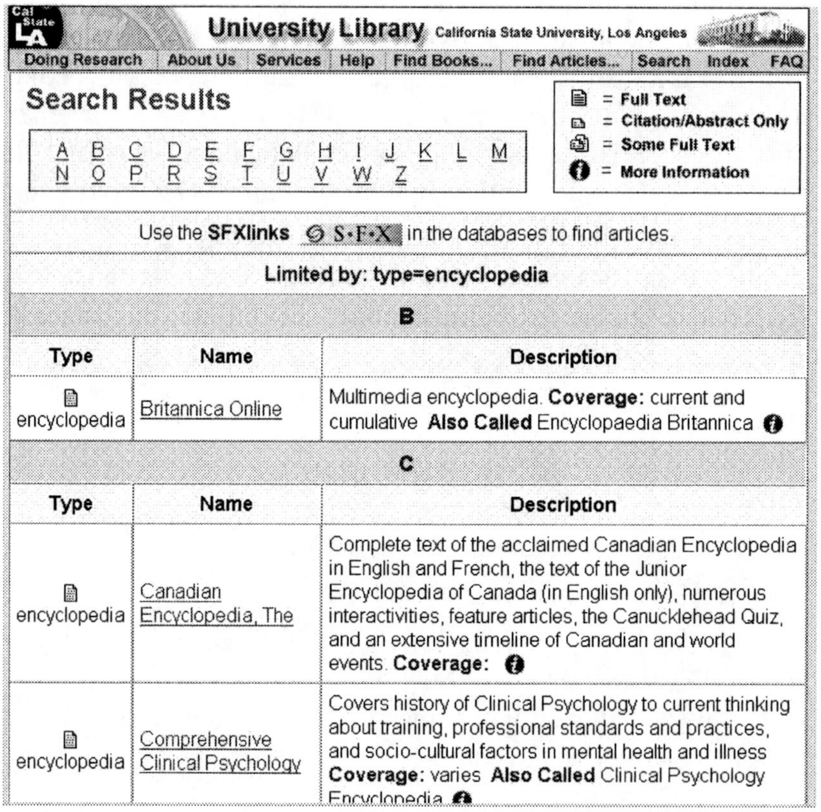

## Coding the Pages

As in a server-side technology such as ASP, Active Client Pages are a combination of HTML code and program segments. In the case of Active Client Pages, the language used for the programs is JavaScript.

Loading the database is done with a JavaScript routine called a "client side include." For example, in the library personnel pages, the code is:

```
<script language="JavaScript" src="/library/cgi-bin/personnel.js"
type="text/javascript"></script><noscript>This page will not work with-
out JavaScript enabled.</noscript>
```

The section between the <script and </script> tags loads the database file. The section between the <noscript> and </noscript> tags provides an error message that will only display if the patron does not have JavaScript enabled on their browser.

The JavaScript code needed to retrieve, process, and display data will vary for each application. For the library's personnel page, the display code has two parts. The first part alphabetizes the names. This is done in the display code rather than within the database to minimize renumbering. The code for sorting is:

```
var indices=0;
for (i=1;i<=NumPersons;i++)
        {
        if (Name[indices]!="")
                {
                indices++;
                SortNames[indices]=Name[i];
                SortNums[indices]=i;
                }
        }
x=1
do
{
        Switched=0;
        for (Z=1;Z<=indices-x;Z++)
        {
                if (SortNames[Z]>SortNames[Z+1])
                {
                        TempNames=SortNames[Z+1];
                        SortNames[Z+1]=SortNames[Z];
                        SortNames[Z]=TempNames;
                        TempNums=SortNums[Z+1];
                        SortNums[Z+1]=SortNums[Z];
                        SortNums[Z]=TempNums;
                        Switched++;
```

```
            }
        }
x++
}
while (x<indices && Switched>0);
```

Here, the first section of the routine checks to see if there are any entries in the database with blank name fields. If there are, it omits them from the sort. The second section performs a simple "bubble sort," which swaps entries if the name of the current entry comes after the name of the next entry.

The second part displays either the faculty, staff, or all personnel within a table:

```
for (x=1;x<=indices;x++)
{
if (Status[SortNums[x]]==srch || srch=="Personnel")
    {
    document.write("<tr><td><a href=\"");
    document.write(WebPage[SortNums[x]]);
    document.write("\">");
    document.write(Name[SortNums[x]]);
    document.write("</a></td><td>");
    document.write(Job[SortNums[x]]);
    document.write("</td><td>");
    document.write(Ext[SortNums[x]]);
    document.write("</td><td>");
    document.write(Room[SortNums[x]]);
    document.write("</td><td>");
    document.write("<a href=\"mailto:" + Mail[SortNums[x]] + "\">" +
Mail[SortNums[x]] + "</a>");
    document.write("</td></tr>");
    }
}
```

The loop runs through all non-blank names and displays those that match the set criteria (faculty, staff, or all personnel). The overall code for this page is very small. The code does not require special statements to open the database, or statements to create a recordset, or specialized code to retrieve the data from the recordset as do server-based technologies. To retrieve a particular name, Name[i] performs the task. The compact simplicity of the code for this page demonstrates one of the advantages of Active Client Pages.

A common JavaScript program is used for all of the bibliographic database selection display pages. In addition to displaying a set list of bibliographic databases, the display program can also predicate selections depending on a "Type" criteria appended to the page's URL. Figure 5 shows such a display of bibliographic databases which are selected for only encyclopedias. By contrast to the relatively simple program used to display personnel, the bibliographic database display program is fairly complex, taking over 300 lines to perform its tasks. Space does not permit discussion; however, the code is freely available at www.calstatela.edu/library/cgi-bin/dbdisplay.js. Most browsers will prompt you to save the JavaScript program as a file.

# Conclusion

Active Client Pages is a database-driven Web page technology that does not require special, server-based preprocessor programs or complex and expensive databases with their Byzantine security restrictions and susceptibility to hacking. Active Client Technology creates compact databases and Web pages which can be produced without expensive support software.

But Active Client Pages are not for every application. Since the entire database must be downloaded to the patron's computer, Active Client Pages are not appropriate for large, complex databases or for databases with sensitive or proprietary information. Where the information in the database is relatively small and all information is intended for display, Active Client Pages can work well.

JavaScript databases are simple enough to create that they do not require a person with specialized training. Our library's database of bibliographic databases was created by a Library Assistant with no JavaScript experience; however, creating the associated Web pages requires an individual with a solid working knowledge of JavaScript.

For organizations that have not implemented one of the server-based technologies, Active Client Pages offers a method for creating database-driven Web pages with minimal expense and complexity. Active Client Pages works well for applications such as personnel pages, schedules, lists of bibliographic databases, and other Web pages where moderate amounts of changing information need to be displayed on multiple Web pages.

The Active Client Pages technology is free for all to use.

# Supporting Materials

## Questions and Answers

Question: What are the four major implementations for database-driven Web pages?

Answer: ASP, JSP, ColdFusion, PHP

Question: How can a JavaScript array be used to simulate a database?

Answer: The array subscripts act like the database record numbers, and the array variable name acts like the database field name.

Question: What is the primary difference between HTML pages and database-driven pages?

Answer: Database-driven pages contain small program segments in addition to standard HTML code. This allows the page to react dynamically to input data.

Question: What is the only piece of software required to create Active Client Pages?

Answer: A text editor

Question: What are the major advantages of Active Client Pages?

Answer:

- simplicity of creation
- simplicity of coding
- does not need specialized software
- does not require access to a server

Question: What are the major disadvantages of Active Client Pages?

Answer:

- Download speed
- Program segments are executed on the client's computer which may be slower than a server.
- All data in the database are transmitted, therefore, the database cannot contain sensitive data.

**Chapter IX**

# Tactical Electric Power Digital Library

Anne Marie Donovan
Independent Consultant, USA

Michael Nomura
University of Texas Institute for Advanced Technology in Austin,
USA

## Abstract

*This case study traces the development of the Tactical Electric Power Digital Library (TEPDL), a special-purpose document repository and information resource Web site. Discussion focuses on content management considerations and their effect on project planning, Web site design, and Web site maintenance. Also described are the process and challenges associated with implementing the content management and content delivery features of TEPDL. The case study is intended to highlight the importance of addressing content management issues early in the digital library Web site planning and design process, and to illustrate how a content management needs analysis can be translated into the selection and development of specific content management tools and processes.*

# Introduction

The Tactical Electric Power Digital Library (TEPDL) is a special-purpose, online information resource that was developed as part of a research project conducted at the Institute for Advanced Technology (IAT) under the auspices of the University XXI program, "a joint effort by the University of Texas at Austin and Texas A&M University to provide digitization research to the U.S. Army" (University XXI, 2003). TEPDL's parent project, *Power Management on the Digital Battlefield*, was a broad investigation into the challenges related to supporting the Army's next-generation "digital force" with sustainable, high-quality electric power. TEPDL was conceived to fulfill one of the *Power Management* project's primary goals, which was "to build a comprehensive body of knowledge regarding electric power generation and consumption on the tactical battlefield" (Leedom, n.d., Section 1, Paragraph 1).

Intended to stimulate information exchange on tactical electric power issues within the Army, TEPDL supports the collection, dissemination, and management of online digital and digitized information resources. TEPDL is a digital library Web site composed of three primary information resource tools: a Document Collection, a Subject Matter Expert (SME) Directory, and a Web Resources Guide.

## Document Collection

The Document Collection is a repository of born-digital and digitized documents. Document types include, but are not limited to, research reports, project briefings, project papers, technology and tactical system descriptions and specifications, lessons learned and best practices information, and test and evaluation results. To encourage content reuse, items in the Document Collection are stored and provided to users in native (original) formats whenever possible. Commonly used formats include Adobe Acrobat Portable Document Format (PDF), Microsoft Word, Microsoft PowerPoint, and Joint Photographic Experts Group (JPEG) image format. Users can view documents online, print them, or download them.

## SME Directory

The SME Directory contains contact information for individuals who have professional expertise related to the production, storage, distribution, or use of electric power in tactical environments.

## Web Resources Guide

The Web Resources Guide is a categorized, annotated directory of evaluated Web site links. The selected Web site links provide access to a broad range of U.S. Army and Department of Defense organizations that have a role in the production, management, or use of electric power on the tactical battlefield. The Guide also includes links to Web sites that contain reference resources, publications, and research and technical information related to electric power generation, distribution, storage, and consumption.

# Background

The Institute for Advanced Technology (IAT) is an autonomous research unit of the University of Texas at Austin, a major research university with approximately 50,000 students, 2,700 faculty, and 17,000 staff members (University of Texas at Austin, 2003). IAT participates in a wide range of research and education programs, but its primary focus has been to support the U.S. Army with basic and applied research in electrodynamics, hypervelocity physics, pulsed power, and education in critical technologies related to those fields (Institute for Advanced Technology, 2003a).

In 1999, IAT initiated the Advanced Training Technology (ATT) team, a special research program to examine the complex information and technology challenges the Army faces in its development of digital training programs (Institute for Advanced Technology, 2003b). The ATT team conducts Army digitization-related research and development under the auspices of the University XXI program, a Congressionally funded initiative to support the U.S. Army that is renewed on an annual basis. *Power Management on the Digital Battlefield*, the parent project for TEPDL, was one of six University XXI research and development efforts approved for Fiscal Year 2002.

# Setting the Stage

Since its inception, IAT has been involved in the development and application of highly complex emerging technologies for a variety of customers. Information and knowledge management technologies, in contrast, seem to have been embraced more slowly than have other technology tools. The fragmentation of IAT into small, semi-independent research units appears to have precluded the establishment of sophisticated systems for organization-wide information sharing. Much collaboration is done face-to-face, and there is heavy reliance on e-mail for project communication. The TEPDL development effort exposed IAT to a number of information management technologies and concepts that might be applied to IAT's own processes and infrastructure.

An in-house information technology (IT) department with two full-time and one or more part-time personnel provides technical support and system administration services for IAT's approximately 150 desktop/laptop computers and 10 network servers. In addition, the head of IAT's Technical Library, assisted by one part-time student employee, maintains IAT's public Web site and a limited organizational intranet.

The TEPDL development team initially comprised two graduate students from the School of Information at the University of Texas at Austin working part time. The team members were chosen primarily for their knowledge as graduate students in an Information Studies program, but also because of their previous active duty military experience. These core team members were assisted on an as-needed and as-available basis by IAT's information technology support staff and the Technical Library's part-time student Web developer. During the later stages of the project, the core development team was expanded to include a full-time IT professional.

The small scale of the TEPDL project permitted most project development, management, and evaluation to be conducted through informal team meetings. For the first six weeks of the project, the core development team met with the *Power Management* project manager twice a week to discuss the direction and status of the TEPDL project. Once the project's government sponsors reviewed and approved the team's proposed implementation concept, these regularly scheduled meetings were reduced to once per week.

Budgetary concerns affected TEPDL development in two ways. First, TEPDL was just one of several ongoing efforts vying for the shared funds of the larger *Power Management* project. Consequently, the TEPDL team sought to minimize development and implementation costs whenever possible. Second, since the final hosting organization for TEPDL had not yet been identified, hosting TEPDL would represent an unplanned expense for the selected organization. The eventual host would most likely have to rely on existing resources (money, people, and technology infrastructure) to support TEPDL for at least one fiscal year. For this reason, minimization of system deployment and maintenance costs was an important consideration during the design effort.

# Case Description

The TEPDL team members were familiar with system development and project management principles and, in the first days of the project, decided to adopt a standard information system development methodology as the framework for the project plan. The team identified six major phases in the development process:

- Phase I: Project Definition and Planning
- Phase II: Data Collection and Analysis
- Phase III: Design
- Phase IV: Construction
- Phase V: Testing and Redesign
- Phase VI: Maintenance

## Phase I: Project Definition and Planning

At the beginning of the project, the development team knew only that it had been tasked to build a knowledge base (the term "knowledge base" is used here in a generic sense and is not intended to imply the use of formal knowledge representation or artificial intelligence) representing "a comprehensive body of knowledge regarding electric power generation and consumption on the tactical battlefield" (Leedom, n.d., Section 1, Paragraph 1). No written specifications for the form or content of the knowledge base had been developed. The team did, however, have access to two source documents from the parent *Power Management* project that proved useful in developing the knowledge base concept. The first document, the original *Power Manage-*

*ment* project proposal, described the general assumptions, goals, tasks, structure, timeline, and resources for the overall project. Some of this information was applicable to the development of the knowledge base concept. The second document, an unpublished slide presentation outlining an initial *Power Management* project strategy, described the "Knowledge Acquisition" phase of the *Power Management* project in some detail. The idea for building a knowledge base had been an outcome of this presentation. This document also identified potential knowledge base users, including tactical system requirements developers, tactical system designers, simulation developers, trainers, and tactical system operators. Armed with insights gleaned from these two documents, and after extensive discussions with the project manager and government sponsor, the development team began to distill the relatively abstract concept of a knowledge base down to a more useable project definition.

As a starting point, the team clarified and confirmed the overall goals and purpose of the proposed knowledge base. The knowledge base was to serve as a centralized, easily accessible, unclassified repository for the formal findings, reports, and other information products produced by the *Power Management* project. Further, the knowledge base was to be an enduring, evolving, and growing information resource and a catalyst for stimulating greater sharing and better dissemination of information regarding tactical electric power.

The team made an early decision that the knowledge base would be Web based. The Web has several characteristics that made it a good fit for this project. First, the Web is an open-ended, fluid medium. A Web-based implementation would provide the flexibility needed to evolve and grow the knowledge base over time. Second, the Web is an efficient way to deliver and manage information across widely dispersed geographic locations. This characteristic is particularly important for an organization like the U.S. Army, which has personnel located throughout the U.S. and around the world. Finally, the Web is relatively easy to access and use. This characteristic of the Web would make the knowledge base accessible to the greatest number of its target audience members in the most time-, cost-, and technology-efficient manner.

Just as the proposed knowledge base had no predefined form, it also had no predefined content. In other words, there was no extant collection of documents or other readily available examples of desirable information resources that might be used as a basis for defining the scope of the project. The development team members, who themselves were not experts in tactical electric power, knew that the identification and development of meaningful content would depend heavily on outside input. Members of the knowledge base's target user audience, which included many different stakeholder groups concerned with tactical electric power, were considered to be the best initial and continuing resource for identifying and providing useful content. As a result, the first and most fundamental content management premise established for the knowledge base was that end users would be among the primary contributors of content. This content management consideration would eventually influence many of the content and functionality requirements for the Web site.

To expedite the design phase of the project, the development team made some general assumptions regarding the basic forms of content that would be included in the knowledge base. First, the team concluded that most of the content would be in the form of self-contained documents. Examples might include journal articles, research papers, technical specification sheets, and after-action reports, as well as some less traditional documentary forms such as slide presentations, images, and video and sound clips. Second, the team had already determined that certain individuals (SMEs) would serve as invaluable sources of domain knowledge. These individuals would be represented in the knowledge base with descriptions of their expertise and related contact information. Finally, and as a natural extension to the idea of the knowledge base as a Web-based resource, it seemed appropriate for the knowledge base to include a collection of links to other Web-based resources. The resulting knowledge base concept document specified the development of a stand-alone, digital library Web site comprising three main information resource components: a digital document repository, an SME Directory, and a Web Resources Guide.

With a basic concept for the knowledge base established, the team developed a high-level work plan, setting target completion dates for major development tasks. From a starting point of mid-September 2002, the project had a final product delivery date of September 2003. Academic deadlines imposed upon the two graduate student team members dictated a relatively compressed timeline of three months to complete the first three phases of the project, which included: scoping and defining the project; completing a user analysis, technology survey, and content survey; and developing an initial system design specification. This compressed development timeline was also influenced by the need to field a working mock-up of the Web site by February 2003 and to roll out a fully functional prototype by early March 2003. The period from March to September 2003 would be used for system testing, redesign, and documentation development. The identification, creation, and collection of content would constitute a primary task throughout the project.

## Phase II: Data Collection and Analysis

The defined tasks for this phase of the project included the verification of primary stakeholders and users, collection and analysis of user data, and identification of system requirements. Verifying primary stakeholders and users was completed through a review of project documentation and consultation with the project sponsor. The collection of primary user data was to be carried out using a variety of methods, including contextual inquiry, user participation, and survey questionnaire. Time and budget constraints, however, ultimately barred the use of preferred methods for user data collection, such as contextual inquiry (on-site observation and interview). The team discussed the problem of user data collection and analysis at length and decided to proceed using only the exploratory user survey data that had been developed.

The idea that management and delivery of all knowledge base services would occur over the Internet through a Web-enabled interface was fundamental to the TEPDL concept. In arriving at that decision, the development team members had made some assumptions—based on their own experiences in military service—regarding target users' computer skills and access to technology. The legitimacy of those assumptions would have to be verified, so the task of collecting and analyzing data on potential users' computer skills and organizational information technology infrastructures was considered a high priority. Accordingly, the exploratory survey questionnaire included several technology use questions.

In addition to distributing the survey questionnaire to a set of target users and organizational leaders via e-mail attachment, the team also made the questionnaire available through a Web interface. This decision proved to be fortuitous. The majority of users responded through the online version of the questionnaire, thereby providing presumptive evidence that users' computer skill levels and their organizational technology infrastructures would be sufficient to enable use of a Web-based knowledge base. The development team recognized that the methods used to distribute and provide access to the survey questionnaire may have skewed the responses in favor of users with above-average computer skills and technology access. The purpose of the survey, however, was not to profile the computer skills and technology access of all possible users, but to confirm that a reasonable segment of the target user population had appropriate skills and technology access. The resulting user survey data, supplemented with technology infrastructure information provided by the users' organizations, was sufficient to develop a baseline user and technology infrastructure profile. The typical target user respondent was found to have the following characteristics:

- Reasonable proficiency and experience using personal computers, office productivity software, e-mail, the Internet, and the World Wide Web
- Lack of significant programming experience (including Web programming or coding)
- Use of Microsoft Internet Explorer 5.x or higher to access the Web
- Access to a T1 or better network connection at work, but possibly a 56k dial-up connection at home

The exploratory survey questionnaire also included several questions about the types of information resources that respondents used in their work. The responses to these questions enabled the development team to identify an initial set of information resources that the target user groups deemed worthwhile. The team immediately began to collect, organize, and evaluate these resources for inclusion in the knowledge base. The resource list also helped the team to develop a sense of the functionality (or lack thereof) embodied in users' preferred electronic resources. The team used this knowledge to formulate functionality requirements for TEPDL.

Based on the basic design concept and an analysis of user data, the team developed a set of high-level system requirements, including several requirements related to content management. These requirements addressed the functionality needed to directly support the three primary information resource components of TEPDL: the Document Collection, SME Directory, and Web Resources Guide. Among the primary content management considerations were the following:

- Content would be subject to frequent changes including:
  - addition of new documents to the repository;
  - addition of new Web resources and changes to existing Uniform Resource Locators (URLs); and

- addition of new SME contacts and deletion of outdated SME contacts.
- Content management would involve the participation and interaction of multiple, frequently changing players.
- End users would be among primary providers of content.
- Formally assigned content managers would more likely be end users or SMEs rather than trained information professionals or Webmasters.
- Content providers/developers/managers would not necessarily be collocated with the TEPDL hosting organization.
- Content providers/developers/managers might be widely geographically dispersed.
- Most end users and content providers/developers/managers would lack programming/Web authoring skills.
- Content management workflow control mechanisms would be required and would have to enable, at a minimum, steps for submission, review, and approval of content.
- Document Collection descriptive metadata, Web resource information, and SME Directory information would be displayed in multiple ways.

The team then translated these considerations into the following content management-related system requirements:

1. A convenient, Web-enabled method for users to submit or recommend content.
2. Functionality to enable content providers/developers/managers who may have limited Web authoring/programming skills to quickly and easily add, update, delete, and publish content to the Web site.
3. Mechanisms to support a content management workflow that will accommodate separate submission, review, and approval steps.
4. A platform-independent method for managing content (to maximize geographic, personnel, and system flexibility for performing content management functions).
5. Mechanisms for separating content from presentation format (to facilitate content reuse, reduce content duplication, and prevent copying errors).

No specific requirements were developed for implementing content management functionality to manage the more static supporting content of the Web site, such as the content appearing on the Home, About, and FAQ pages. The team believed that changes to the basic structure or static content of the Web site would be infrequent and that implementing content management functionality similar to that identified for the more dynamic content areas of the site was too costly relative to any potential benefit.

## Phase III: Design

The goal of the design phase was to codify the basic system concept and set of requirements into a formal system design document to be used as a blueprint for building the actual TEPDL Web site. Included in the design document were both a functional and a technical specification for TEPDL. The functional specification, as the name implies, described what the proposed Web site should do or should enable a user to do. Roughly speaking, the functional specification represented a technology-independent view of the system design. Conversely, the technical specification provided a technology-dependent view of the design. The purpose of the technical specification was to describe the technology tools and methods that would be used to implement the functional specification.

Many of the content management features included in the original functional specification addressed the proposed end user content submission mechanisms for each of the three information resource components (Document Collection, SME Directory, and Web Resource Guide) of the site. For example, an online form was specified that would allow end users to recommend/upload digital document submissions to the Document Collection. Another form was described that would allow users to nominate themselves or others for inclusion in the SME Directory. Finally, an e-mail link was specified to enable end users to submit Web site recommendations for the Web Resources Guide. The following is an example of a functional specification for the Submit Document Form:

> By completing an online form, the user may describe and submit (or recommend) a digital document for inclusion in the Document Collection.
>
> Form includes multiple labeled fields for the user to enter descriptive metadata for a document and submit contact information.

User may reset all form fields.

Form permits the user to upload a digital document file.

Upon submitting the initial input form, the user is directed to an intermediate form page that shows all information entered. From the intermediate page, the user has the option to cancel submission, return to the initial input form to make changes, or submit the data as shown. (Note: This intermediate page serves as a data verification step.)

If final form submission is successful, the user is directed to a status page showing a receipt confirmation message. If final form submission fails, an appropriate error message is displayed to the user.

Submitted information and digital document files are stored, but are not automatically added to the Document Collection repository for display.

(Note: As a quality control measure, an authorized content manager must review and process all submissions, and load new documents and bibliographic data into the official Document Collection repository).

Figure 1 shows the resulting Submit Document Form page.

Specifications for a basic content management administration interface or content management system were also included in the functional specification (addressing content management-related Phase II requirements 2-5) (see Figures 2 and 3). The content management system was intended to enable form-based management for all content displayed in the Web Resources Guide and SME Directory components of the Web site. In addition, the content management system would provide an interface to the data and documents submitted by end users (via the Submit Document Form) for inclusion in the Document Collection.

Implementing the content management features identified in the functional specification would require the interaction of various technologies described in the technical specification. The centerpiece of the implementation solution lay in the use of dynamically generated, database-driven content. Enabling this functionality would involve three elements: a database back-end, a Web-enabled front-end, and an interface between the two.

A relational database would serve as the basic foundation for content management system functionality. The database would store and organize the principal content comprising the Web Resources Guide and SME Directory components of the Web site. Web templates would provide the main views and access into the stored content. The templates would be used to display database content

*Figure 1*

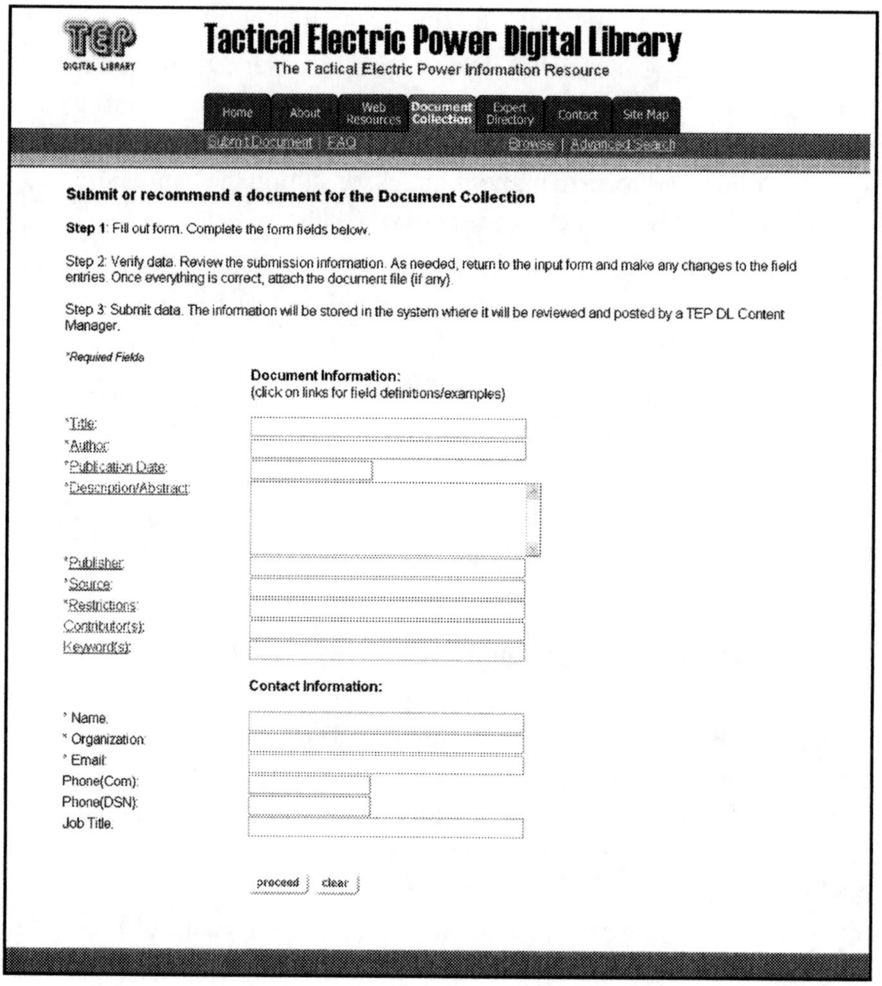
Tactical Electric Power Digital Library
The Tactical Electric Power Information Resource
Home
About
Web Resources
Document Collection
Expert Directory
Contact
Site Map
Submit Document | FAQ
Browse | Advanced Search
Submit or recommend a document for the Document Collection
Step 1: Fill out form. Complete the form fields below.
Step 2: Verify data. Review the submission information. As needed, return to the input form and make any changes to the field entries. Once everything is correct, attach the document file (if any).
Step 3: Submit data. The information will be stored in the system where it will be reviewed and posted by a TEP DL Content Manager.
*Required Fields
Document Information:
(click on links for field definitions/examples)
*Title:
*Author:
*Publication Date:
*Description/Abstract:
*Publisher:
*Source:
*Restrictions:
Contributor(s):
Keyword(s):
Contact Information:
* Name:
* Organization:
* Email:
Phone(Com):
Phone(DSN):
Job Title:
proceed
clear

on the public digital library Web site and would also be used to add, edit, delete, and display database content on the access-controlled content management system interface. A software code interface would connect the database back-end to the Web template front-end. This code would be written in one of several so-called "scripting languages," many of which have been specially designed and optimized for Web programming. Most of this code or script would be embedded within the Web templates and would run whenever those templates were accessed over the Web.

Using Web templates to dynamically retrieve and display content stored in a relational database repository would achieve the design objective of separating content from presentation format and provide the following advantages:

*Figure 2*

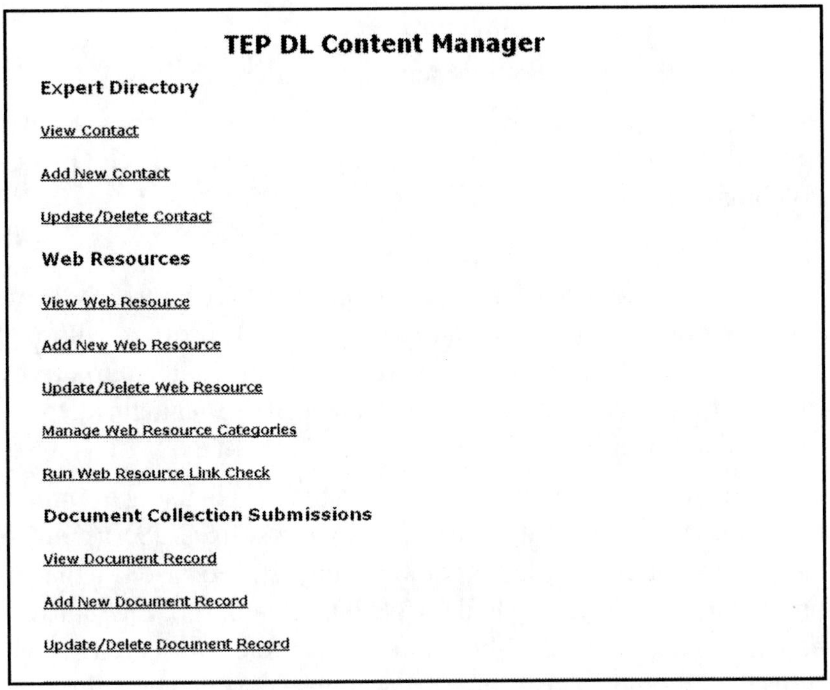

**TEP DL Content Manager**

**Expert Directory**

View Contact

Add New Contact

Update/Delete Contact

**Web Resources**

View Web Resource

Add New Web Resource

Update/Delete Web Resource

Manage Web Resource Categories

Run Web Resource Link Check

**Document Collection Submissions**

View Document Record

Add New Document Record

Update/Delete Document Record

*Figure 3*

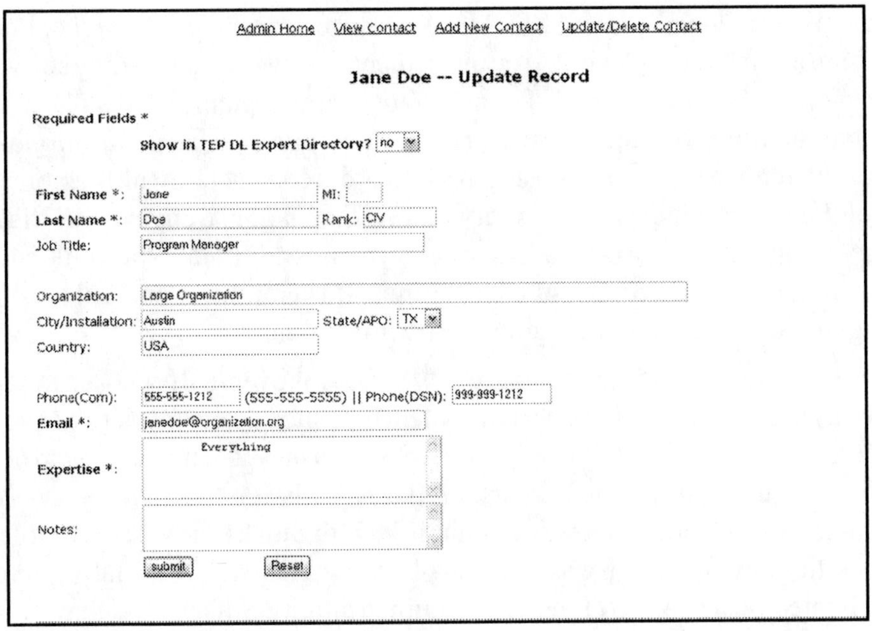

Admin Home    View Contact    Add New Contact    Update/Delete Contact

**Jane Doe -- Update Record**

Required Fields *

Show in TEP DL Expert Directory? no

First Name *: Jane          MI:
Last Name *: Doe           Rank: CIV
Job Title: Program Manager

Organization: Large Organization
City/Installation: Austin          State/APO: TX
Country: USA

Phone(Com): 555-555-1212    (555-555-5555) || Phone(DSN): 999-999-1212
Email *: janedoe@organization.org

Expertise *:     Everything

Notes:

submit          Reset

- simplify the Web site edit/update process;
- improve content and display consistency;
- reduce duplication of both content and effort; and,
- allow content providers without Web coding skills to quickly and easily publish content to the Web site, thus circumventing the proverbial Webmaster bottleneck.

Several database and scripting language options were considered before a suitable combination was selected for the TEPDL project. Although no formally defined selection criteria were used to evaluate alternatives, the informal decision-making process was influenced by four main factors: cost, ease of acquisition, ease of transferability, and ease of use.

Almost from the outset, the team dismissed the idea of using a commercial enterprise-class relational database, such as Microsoft SQL Server or Oracle, because the cost of those systems could not be justified based on the modest performance demands anticipated for TEPDL. Among commercial desktop databases, FileMaker Pro and Microsoft Access were considered as potential solutions. IAT already had an enterprise license for FileMaker Pro, and the software had a reputation for being very easy to use. Moreover, IAT also had a license for Lasso, a commercial scripting language and engine that could be used with FileMaker Pro. On the negative side, virtually no Army organization that might eventually host TEPDL was likely to have either FileMaker Pro or Lasso on hand. The selected Army host, therefore, would have to buy software licenses for both programs. In contrast, most Army organizations already own copies of Microsoft Access. Also in favor of Access was that the development team had previous experience using the database in conjunction with Macromedia ColdFusion, a popular commercial scripting language and engine. IAT did not use or support Microsoft Access, however, and the IT staff was reluctant to install the software on any of its machines. It was at this point that the team began to consider non-commercial software options.

An open source relational database, MySQL, was eventually chosen to serve as the content management system content repository. Several factors favored the selection of MySQL. First, it was free, which meant that there would be no initial acquisition or transfer costs. In addition, MySQL was widely used and extensively tested, and it was compatible with Sun Microsystems' Solaris operating system, which was necessary because TEPDL was initially going to be hosted on a spare IAT server machine running Solaris. Because of the database's widespread popularity, many software scripting languages had MySQL interface functionality already built in. In short, as a highly capable, enterprise-class database management system, MySQL far exceeded the feature and performance requirements of the TEPDL project.

To create the Web templates and provide Web-enabled connectivity to the database, the team elected to use the PHP: Hypertext Preprocessor (PHP) scripting language. PHP had many advantages very similar to those of MySQL. PHP was freely available, open source software, was widely used and tested, and it provided much more capability than was needed for TEPDL. Additionally, PHP was optimized for use on the Web and had a large number of built-in MySQL interface functions.

Compared to the SME Directory and Web Resources Guide, the Document Collection display and content management requirements were much more complex. Only one primary functional requirement (submission of a document to the Document Collection administrator) could be easily incorporated into the development team's homegrown content management system solution.

Although the team expected the Document Collection to be administrated by a fairly small, albeit geographically separated, group of SMEs, the repository's content would be collected from and distributed to a large, diverse, and widely dispersed user group solely through a Web interface. The repository would contain a variety of digital file formats (including text, images, audio, and video) and document types, not all of which would be amenable to full-text search. The repository's content management functionality would have to include a bibliographic toolset to enable resource description and discovery, as well as the ability to manage multiple collections for multiple user groups. In addition, the sensitive nature of some documents would require both user and file access control functionality at the collection and document level. Finally, the team's decision to simplify reuse of TEPDL content demanded that the repository's digital documents and their associated bibliographic data be exportable, preferably in Extensible Markup Language (XML) format. Building the required Document Collection functionality from scratch was well beyond the capability of the core development team members, so a pre-packaged software solution would have to be pursued.

Selection of a suitable software package was driven by multiple factors, including the functionality requirements listed above, ease of integration with the other components of TEPDL, software availability and acquisition costs, license transferability, and projected long-term maintenance costs. System design requirements demanded that the software package support Web delivery of content and platform independence for users. The software would also have to be scalable and extensible. The team considered three types of commercial information management software products: enterprise collaboration, document management, and digital library. An evaluation matrix was compiled to aid the selection process (see Table 1).

All of the products met some of the requirements for the document repository, but all had limitations as well. The enterprise collaboration and document management software packages had very similar characteristics and functionality. Both types of software included user/document access controls, full-text searching capabilities, and support for multiple file types/formats. However, these products also had many other features, such as robust cooperative work functionalities, that were not needed for the creation and management of the TEPDL document repository. Further, since most users of TEPDL would have access to a comprehensive suite of collaborative work tools through the Army's institutional Web portal, *Army Knowledge Online*, purchase of these functionalities for TEPDL was deemed redundant. Sophisticated bibliographic tools were generally lacking in the enterprise collaboration and document management products. In addition, these packages commonly involved per-seat charges, the use of proprietary client software, and the need to purchase add-on components to achieve the desired level of functionality. Of the digital library software suites, few supported the conversion of non-text formats (such

*Table 1*

| Product Type | Platform independence | Multiple digital formats | Archival management tools | Full-text search | Full-featured bibliographic toolset | Scalable and Extensible | XML base | Cost factors |
|---|---|---|---|---|---|---|---|---|
| Enterprise Collaboration | SOME | YES | ADD ON | YES | NO | YES | YES | Per Seat Charge |
| Document Management | SOME | YES | ADD ON | YES | NO | YES | YES | Per Seat Charge |
| Digital Library | YES* | YES | YES | YES | YES | YES | YES | No Seat Charge |

as PDF) for full-text search, but all provided full-featured toolsets for bibliographic description, resource discovery, and collection and document management. The digital library products also supported online display and delivery of multiple file types, and the export of bibliographic data (sometimes in more than one format). In addition, these software packages offered platform independence for end users and levied no per-seat charges.

Having concluded that digital library software was the best vehicle for the TEPDL Document Collection, the team reviewed the small list of available products, keeping cost considerations foremost in mind. Though less expensive than enterprise collaboration or document management software, commercial digital library software products, typically priced at several thousand dollars, were by no means inexpensive. The team opted, therefore, to turn first to an open source software solution and quickly focused on Greenstone Digital Library software.

Greenstone is a product of the New Zealand Digital Library Project at the University of Waikato, and is being developed and distributed in cooperation with the United Nations Educational, Scientific, and Cultural Organization (UNESCO) and the Human Information for All Non-Governmental Organization (Human Info NGO) as open source software under the terms of the GNU General Public License (Greenstone.org, n.d.). Greenstone software was easy to install and was not overly difficult to use, but the evaluation process quickly revealed some unexpected limitations in the software's functionality. For example, input of large documents was time consuming (taking several hours in some cases), and the team was unable to pinpoint the root cause. In addition, it was not possible to delete individual documents from aggregated collections, and there appeared to be no provision for easily customizing the pre-loaded presentation templates.

Although the Greenstone Digital Library software package was zero-cost to acquire and performed largely as advertised, it did not meet all of the functionality requirements for the TEPDL digital document repository. Furthermore, because the team did not have the skills to modify the software, Greenstone could not be integrated with the TEPDL Web site without hiring a professional programmer to write new code—a prohibitive time and cost factor for the project. Based on the team's lack of expertise for modifying complex open source software, the project manager directed the team to pursue a commercial software package for the Document Collection. The presumed advantage of a commercial solution over an open source product was that the commercial contract could be written to include vendor-provided operation and maintenance support, which the team was very likely to need when integrating the software with the other components of the TEPDL Web site.

The team elected to test CONTENTdm, a commercial digital library product distributed by DiMeMa, Inc. The decision to evaluate CONTENTdm was made because it was available on a 60-day, free-trial basis and because it incorporated many attractive content management features. CONTENTdm's Web-enabled collection administration toolset allowed user and collection management to be conducted by multiple individuals, and documents to be processed into the repository from as many as 50 separate locations. CONTENTdm also supported common data interchange protocols such as Z39.50 and Open Archives Initiative (OAI) harvesting, and resource descriptions were based on the Dublin Core and the Visual Resource Association Core. To enable content reuse, all resource descriptions could be exported in XML. CONTENTdm's content management capability required a proprietary client, so it was not possible to integrate this interface with TEPDL's other content management system tools. As a result, implementing CONTENTdm to support the Document Collection meant that Web site content would have to be maintained using two separate content management interfaces. Given the advanced functionality of CONTENTdm, however, this limitation was deemed a minor issue, especially since it would affect only Web site administrators and not end users. Overall, the team was impressed by the features and performance of CONTENTdm during the trial period, and IAT subsequently contracted to purchase the software for TEPDL.

## Phase IV: Construction

Construction was the most labor-intensive phase of the project, requiring additional people and skills to augment the core development team. The Technical Library's part-time Web developer, for example, proved instrumental throughout the construction phase. In close coordination with the core development team, the Web developer created almost all of the visual design elements of TEPDL and did most of the Hyper Text Markup Language (HTML) coding for the Web site. The core development team members handled the PHP scripting, database creation, CONTENTdm toolset configuration, and content processing and maintenance. When a full-time IT professional was eventually added to the team, she assumed system administration duties for the TEPDL server machine.

Building the content management system from scratch proved to be a challenge. The team members had no formal training as software programmers, though they did have some experience coding in HTML and ColdFusion. Being far more accustomed to Graphical User Interface (GUI) operating system environments, the team members were initially tentative as they learned to navigate the Solaris (and later Linux) operating system and to manipulate the Unix-style application tools by command line. As these tasks became easier with practice, however, the work began to flow smoothly.

The team's familiarity with relational database design and Structured Query Language significantly eased the learning curve for understanding and using the MySQL database software. The online documentation available on the MySQL Web site was excellent, and the team referred to it frequently during the process of building, modifying, and populating the database. Manipulating MySQL by command line was decidedly tedious, but fortunately the TEPDL database was neither large nor complex.

The most difficult aspect of the construction process was the PHP script writing. The team conducted extensive research in books and on the Internet, and invested countless hours in trial-and-error coding in attempts to get scripts to work as desired. Although the online documentation available on the PHP Web site was quite good, the abbreviated examples given in the documentation did not always provide enough detail to help programming novices like the team members properly construct and troubleshoot their code. When they could be found, the reference resources that included fully constructed code examples for building commonly used Web site functionality components provided the most help. All told, the team was able to implement about 90% of the planned content management system functionality.

Integrating the CONTENTdm-driven Document Collection displays into TEPDL did not pose any major problems. CONTENTdm supported the customization of display templates, and in the few cases where problems arose, the software vendor was very responsive, providing a suitable patch or workaround when necessary. Through the exemplary efforts of IAT's part-time Web developer, the Document Collection displays looked nearly identical to the rest of the TEPDL Web site.

CONTENTdm provided extensive content management tools, including user and collection access controls, the ability to create multiple collections with customized metadata sets for each collection, and controlled vocabularies for specific metadata fields. Since the final hosting organization for TEPDL was not known and no pre-existing collection of documents was available, the team decided to create two small test collections (100+ documents total) to demonstrate the functionality of the CONTENTdm software suite. One collection contained documents related to the development of TEPDL and the other contained a sample collection of multi-media documents related to tactical electric power.

Each collection was created using a metadata set mapped to Dublin Core (Title; Author—DC Creator; Date; Description/Abstract; Index Terms—DC Subject; Publisher; Contributor; Identifier; Related Documents—DC Relation; Restrictions—DC Rights; Language; Format; Source). Since many of the documents covered similar topics and had corporate authors, an additional, unmapped metadata field, Keywords, was also added to improve resource discovery. All metadata fields were made searchable.

To assist collection administrators in the development of document metadata, the TEPDL online document submission form included fields for users to enter basic descriptive information (e.g., author, date of publication) for each submitted document. Also, a strictly defined set of metadata entry formats was established to promote search and display consistency. In addition, a controlled vocabulary list was adapted from the Defense Technical Information Center (DTIC) thesaurus and was enabled in an Index Terms field within CONTENTdm. This set of index terms was made available to collection administrators through a drop-down menu. All together, these measures were intended to enhance resource discovery and simplify document collection maintenance.

## Phase V: Testing and Redesign

When the TEPDL project entered the testing and redesign phase, a permanent host for the knowledge base still had not been identified. The development team members continued to perform primary content management duties for TEPDL, and, by default, conducted most of the usability and bug testing for the Web site. In their roles as de facto primary end users and content administrators for the Web site (not an optimal situation), the development team members identified and implemented many minor interface and functionality improvements to TEPDL.

Time, budget, and personnel constraints frustrated plans to conduct a formal usability test of the prototype design. However, the project manager recruited a small number of potential end users to test-drive the Web site. In addition, two months before final delivery, the team took advantage of an opportunity to demonstrate TEPDL at a trade show that was heavily attended by military personnel, many of whom were within the target user group for TEPDL. Informal feedback from potential end users was almost universally positive.

## Phase VI: Maintenance (Content Management)

As designed, the TEPDL content management system provided much capability with few restrictions. This characteristic made the content management system extremely flexible in the workflow regimes that it could support, but it also meant that the content management system would need to be supplemented by well-defined content management processes, procedures, and strategies. Correspondingly, a significant portion of the TEPDL Operator Manual was devoted to content management processes and planning. The following excerpt from the manual illustrates some of the content management guidance it provided:

### Choosing a Management Level

Content management comprises three primary efforts: acquisition, ingest, and maintenance. To determine a suitable level of management effort, each part of the DL [digital library] (the Document Collection, the Expert Directory, and the Web Resources Guide) should be considered individually. Management can be carried out in a "passive" or an "active" manner, or through a combination of active and passive methods. Some examples of passive and active methods for content management are described below. In general, active content management is more labor intensive than passive measures, but results in more useful content.

### Content Ingest

**Passive**: DL Content Manager accepts all materials that are submitted [after administrative review of material to eliminate those with classified or proprietary content]. Document description information (metadata) is derived from document input form. DL Content Manager makes no effort to verify or expand document description information. DL Content Manager accepts all self-nominated SMEs and all suggested Web resources for inclusion in the respective directories.

**Active**: SME reviews/appraises all documents before they are input to the DL. SMEs would have authority to exclude submitted documents or add comments to the document description, document structure, or content. DL Content Manager reviews metadata for validity and pursues additional document metadata when deemed necessary. DL Content Manager reviews all nominated Web resources and may exclude those that he/she deems unsuitable. DL Content Manager contacts all SMEs to explain/describe SME role and to verify expertise information.

**Combination**: A mix of passive and active measures, e.g., a SME would review submitted materials only upon request of the DL Content Manager. DL Content Manager pursues additional document information only to complete metadata fields for title, author, publisher, and publication date. DL Content Manager assesses nominated Web resources only for functionality, not content (Donovan, 2003, pp. 11-12).

Four notional Web content management (WCM) scenarios illustrating some of the functionality and flexibility of the TEPDL content management system are presented below. These scenarios are intended not only to highlight features of TEPDL, but to provide insight into the ways this type of content management functionality might be applied more generally to the design of library and other information resource Web sites.

## WCM and Workflow Scenario 1

The Tactical Electric Power Digital Library is being hosted at IAT in Austin, Texas. A project officer at Fort Belvoir, Virginia, accesses the TEPDL Web site and uses the online "Submit Document" form to submit a digital copy of a generator test report document. The submitted document and associated metadata are stored in the TEPDL content management system database. Simultaneously, an automatically generated e-mail message is sent to the TEPDL content manager, alerting him to the fact that a new record has been added to the Document Submission portion of the content management system database. The content manager accesses the content management system Web interface and selects a link that allows him to view all document submissions stored in the database. He locates the appropriate record by title and submission date, and downloads the document file to a directory on his computer. He then reviews the descriptive information (metadata) provided by the submitter. It appears to be accurate and complete, so he opens the CONTENTdm content management client and uploads the document file to the document repository. In the client, he enters additional descriptive metadata into the bibliographic record for the document, including a few controlled vocabulary terms available from a drop-down display list. He processes the submission and then approves the document for display and delivery through the Document Collection section of the TEPDL Web site.

## WCM and Workflow Scenario 2

The Tactical Electric Power Digital Library is being hosted at Fort Hood, Texas. A TEPDL content manager who is stationed at Fort Monmouth, New Jersey, and who is herself listed in the SME Directory, has a hydrogen fuel cell question for an SME located in Maryland. Based on the contact information listed in the SME Directory, the content manager sends the fuel cell expert an e-mail message that is immediately returned as undeliverable. She then calls the listed work phone number of the SME and receives an "out of service" message. The content manager notes that the fuel cell SME's contact information was last updated over six months ago. She opens the TEPDL content management system Web interface and selects a link allowing her to view a complete listing of all SME records. She enters the last name of the fuel cell SME into a search box and quickly locates his record. Using a drop-down menu on the content management system interface, the content manager changes the status of the fuel cell SME's record from "Show" to "Do Not Show" until she can find time to verify the contact information. The record is now no longer visible on the public TEPDL Web site, but remains visible and accessible through the content management system interface. Later, the content manager learns that the fuel cell SME has recently retired. The content manager again opens the content management system interface, but this time, after locating the record for the retired SME, the content manager selects the Delete Record button and permanently expunges the record from the content management system.

## WCM and Workflow Scenario 3

The Tactical Electric Power Digital Library is being hosted at Fort Leonard Wood, Missouri. A content manager responsible for maintaining the TEPDL

Web Resources Guide is on a business trip from Missouri to Austin, Texas. The content manager has a free half-hour and decides to perform his weekly TEPDL Web Resource link verification check. Using his laptop computer and a wireless Internet connection, he opens the TEPDL content management system Web interface and selects the link labeled, Run Web Resources Link Check. An automated script begins checking every URL listed in the content management system database. After about 10 minutes, the script has run through all 83 URLs. Two of them appear to be giving error messages. The content manager clicks on the first bad link shown on the Link Check results page of the content management system. The response is slow, but the link works. The content manager then moves on to the next link error. The second bad link does not seem to work at all. The content manager performs a quick Web search looking for the site in question. He finds it and confirms that the URL has been changed. In the TEPDL content management system, the content manager searches the Web Resources list to find the affected Web site record. He opens the Update Record form for the Web site and pastes the new URL into the appropriate form field. He submits the change, and the new URL is immediately reflected in the content management system and on the TEPDL Web site.

## WCM and Workflow Scenario 4

TEPDL is being hosted at IAT in Austin, Texas. The Military Energy Committee, which provides operational oversight for TEPDL, would like to have a new display feature added to the Web site. The committee is interested in keeping abreast of the newest additions to the SME Directory. Currently, the browse page of the SME Directory shows an alphabetically ordered list of all SMEs, which includes their names and brief descriptions of their areas of expertise. The committee would like to keep this a standard browse page, but would also like to have a New Experts page added to the site that shows the 10 most recent listings in the SME directory. On the New Experts browse page, rather than names and descriptions of expertise, the committee members would like to see names, organizational affiliations, and the dates the Subject Matter Experts were added to the directory. In addition, rather than alphabetical order, the committee would like to see the entries sorted by date, from newest to oldest. The TEPDL Webmaster creates a new Web template and uploads it to the server to accommodate the committee's request. She then adds the template to the SME Directory section of the TEPDL Web site through a New Experts hyperlink. The digital library now has a new Web page that will be dynamically populated with content using data that already exists in the TEPDL content management system database. In addition, neither the Webmaster nor the content manager will have to perform future updates to this page manually because the content displayed will automatically always be the most current information available in the system.

# Current Challenges Facing the Organization

As an information resource that is vitally dependent upon end user contributions to achieve the critical mass of content necessary to become a beneficial, self-perpetuating system, TEPDL faces a significant uphill battle. Despite being an issue of great importance, tactical electric power, as broadly applied within the context of TEPDL, does not engender or represent a naturally occurring community of interest or practice. As a result, in the normal course of their work, members of the Web site's target user audience are not likely to seek out or even surmise the existence of such a resource, and thereby contribute to its growth. It is clear that the continued viability of TEPDL will depend upon the patronage of a high-level organizational sponsor with a vested interest in addressing overarching tactical electric power issues. This sponsor will need to actively publicize and promote TEPDL and, ideally, will have enough positional power to encourage or direct the type of broad participation that will be needed to sustain the knowledge base with a steady flow of useful, current content.

# References

DiMeMa. (2003). CONTENTdm. Retrieved August 25, 2003, from *www. contentdm.com/*

Donovan, A.M. (2003). *Tactical electric power digital library operator manual.* Unpublished manual.

Greenstone.org. (n.d.). Greenstone digital library software. Retrieved August 25, 2003, from *www.greenstone.org/*

Institute for Advanced Technology. (2003a). Institute for Advanced Technology homepage. Retrieved August 25, 2003, from *www.iat.utexas.edu/*

Institute for Advanced Technology. (2003b). IAT—Advanced training technology. Retrieved August 25, 2003, from *www.iat.utexas.edu/att.html*

Leedom, D. (n.d.). *Power management on the digital battlefield.* Unpublished paper.

MySQL AB. (2003). MySQL. Retrieved August 25, 2003, from *www.mysql.com/*

Nomura, M. (2002). *Analysis and design, tactical electric power knowledge base.* Unpublished document.

PHP Group. (2003). *PHP.* Retrieved August 25, 2003, from *www.php.net/*

University of Texas at Austin. (2003). *About UT.* Retrieved August 25, 2003, from *www.utexas.edu/welcome/*

University XXI. (2003). University XXI homepage. Retrieved August 25, 2003, from *www.uxxi.org/*

# Supporting Materials

Questions and Answers

Question: What is the overall problem in this case?

Answer: The developers have been tasked to create a knowledge repository for which there is no existing collection of documents or other information resources.

Question: What are some of the main challenges in the case?

Answer: All phases of the project, but especially user data collection, are negatively affected by funding constraints and the very short time period allotted for prototype development. Additionally, the potential user group has been defined, but not clearly identified, and possible information sources are scattered and not readily identifiable.

Question: What are some of the enabling technological and organizational factors in this project?

Answer: Among the enabling factors are widespread computer literacy among potential users and the existence of a highly developed IT infrastructure across potential user organizations. The project also benefits from its affiliation with a large research university. In addition, the small size of the project team greatly simplifies coordination and decision making.

Question: What are some of the specific design and implementation challenges in this case?

Answer: The initial design challenge is the lack of an extant document collection to suggest a scope or form for the repository. The team cannot validate some design decisions because a host for TEPDL has not been identified. Design implementation is impeded by the team's lack of a programmer.

Question: What are some emerging technologies that should be considered in solving the content identification and collection problems in this case?

Answer: Content identification and collection could be simplified through the use of Web spiders (to find Web content); content-filtering, auto-classification, and indexing software (to collect/describe documents); and knowledge network mapping tools (to identify subject matter experts). Other potentially useful tools include neural network and pattern matching technology and Knowledge Discovery in Databases (KDD) software.

# Epilogue

The Tactical Electric Power Digital Library (TEPDL) project has been a qualified success. While the TEPDL development team successfully achieved the goal of creating a flexible, platform-independent method for managing and delivering Web site content, TEPDL itself remains without a permanent home or sponsor. As a positive side effect of this project, however, the University XXI team at the Institute for Advanced Technology is now interested in pursuing a capability like TEPDL to capture, manage, and disseminate the intellectual work product and final deliverables associated with the University XXI program. To that end, in the near future, a similar but simpler version of a tool like TEPDL will be constructed for use by the University XXI community.

# Lessons Learned

No ground-breaking lessons learned resulted from this project, but a few old lessons were reinforced:

1.  Although technology can facilitate the exchange of information within an existing community, technology alone is not sufficient to establish a community of interest or a culture of information sharing.

2.  Comprehensive user studies, including detailed user needs analyses, are a crucial part of any information system development project. User representatives should be fully integrated into the system design, development, and deployment processes.

3.  Resource discovery and reuse can be enhanced by the use of common data interchange protocols (e.g., Z39.50 and Open Archives Initiative (OAI) harvesting), metadata standards (e.g., Dublin Core), and controlled vocabularies (e.g., Medical Subject Headings (MeSH)).

# List of Additional Sources

Biblarz, D., Bosch, S., & Sugnet, C. (Eds.). (2001). *Guide to library user needs assessment for integrated information resource management and collection development: Collection management and development guides, No. 11.* Lanham, MD: Scarecrow Press.

Bradburn, N.M., & Sudman, S. (1979). *Improving interview method and questionnaire design.* San Francisco: Jossey-Bass.

Cedars Project. (2002). The Cedars guide to digital collection management. Retrieved February 2004 from *www.leeds.ac.uk/cedars/guideto/collmanagement/guidetocolman.pdf*

DuBois, P. (2003). *MySQL cookbook.* Sebastopol, CA: O'Reilly.

Friedlein, A. (2000). *Web project management: Delivering successful commercial Web sites.* San Francisco: Morgan Kaufmann.

Greenstein, D., & Thorin, S.E. (2002). *The digital library: A biography.* Washington, DC: Digital Library Federation and the Council on Library and Information Resources. Retrieved February 2004 from *www.clir.org/pubs/reports/pub109/pub109.pdf*

Hurley, B.J., Price-Wilkin, J., Proffitt, M., & Besser, H. (1999). The making of America II testbed project: A digital library service model. Retrieved February 2004 from *www.clir.org/pubs/reports/pub87/contents.html#about*

Jolliffe, F.R. (1986). *Survey design and analysis*. New York: Halstead Press.

Niederst, J. (2001). *Web design in a nutshell* (2nd ed.). Sebastopol, CA: O'Reilly.

Pitschmann, L.A. (2001). *Building sustainable collections of free third-party Web resources*. Washington, DC: Digital Library Federation. Retrieved February 2004 from *www.clir.org/pubs/reports/pub98/pub98.pdf*

Shneiderman, B. (1998). *Designing the user interface: Strategies for effective human-computer interaction* (3rd ed.). Reading, MA: Addison-Wesley-Longman.

Sklar, D., & Trachtenberg, A. (2002). *PHP cookbook*. Sebastopol, CA: O'Reilly.

VanDuyne, D., Landay, A., & Hong, J. (2003). *The design of sites: Patterns, principles, and processes for crafting a customer-centered Web experience*. Boston: Addison-Wesley.

Van House, N.A., Butler, M.H., Ogle, V., & Schiff, L. (1996). User-centered iterative design for digital libraries: The Cypress experience. *D-Lib Magazine*, (February). Retrieved February 2004 from *www.dlib.org/dlib/february96/02vanhouse.html*

Chapter X

# Developing Committees to Create a Web Content Management System

Sarah Robbins
University of Oklahoma Libraries, USA

Debra Engel
University of Oklahoma Libraries, USA

## Abstract

*This case study examines the use of committees to develop a Web content management system in an academic library. It explains the process undertaken at the University of Oklahoma Libraries (libraries.ou.edu) to move from an HTML to a database-driven Web site and the issues involved with using committees to steer such projects. Creating a framework where librarians use locally developed content management tools to control Web site content while the systems office retains control of the presentation of content is also discussed. Another aspect of the case study includes the evolution of Web committees in the organization, the development of a system-wide philosophy, and the gradual acceptance of the Web site as a service that demands continual attention. The authors hope readers will benefit from these experiences when implementing similar projects.*

# Introduction

The University of Oklahoma (OU) is a doctoral degree-granting research university serving the educational, cultural, economic, and health care needs of the state, region, and nation. OU enrolls more than 30,000 students and has 2,000 full-time faculty members in 19 colleges that offer 150 majors at the baccalaureate level, 142 majors at the master's level, 76 majors at the doctoral level, 30 majors at the first professional level, and five graduate certificates.

The University of Oklahoma Libraries, the largest research library system in the state, contains 4.2 million volumes, subscribes to 18,000 unique periodicals, and provides access to more than 170 databases. University Libraries (UL) includes Bizzell Memorial Library (main library), six branch libraries, and four special collections. UL is composed of three main administrative units: systems, public services, and technical services. UL employs approximately 55 professional staff members, 84 support staff members, and 61 FTE student workers. The organizational culture of UL combines a traditional hierarchical model of administrative organization with committees appointed based on need or functionality, such as committees for strategic planning or circulation services and search committees. The library budgets the salaries of all library staff including systems personnel, as well as materials and collections, and hardware and software applications. Although the University of Oklahoma does not prescribe specific style guidelines for the UL's Web site, they do provide basic guidelines on official OU colors for Web sites and strategies for ADA compliance. In addition, the university administration places a high priority on equitable services for all students served at three geographically distinct campuses, as well as distance education students, which has influenced the development of the UL Web site.

# Setting the Stage

## Trends in Library Web Site Development

Librarians have been content managers for centuries. With the rapid growth of the Internet, many organizations of every size are focusing on content management issues. Forrester Research defines content management as "a combination of well-defined roles, formal processes, and supporting systems architecture that helps organizations contribute, collaborate on, and control page elements such as text, graphics, multimedia, and applets" (Guenther, 2001b, p. 81). Boiko (2001) suggests a broader definition of content management, and claims that content management "is the process behind matching what you have to what they [users] want" (p. 8). Regardless of how content management is defined, it is clear that libraries are now in the business of managing content beyond the traditional library catalog, and library Web sites are playing a critical role in helping libraries do this.

Using committees to develop Web sites is not a new phenomenon in libraries. A survey of the literature reveals that libraries have relied on committees or teams to complete projects for years and have continued to use this model in developing library Web sites. As written in the article "Make It a Team Effort," successful teams depend "upon support from library administrators as well as on the achievement of a library-wide consensus" (Smith, Tedford, & Womack, 2001, p. 19). As Web sites assume more prominent roles in marketing library services and resources, administrators have increased interest in the appearance of Web sites and, thus, will need to fully support the work of committees charged with managing the Web site. If the committees are not supported by administrators, the committees' work will be for naught, and committee members will grow to resent the process.

Library Web site development within the academic environment has changed significantly in the past decade. Since library patrons utilize the library Web site as a portal to access the library's services and resources, the Web site has become an integral part of marketing library operations. In her article "Getting out of the HTML Business," Antelman (1999) suggests that library Web sites have grown in size and complexity since the mid-1990s. One trend in library Web site development is the creation of a database-driven content management system, particularly if the Web site has grown beyond the ability of library personnel to manage it as a collection of static HTML pages (Guenther, 2001b). While the number of HTML pages that are manageable will vary depending upon the size of the institution, the depth of literature on this topic indicates that there is certainly a point where it is simply no longer feasible to continue HTML Web sites, and organizations should migrate to the database-driven format to improve efficiency. The migration from an HTML site to a database-driven site requires significant planning and work.

Designing a database-driven content management system places the power of content generation in the hands of the librarians or subject content experts while placing the technology experts in control of Web page coding, design, and layout (Brown & Candreva, 2002). Brown and Candreva assert that as library Web sites continue to grow "the more sense it makes to build a dynamic Web site" (p. 25). In "Designing a Database-Driven Web Site, or the Evolution of Infoiguana," Roberts (2000) encourages the creation of a database-driven Web site for content management and states, "When the content on a site reaches critical mass, it's time to stop managing it as a list of resources embedded in static HTML and start using the Web as an interface to a database containing bibliographic information" (p. 27). The database-driven approach allows the decentralization of creating and updating content while retaining a consistent style for the Web site.

Using a committee may not be the easiest or most expedient way to develop a library Web site, but the long-term benefits may far outweigh the short-term costs. Smith, Tedford, and Womack (2001) write, "When all areas of a library are represented on a team, there are increased feelings of ownership by the entire organization" (p. 19). This sense of ownership can lead to a better product and commitment to maintaining the Web site. Another benefit of a team approach to Web site management is that "[t]eamwork distributes the labor of Web site management, which makes a more comprehensive Web site feasible" (p. 20). With representatives on a Web committee from every library unit, Web content can be controlled by those most knowledgeable about the content. This will improve the quality of the overall Web site.

In the article "Cooperative Web Weaving: The Team Approach to Web Site Development at Illinois State University," the authors give four lessons they learned through the process of using a committee to develop a Web site. In describing these lessons, they note that the "committee required more time to accomplish the work, but developed a better product," that "not everyone would agree to participate," that they assumed a stronger editorial role than they had anticipated, and that there "was the need to be flexible" because the site did not develop as expected despite planning (Jagodzinski, Cunningham, Day, Naylor, & Schobernd, 1997, pp. 10-11). The general principles of these lessons could be applicable to committee work in any library situation, not just Web site development.

While the committee or team approach to Web site development may not work for every organization, Guenther (2001a) warns, "Without a strong governance structure and process in place, Web development priorities are based on a strategy of 'who yells the loudest,' not necessarily on which priorities have the greatest strategic impact for the organization" (p. 70). Whether it is a single Webmaster working in conjunction with library departments or a formally appointed library committee, there needs to be a structure that looks at the big picture of Web site development within the organization and within the campus environment that can establish priorities.

## Technology Utilization at University Libraries

University of Oklahoma Libraries uses technology to provide resources and services to faculty and students. The technologies available to patrons within the libraries include public computers, circulating laptops, and hardwire data ports and wireless connectivity for students and faculty with their own laptops. Technology has played an increasingly vital role for UL and expands the array of library resources available to patrons via library facilities and through the Web site, 24 hours a day, seven days a week.

The number of electronic databases has grown dramatically in the past four years, from less than 100 databases in 2000 to over 170 databases in 2004. In some cases, the increasing availability of online resources has changed librarians' search strategies. Many librarians will utilize the electronic resources first and the library online catalog second when assisting patrons. To improve access to electronic resources, University Libraries subscribed to Serials Solutions in 2003 to help with URL maintenance for both the library Web site and catalog. In addition, library personnel are currently investigating a URL resolver with federated searching functionality for the future.

A new emphasis on patron service has been moderately successful within the traditional management and governance of UL. Areas of success include: improved service via the library Web site, increased financial resources for collection development, expanded library hours, heightened awareness of library services for students and faculty, and an increased number of computers available to patrons. Areas that need further attention include: staff development and training, building a team management perspective, and benchmark evaluation and assessment of services and resources. The newly developed University Libraries' strategic plan provides a structure and impetus for addressing many of these issues.

# Case Description

University Libraries has undergone several iterations of library Web site management. Initially, the library Web site was maintained by the library systems office while units within the library maintained sites for their areas. UL progressed to a model of Web site management that utilized committees. Since the committee structure was first used to manage the library Web site at UL, there has been an Advisory Web site Committee, a Web Committee for Research and Development, a Web Liaison Committee, and a Web Steering Committee. These committees have been responsible for the migration of the library Web site from purely HTML pages to a database-driven site, as well as for the development of content management tools that allow librarians to manage content while the systems office control display and presentation.

## Advisory Web Site Committee

### The Committee Structure

The Dean of University Libraries appointed an Advisory Web Committee to serve from June 2000 to May 2001. The committee included eight representatives from systems, public services, and administration. This was UL's first attempt to use a committee structure to manage the Web site. According to the appointment letter, the committee's charge was to "solicit and review comments and suggestions about the Web page and make recommendations to the Director of Public Services and Library Systems on format and functions of the Web page." The Assistant Director of Library Systems chaired the committee, which met infrequently. The committee members' lack of investment in the committee, and the Web site, would be an obstacle for future committee efforts.

### Status of the Web Site

At that time, the UL Web site had hundreds of static HTML pages filled with outdated information, no subject or keyword access to databases or e-journals, an inconsistent style between library units' Web pages, and inadequate navigation. Each unit maintained the Web pages for its area and simply uploaded HTML files to a network folder to publish the pages on the library

Web site. Many of the Web pages contained the same types of information such as circulation periods, policies, and contact information. Any time this information changed for whatever reason, each of the pages containing this information needed updating. Needless to say, many units did not update their Web pages in a timely manner, and consequently, the comprehensive library Web site contained both misinformation and contradictory policies.

Looking at the Web site in its entirety, it was evident that many units did not touch their Web pages after the initial posting of the page and that the Web pages did not accurately reflect the dynamic nature of the organization. Organizationally, University Libraries acknowledged that maintaining the Web site manually using static HTML pages was not a good investment of library personnel's time. Approximately 30 library staff members created and maintained HTML pages. Content management was decentralized, and there was no cohesive policy driving the development of new content or the maintenance of current content. Systems staff posted guidelines on the library intranet, but few people knew of their existence and even fewer adhered to these guidelines in the creation of new Web pages. Since the committee members had a purely advisory role, they lacked enough power to be truly effective as collaborators in an overhaul of the existing HTML Web site structure. While purely HTML Web sites were not uncommon for libraries at the time, the national trend was moving towards database-driven Web sites (Antelman, 2002).

## User Feedback

In June 2001 library staff met with students in a library school course entitled "Design and Implementation of Networked Information Services" to evaluate the current UL Web site. The students taking the course focused on evaluating library Web sites and on usability testing. These evaluations were the basis for weekly class discussions. The student feedback on the design of the University of Oklahoma Libraries' Web site included comments that the front page of the Web site was too busy, that there was no uniform navigation between the units of the library within the Web site, and that there was no subject searching for electronic resources.

# Web Committee for Research and Development

## *The Committee Structure*

During the fall of 2001, the Dean of University Libraries appointed a Web Committee for Research and Development to completely redesign the library Web site. The 15-member committee included representatives from systems, public services, and technical services. Operating principles for the group focused on taking action, performing test marketing, and placing the control of content in the hands of the librarians while the control of the technology remained in the hands of the systems staff. The committee practiced a new method of operation by organizing itself around tasks that needed to be accomplished through the establishment of workgroups, setting action plans with short timetables, and making a decisive break with tradition by generating a product, an updated Web site, at the end of four months.

The committee divided into three workgroups: Web site design, content development, and subject access to electronic resources. These workgroups maintained a high momentum and generated many ideas during the fall semester. The workgroups fine-tuned content for the Web site; chose colors, fonts, and the general navigation style; and developed an electronic resources management system. Though the committee structure was not without flaws, overall, the committee sensed that progress was being made in a positive direction.

## *Status of the Web Site*

The redesigned Web site that launched in January 2002 was the first of several phases progressively moving the library towards a database-driven Web site. A result of this Web site launch was that the content of the Web site was now controlled by the librarian or staff member whose job responsibilities most directly related to the content to be managed, while systems staff retained control of the technological and design aspects of the library Web site. Klein (2003) shares this sentiment when he comments, "Hell hath no fury like an instructional librarian whose schedule you've messed up. I've learned my lesson: Don't manage other people's information. Let them manage it themselves" (p. 28).

Subject librarians managed their subject areas' database and e-journal lists and maintained subject-related Internet links and search engine lists. Administrative assistants maintained the libraries' hours and personnel rosters, while the Director of Public Services updated announcements. The Electronic Services Coordinator kept the knowledge base and online tutorials current. Each of these areas was maintained using Web interfaces accessible through the library's intranet. After the systems staff had locally developed the Web interfaces, they focused their attention on future developments that required their technical expertise, leaving content management to other library personnel.

## User Feedback

Members of the Web Committee for Research and Development met again in July 2002 with students taking the library school course entitled "Design and Implementation of Networked Information Services." The students evaluated the newly launched library Web site and provided feedback. Comments were more favorable than they had been previously. Students noted improvements such as subject access to the electronic databases and the consistent navigation style that brought cohesion to the library system. Not knowing where to begin searching for databases was one issue the students noted as problematic with the new Web site. This concern was addressed in a future iteration of the Web site. To test ADA compliance, the library systems staff used Bobby (bobby.watchfire.com), a free, online application designed to help expose and repair barriers to accessibility.

# Web Steering Committee and the Web Liaison Committee

## Structure of the Web Steering Committee

After the launch of the redesigned Web site in January 2002, a four-person Web Steering Committee was formed to provide leadership for the next phase of Web site development. The Web Steering Committee met as needed to discuss the concerns of patrons and library personnel with the recently released Web site. The Web Steering Committee continually set and juggled priorities. These priorities included which Web site interfaces would be developed and the timeline for implementation. The Web Steering Committee communicated these priorities and timelines to the members of the Web Liaison Committee through e-mail updates and occasional meetings.

## Structure of the Web Liaison Committee

The Web Liaison Committee included 20 representatives—one from each department, special collection, or branch within the library system. The Web Liaison Committee was established primarily for communication purposes. The Web Steering Committee met periodically with the Web Liaison Committee to inform the liaisons of the direction of the Web site and to seek feedback. Liaisons received e-mail updates to disseminate to their units. The Web Liaison Committee met sporadically during 2002 and 2003.

The liaisons met individually with members of the Web Steering Committee to communicate their units' needs and to approve changes in design and content. This one-on-one communication was vital during the planning and implementation phase of the Web site development. Although each of the liaisons provided feedback to the Web Steering Committee through these personal interactions, the Web Liaison Committee as a group lacked investment because there were few large group meetings and no workgroups with assigned tasks as there had been on the previous Web Committee for Research and Development.

Because many of the liaisons had served on the previous Web Committee for Research and Development and had participated in highly productive workgroups, there was a necessary change of pace and expectations that came as a part of the shift from the workgroup model to the liaison model. For some liaisons, this change of pace made them feel less informed about the Web site development and even disengaged from the entire process. In retrospect, the Web Steering Committee should have invested more time communicating the aims of the new liaison committee to the liaisons so that they would more fully understand their role in the Web site development process. The chair of the Web Liaison Committee did not communicate the purpose of a database-driven Web site and content management system in terms that the Web Liaison Committee members understood.

## Status of the Web Site

Many external forces pressured the library to launch the redesigned Web site in June 2003, before content management tools were developed. The university administration wanted to present a unified campus to the students and faculty; this highly charged political environment resulted in a strong push to support an authentication system that is compatible for both the University of Oklahoma Norman Campus and the University of Oklahoma Health Sciences Center. The purchase of Serials Solutions data to create consistency between the Web site's e-journal lists and the library catalog provided an additional impetus to launch the new Web site. A migration from an Access database to an Oracle database was also a factor. This migration was necessary to prevent the locking and concurrency issues that arise when many people have editing capabilities in Access-backed interfaces (Robbins & Smith, 2004, p. 244). In addition to these many motivations, it is common practice at UL to change the Web site only during student holidays. If UL had not launched in early June, then the next acceptable time to launch the new Web site would have been August, right before the start of the fall semester. This was unacceptable. Library personnel dislike major changes to the Web site prior to the start of the semester and prefer having summer months to work out potential problems and plan for library instruction.

While patrons reacted favorably to the Web site, many of the library personnel found fault with various features of the new Web site. After the launch of the redesigned Web site in June 2003, losing the ability to control and update content on the Web site frustrated many of the library staff members. Much of the libraries' Web site was frozen in March 2003 to give the systems staff time to migrate data from Access to Oracle. This meant that by June 2003, many subject librarians were eager to have control of their subject area content again and to update URLs, add databases, and so forth. To their dismay, the Web interfaces previously used to update the Web site no longer worked because of the migration from Access to Oracle, and the new interfaces had not yet been developed. It was uncertain when these new interfaces would be completed and ready for use. The Web Steering Committee worked to develop a temporary system for getting changes made on the Web site while systems staff developed the interfaces. The temporary solution was less than ideal from the perspective of the subject librarians because they had to rely on those in the systems office to make changes. In addition, when the subject librarians utilized these temporary solutions for updating content, it meant that systems personnel used their time on makeshift measures rather than on developing long-term solutions.

In March 2004, content management tools for the library Web site were launched. The new locally developed content management tools allow the subject bibliographers to manage content on their subject area pages and allow all designated unit liaisons to edit and update the Web pages for their units. In addition, administrators have control of the library announcements, front page content, and personnel information. The librarians were pleased to regain control of their content after a year of waiting.

## User Feedback

Although no formal evaluation of the most recent Web site launch has been done, informal contact with library patrons has indicated a favorable impression of the site. Each semester a presentation is made to the undergraduate Student Congress about library services. At the fall 2003 meeting, the student representatives provided overwhelmingly positive feedback about the newly launched Web site. The reporter from the student newspaper was also enthusiastic about the changes and wrote a feature story including a screenshot of the electronic resources management system. Individual patrons have commented via Web feedback forms about their discoveries in using the updated Web site. Future evaluation of the Web site includes the planning and implementation of usability studies, as well as using focus groups to identify the strengths and weaknesses of the Web site.

# Current Challenges Facing the Organization

## Evolution of Web Committees

Using committees to manage and direct a complex project, such as revitalizing a Web site, can be daunting. A committee approach was implemented to organize the work with input from a diverse library staff representing a variety of public service and technical service units. The success or failure of any committee is greatly impacted by the mode of operation, committee structure, and group process. In the case of UL, the Web committees changed over a period of time as part of a gradual organizational evolution.

While the Advisory Web Committee had sufficient representation from the various library units and had a specific charge, it lacked the power to make some of the major revisions of the Web site that later committees would accomplish. With a purely advisory role, committee members did not necessarily invest themselves in creating or managing content. Systems staff continued to control the look of the Web site's front page, while units controlled the look of their units' pages. The advice of the committee had little impact on the actual appearance of the Web site. While the Advisory Web Committee introduced the concept of using committees to manage the library's Web site, its lack of authority made committee members leery of the process.

The Web Committee for Research and Design had a strong commitment to improving the Web site. Motivation provided momentum; as a result, committee members as stakeholders felt a high degree of ownership and investment in the success of the Web site project. Since each committee member served on a workgroup and these workgroups were assigned specific tasks to complete, members could easily see their ideas and suggestions come to life and manifest themselves on the library's Web site. This momentum would have been difficult to sustain for a prolonged period of time, but the workgroup model proved effective for the targeted initial revitalization of the Web site.

The migration from the Web Committee for Research and Design to the Web Steering Committee/Web Liaison Committee model was difficult for some committee members. The charge of the Web Steering Committee/Web Liaison Committee was not as clear as the charge had been for the Web Committee for Research and Design, because the Web site revisions needed were more behind the scenes than those that affected the public appearance. The Web Liaison Committee structure was designed for communication with every library unit represented on the committee. The liaisons did not have specific development assignments nor were they consulted in the development of the implementation timetable. This lack of involvement made the liaisons feel removed from both the Web site revision process as well as the final product.

Members of the Web Steering Committee sensed that the liaisons felt undervalued and that the liaisons preferred the previous workgroup model so that they could be more involved in the process and final product. In an evaluation of the Web development process utilizing the Web Liaison Committee, one liaison expressed:

"The process for communicating change works, but I would like to see the Web Liaison Committee meet more often and maybe have a heads-up about planned changes so we can discuss them. Although I know it's really the [Web] Steering Committee's job to plan and discuss changes, I do miss the sense of involvement we had with the large group when we first started the project."

While this statement typified how the Web Steering Committee perceived the liaisons to feel, the majority of the committee liaisons indicated they were satisfied with the new liaison model. One evaluation read, "I think the [Web] committees that are in place work well," while yet another committee member succinctly expressed, "Impressive result, sound process."

Web site initiatives generated by committees may falter if the change process is not paced comfortably enough to promote ongoing participation. Web site changes must also be punctuated with opportunities for both small successes and long-term projects that only yield significant results over time. The chair of the Web Liaison Committee felt that the committee members were dissatisfied with the progress of the Web initiatives in the past year, particularly since the bibliographers did not have access to their subject pages in a year. Nevertheless, the committee evaluations from the Web Liaison Committee members did not support this hypothesis. The evaluations indicated that for the most part, the committee members were satisfied with the development of University Libraries' Web site, as well as the committee process.

The Web Steering Committee committed a management mistake: over-promise and under-delivery. The Web Steering Committee had planned for the Web content management tools to be ready by the end of Summer 2003 at the latest. Unfortunately, a number of factors resulted in delaying the development of content management tools until March 2004. Setting goals and deadlines for taking concrete steps is essential to the successful implementation of any committee project. Because of delays in the development of content management tools for the library's Web site, the chair felt that the liaisons would be eager to disband the Web Liaison Committee in favor of a different model. It was a surprise to discover that many committee members felt the model was working and appropriate for UL.

## Development of the University Libraries' Strategic Plan

University Libraries is implementing a new system-wide strategic plan created in 2003 which includes objectives involving the development of the library's Web presence. In light of the implementation of the strategic plan, the Web

Steering Committee asked itself, "Should the Web Liaison Committee continue to function as it has in the past year or evolve into a new Web committee structure?" One recommendation from the Strategic Plan Implementation Committee is to introduce a technology committee. If UL decides to implement a technology committee, a new Web governance structure may evolve. It is possible that the Web Liaison Committee could evolve into the technology committee that would serve as a communication tool for all technology-related issues rather than narrowly focusing on Web site development. From within the technology committee, a Web-focused workgroup or steering committee would likely emerge.

## Personnel Issues

The staffing level within the Systems Office is minimal. The systems personnel include two librarians, two program analysts, one support staff member, and five student workers and graduate assistants. One person acts as the UL Webmaster, but is also responsible for system security, server maintenance, and training the systems office staff. He cannot devote his full attention to Web site development. Without content management tools in place that allow librarians to control content and with the systems staff's time divided among multiple projects, the Web site quickly becomes outdated.

The library systems staff supports traditional library services such as the catalog, circulation, and departmental technological needs as well as new and emerging service areas including digitization projects and off-campus access to electronic resources. With a limited number of employees in the systems office, the day-to-day operations such as server maintenance, upgrades to existing technology, and basic hardware and software repairs and installations keep all of the systems personnel fully occupied. Add unexpected technological problems (worms, viruses, power outages) to the already strained personnel resources and a tense environment develops at times. It is difficult to make progress on Web site development when any crisis, small or large, interferes with the necessary work.

A key issue within the organization is how to develop a library-wide awareness that additional staff in the systems department needs to be a priority for the library as a whole. All library areas—public service departments, technical service departments, branch libraries, and special collections—are minimally staffed. A branch librarian has difficulty thinking "system" when he or she is trying to keep the doors open to a facility that operates 76 hours a week with limited staff and student hours. Each library unit has priorities that depend on systems' architecture and personnel to develop and implement, so a backlog of work in systems affects every library unit.

The long-range impact of using committees to develop a Web content management system is significant. The progression has set a precedent at University Libraries for productive committee work within the organization. The lessons learned from an organizational commitment to the use of committees for Web site development has improved library services.

# References

Antelman, K. (1999). Getting out of the HTML business: The database-driven Web site solution. *Information Technology and Libraries, 18*(4), 176.

Antelman, K. (2002). *Database-driven Web sites.* New York: Haworth Information Press.

Boiko, B. (2001). Understanding content management. *Bulletin of the American Society for Information Science and Technology, 28*(1), 8.

Brown, K.L., & Candreva, A.M. (2002). Managing database-driven Web content. *School Library Journal NetConnect, 48*(11), 24.

Guenther, K. (2001a). Web site management: Effective Web governance structures. *Online, 25*(2), 70-72.

Guenther, K. (2001b). What is a Web content management solution? *Online, 25*(4), 81.

Jagodzinski, C., Cunningham, J., Day, P., Naylor, S., & Schobernd, E. (1997). Cooperative Web weaving: The team approach to Web site development at Illinois State University. *Journal of Interlibrary Loan, Document Delivery & Information Supply, 8*(2), 1-20.

Klein, L.R. (2003). Mixing up Web site management. *Library Journal NetConnect, 128*(7), 28.

Robbins, S., & Smith, M. (2004). Managing e-resources: A database-driven approach. In D.C. Fowler (Ed.), *E-serials collection management: Transitions, trends, and technicalities* (pp. 239-251). New York: Haworth Information Press.

Roberts, G. (2000). Designing a database-driven Web site, or the evolution of the Infoiguana. *Computers in Libraries, 20*(9), 27.

Smith, S., Tedford, R., & Womack, G. (2001). Make it a team effort. *NetConnect,* (Winter), 18-20.

# Supporting Materials

## Questions and Answers

Question: Why were committees used to develop a Web content management system?

Answer: Using committees to redesign a Web site provides library staff with a sense of ownership for the changes that are made to the Web site. A variety of viewpoints, including those from public services, technical services, and systems staff, is important for providing diversity of opinion and creating a product that represents the needs of all users.

Question: How can you develop a committee structure that will be productive for a library organization in Web site development?

Answer: Assess your organization's capacity for utilizing committees. Investigation should include previous use of committees within the organization, the effectiveness of committees in past projects, and the organizational support for changes recommended by committees. Successful delegation occurs when every member of the committee feels involved with the process and feels that they are making a contribution. Evaluating the productivity of the committee's progress is vital for success.

Question: What would have improved the Web committees' processes in this case?

Answer: Developing a system-wide perspective would help individual committee members understand the overall goals of Web site development. More frequent committee evaluation of the group process would help promote a better understanding of the group's function and goals. Decreasing the amount of time between planning of the Web content management tools and implementation would have decreased frustration. It is difficult to maintain enthusiastic commitment of committee members' time and energy over an extended period of time. Some committees need greater flexibility while others require greater structure.

Question: How do you measure the success or failure of a Web committee in developing a Web site?

Answer: A committee's success is largely a reflection of the proportion of the participants who take responsibility for its success. Committee members should continually ask themselves assessment questions about effective committee and group process. A Web committee should establish expectations with objectives, governance structure, timetables, and periodic benchmarks that indicate progress. A committee planning process that incorporates assessment, planning, implementation, and evaluation is essential. Evaluating a Web committee also involves evaluation of the final product: the Web site itself. The Web site evaluation process should incorporate a variety of feedback mechanisms, including Web site usability studies, focus groups, and direct feedback.

Question: What are some of the emerging technologies that should be considered in solving the problem(s) relating to the case?

Answer: There are commercially available Web content management systems that should be analyzed by the committee and the library for possible implementation. Vendors that provide Web content management solutions include SIRSI, Innovative Interfaces, MyLibrary, and the Scout Portal Toolkit.

Question: What recommendations could be suggested to the management of the organization described in this case? Provide arguments in support of the recommended solution.

Answer: Library management should consider utilizing the strengths of the two committees. The Web Committee for Research and Design brought a new vitality to the organization with a "can-do" spirit that was contagious. The ideas recommended were implemented quickly. The Web Liaison Committee brought together a more diverse group representing every library unit.

Shorter time between development and implementation needs to be a priority. In addition, the committee chair for the new Web development committee needs to solidly ground committee members in the expectations for the Web development committee including objectives, communication, benchmarks, and training.

## Lessons Learned

Lesson 1: Collective Priorities Supersede Unit Priorities

Web committee members must develop a broad vision of library system priorities. Library staff cannot remain in a pattern of thinking only about what is best for their unit. Developing a system-wide perspective is a complex process involving a commitment from everyone, including the library administration, supervisors, and staff. Utilizing a committee structure to develop a Web site with a system-wide perspective is part of building a system philosophy. Library staff members at all levels need to be consulted during the planning, implementation, and evaluation of the process. Library Web site requirements grow and change through the Web site development cycle, a progression that requires considerable feedback and persistent consultation.

Lesson 2: Long-Term Improvement Is Dependent Upon Changing the Organizational Culture

Organizational culture evolves slowly. Library staff traditionally valued the status quo, even if the status quo was inadequate. With new personnel and with new direction from the Dean of Libraries, the status quo changed quickly during the first Web update. Library employees have acknowledged these changes as improvements. However, many employees express doubt that these changes will be maintained for any substantial amount of time. Some employees tend to view the tremendous productivity of the Web Committee for Research and Development as a fluke rather than as a sustainable model for future committees within the organization.

Creating a culture that will continually assess the library's Web site is difficult to generate when the organizational culture has not implemented service quality evaluation into strategic planning in the past. During 2003, a new library strategic plan was developed that includes assessment and evaluation, and this plan should provide motivation for change. The organizational values of assessment, planning, implementation, and evaluation are the building blocks of the strategic plan.

Lesson 3: Change Is a Journey, Not a Destination

The members of the Web Liaison Committee did not fully understand the nature of the change to a database-driven content management system. As a result, the perspective that the Web site is in a perpetual development cycle was not well accepted. The next iteration of the Web committee will have a distinct advantage because of the experiences of the past year. Learning what not to do in a group process is a valuable lesson learned for the organization and the members of the committee. It is evident from the evaluation that some members of the Web Liaison Committee want to be directly involved in Web site development. Others are satisfied with their role as a liaison for their units and as communicators of change.

The process of utilizing committees to implement Web site redesign and content management requires individual growth, group maturity, and organizational development. Learning how to interpret problems as an opportunity for change takes time. Communicating effectively and making the best use of staff time is an ongoing priority. The ability to incorporate a committee process for Web site problem solving has helped to build a database-driven Web content management system with potential to improve. The library staff has begun to accept that continuous improvement of the Web site is critical to providing quality library services and resources to customers with increasingly demanding expectations.

## List of Additional Sources

Davidson, J., & Rusk, C. (1996). Creating a university Web in a team environment. *Journal of Academic Librarianship, 22*(4), 302-305.

Guenther, K. (2001). Creating cross-functional Web teams. *Online, 25*(3), 79-81.

Guenther, K. (2002) Communicating the value of Web development efforts. *Online, 26*(4), 63-66.

Internet Archive. Retrieved March 9, 2004, from *www.archive.org*

Johnson, B. (1998). Academic library Webteam management: The role of leadership and authority. *Issues in Science and Technology Librarianship, 18*. Retrieved March 3, 2004, from *www.library. ucsb.edu/istl/98-spring/article4.html*

Manning, J. (2002). Customer-obsessed Web team. *EContent, 25*(1), 36-40.

Ryan, S.M. (2003). Library Web site administration: A strategic planning model for the smaller academic library. *Journal of Academic Librarianship, 29*(4), 207-218.

Wilson, A.P. (2004). *Library Web sites: Creating online collections and services.* Chicago: American Library Association.

# Glossary*

## A

**Access Control:** Access control is a system of privileges and permissions that restricts access to a directory or file. In content management systems permissions are assigned to authors, copy editors, graphics editors, and other contributors according to their roles.

**Aggregation:** Aggregation is the merging of several licensed or subscription services into a single area, thereby making otherwise scattered data, information, and services accessible at a single location, usually via a Web page.

**Apache Server:** Apache Server is a cross-platform Web server freely available under an open source license. The current version runs on most UNIX-based operating systems, on UNIX/POSIX-derived, and on Windows 2000. Debuted in 1995, the Apache's continued development is primarily among a set of volunteer programmers known as the Apache Group. The source code can be modified or adapted by developers.

**Application Programming Interface (API):** API is a set of software functions used to initiate contact with network services and the mainframe. One of the primary purposes of an API is to provide a set of commonly used functions—for example, to draw windows or icons on the screen. By making use of its functionality, programmers can save the task of programming everything from scratch.

**Application Server:** The application server is a server program that hosts transaction and interaction logic for an application. An application server runs on both the development and the production servers. Application servers execute the operations necessary to complete transactions and other interactions between end users, databases, and applications. For example, when a Web page is requested by a Web browser, the Web server will "hand off" the page request to the application server for files with particular file extensions. The server provides functionality such as database access classes, transaction processing, and messaging. It is a key publishing engine in the CM environment (see also Development Server, Production Server, Staging Server).

# B

**Blog (Weblog):** Blog is short for Weblog, a combination of Web and log. Blog is a Web site that contains periodic, reverse chronologically ordered posts. Each post has an anchor that allows a hyperlink to the post from anywhere on the Web. A person who maintains a blog is called a blogger. Blogger (www.blogger.com) is a free Web-based tool that facilitates the posting of blogs. Users FTP a template of their Web page to the blogger site and are able to submit content via a Web-based form. Submissions are posted instantaneously to the Web, and the content maintains the look and feel dictated by the template. In short, it is a simple, Web-based CM system.

# C

**Chunk:** In a content management environment, a chunk is an information content element that can carry a meaningful semantic tag. It is the result of an effort to divide information into small enough sections so that they can be managed easily.

**ColdFusion:** Created in 1995 by Allaire and merged with Macromedia in 2001, ColdFusion integrates browser, server, and database technologies into Web applications. ColdFusion Web pages include application tags written in ColdFusion Markup Language (CFML) that simplifies integration with databases and avoids the use of more complex language like

C++ to create translating programs. Using ColdFusion, a developer can combine a content database with a set of templates to create a site that builds and serves pages "on-the-fly." The suite of applications is composed of two pieces: ColdFusion Studio—the development interface; and the ColdFusion server, a cross-platform Web application, which deploys pages to the user. ColdFusion uses its own markup language, CFML, which incorporates elements of HTML and XML.

**Content Management System (CMS):** CMS is application software that manages unstructured content for Web-based access. Once the content has been developed, it can be stored in a relational database, which resides on a content server. The content is then published typically via a template. The publishing module may be capable of handling dynamic content "on the fly." The CMS often includes a security mechanism that grants or denies access to content. An embedded search function might support searches by subject, full-text, author, or other terms. The CMS may also automatically reformat content for other Web-enabled access.

# D

**Database-Driven Web Pages:** "Database-driven" describes Web sites that store and maintain content in a database. The database can be built using a relational database, XML structure, or a structure constructed by other scripting language, such as JavaScript. The database-driven Web pages support information transactions with the user and produce Web pages "on the fly" as users request them.

**Development Server:** The development server is the server computer on which Web site development is performed and tested. This server sits behind the organization's firewall. Ideally, all content development and testing occur on the development server. Final content is published from the development server to the production server (see also Production Server and Staging Server).

**Document Management (DM):** Document management is an application or system designed to organize information and make files accessible to all users regardless of origin or format. A document management system comprises file storage (the physical location of each file), file categorization (file types and groups based on the criteria), metadata (owner, status, creation date, etc.), workflow management (files are routed from person to person based on defined roles and standard), version control (files can be saved as historical series and can be retrieved later), and access points (user can find files through full-text searching, table of contents, and indexes).

**Dublin Core:** The Dublin Core is a set of standards with reference to the Resource Description Framework (RDF), a dialect of XML. It is used to ascribe library metadata to online documents or any Web page in a consistent basis to enhance retrieval. The *Dublin Core Metadata Element Set* consists of 15 metadata elements: title, creator, subject, description, publisher, contributor, date, type, format, indentifier, source, language, relation, coverage, and rights.

**Dynamic Content:** Dynamic content is content that can be generated on the fly from either a file system or a database using one of or all of the following: Server Side Includes, CGI scripts, Java servlets, or an application server. Dynamic content is updated frequently and can therefore be kept current and relevant for its appropriate audience. Dynamic content can include sophisticated JavaScript or Shockwave for an interactive experience or serve as a flat HTML page that is updated frequently.

# E

**Enterprise Content Management (ECM):** Enterprise CM systems encompass the entire content creation and management for the organization and not just the Web site, as is the case with a CMS (see also CMS).

**eXtensible Markup Language (XML):** Put forth by the World Wide Web Consortium (W3C), XML is an offshoot of Standard Generalized Markup Language (SGML), but XML is much easier to use and apply. It was created so that richly structured documents can be described, exposed, shared, and modified over the Web. XML allows Web developers to design their own customized tags to provide functionality that is not available with HTML. The combination of XML and HTML permits powerful and content-rich Web sites. For example, a Web site using XML tags can link to multiple documents using a single HTML hyperlink. Since XML describes the underlying information and its structure, content can be separated from the display.

# F

**Federated Search:** Federated search tools search across a variety of information sources and display results in a single interface. They can be used to consolidate data from multiple sources, while authenticating and de-duplicating results. They can simultaneously search a wide variety of online resources, such as library catalogs, electronic journals, multiple databases, Web resources, as well as locally held materials. Various products have recently been released into the market, which are designed to integrate with portal software or the OPAC (see also Metasearch).

# G

**GNU General Public License:** The GNU General Public License (GPL) is a copyright-free software license or open source license. In contrast to proprietary licenses, the purpose of the GPL is to protect the user's freedom rather than restrict it. The Free Software Foundation (FSF), a non-profit institution, designed the GNU GPL to promote the publication of free software.

# I

**Information Architecture:** Information architecture is the basic design of the system as it relates to the classification and organization of information content in the CMS environment. It encompasses chunking and tagging strategies, template designs, forms for content element entry, metadata collection, reuse, syndication and aggregation feeds, and database models or schemas. Schemas for classifying information, called taxonomies, are often seen as the building blocks for information architecture.

# J

**Java Database Connectivity (JDBC):** Developed by JavaSoft, a subsidiary of Sun Microsystems, JDBC is a Java API that enables Java programs to execute SQL statements. Since Java itself runs on most platforms, JDBC makes it possible to write a single database application that can run on different platforms and interact with different DBMSs. It is also possible to allow Java programs to interact with any SQL-compliant database. JDBC is similar to ODBC, but is designed specifically for Java programs, whereas ODBC is language independent (see also ODBC).

**JavaScript:** Developed by Netscape, JavaScript is a relatively simple scripting language that can be used to integrate with HTML code and add interactivity to a Web page. JavaScript is intended to provide a quicker and simpler language for enhancing Web pages and servers, whereas Java, developed by Sun Microsystems, was built as a general-purpose object language. JavaScript is an open language supported by most current Web browsers.

# K

**Knowledge Management (KM):** Knowledge management is a term associated with the processes for the creation, dissemination, testing, integration, and utilization of knowledge. In contrast to content management systems, KM systems focus on identifying, storing, and maintaining access to key bits of information relevant to an organization's objectives.

# L

**Link Resolver:** Link Resolver is software used to connect a link source with potential target(s). Used primarily to access a range of electronic databases, it accepts the OpenURL from the link source and determines from what target(s) the cited article is available. The link resolver has access to a database, sometimes called a knowledge base, that records what journals particular group users have access to, from which sources, and within which date range.

**Link Source:** Link Source is software that can recognize when a user has a link resolver available, and display a special button or link on citations (such as SFX, Search LinkSource, or more information). When a link is clicked, the link source sends an OpenURL to the user's resolver identifying the selected resource (database, e-journal, library catalog, Web search engine, interlibrary loan system, etc.).

**Link Targets:** Link targets are the resources the resolver can provide links to. These targets can be electronic journals, aggregated databases, interlibrary loan systems, abstracting services, citation indexes, and library catalogs.

# M

**Metadata:** Metadata is data about data. Metadata is commonly used to identify information that describes a Web asset, most typically an **HTML** file. Metadata is data that accompanies a piece of content or an entire document. Written in HTML, metadata describe the content and provide optional information like a caption, abstract, or keywords for search engines. It could include a creation date, publication date, and expiration date. It could include copyright information and terms of use. Document metadata might include the full list of the Dublin Core ontology properties. It is usually stored in a relational database or an object-oriented database. Metadata that describes an HTML file might include the name of the author, the language the file is written in, the source of the file, the keywords that describe the file, and the audience the content is targeted for. Metadata is typically included in the HTML code of a given Web page.

**Metasearch:** Metasearch is a search of other searches. Often found as a feature in some search tools, it can be used to consolidate data from multiple sources. It can simultaneously search a wide variety of online resources, such as library catalogs, electronic journals, multiple databases, Web resources, and locally held materials. Metasearch engines often cluster the results around found terms in order to assist in narrowing the result list (see also Federated Search).

**MySQL:** MySQL is a computer software product, a multi-threaded, multi-user, SQL (Structured Query Language) relational database server. MySQL, as free software, utilizes the GNU General Public License. It is often used in conjunction with freely available programming languages like PHP to provide a platform for developing in-house applications. The PHP-MySQL combination is also cross-platform compatible.

# O

**Open DataBase Connectivity (ODBC):** Developed by Microsoft Corporation, ODBC is a standard database access method that provides a set of functions to enable access to databases. ODBC supports access to both relational and non-relational databases. The goal of ODBC is to make it possible to access any data from any application, regardless of which database management system (DBMS) is handling the data. For this to work, both the application and the DBMS must be ODBC compliant, that is, the application must be capable of issuing ODBC commands, and the DBMS must be capable of responding to them.

**Open Source:** Open source means that the source code is openly available, and refers generally to any computer software whose source code is either in the public domain or, more commonly, is copyrighted by one or more persons/entities and distributed under an open source license such as the GNU General Public License (GPL). Freely distributable means that anyone may duplicate, modify, redistribute, and use freely under a license. Some examples of open source tools are: Apache, *BSD*, Emacs, GIMP, *GNU GNOME*, KDE, *Linux*, *Moodle*, *Mozilla*, *MySQL*, *OpenOffice.org*, *PHP*, *phpBB*, *Postnuke*, *TeX*, *VIM*, *XFree86*, and *Zope*.

**OpenURL:** OpenURL is a uniform format for passing metadata among link sources, link resolvers, and other applications involved in context-sensitive linking. Its primary application currently is to provide persistent linking to journal articles independent of the database housing them.

# P

**Parsing:** Parsing is the process of checking an SGML-formatted document to ensure it has met all the rules of both SGML (Standard Generalized Markup Language) and the DTD (Document Type Definition). Technically, a document is not considered to be SGML until it has been successfully parsed, as defined by the ISO Standard for SGML.

**Personalization:** Personalization is the process of matching categorized content to users' needs. The personalization process occurs upon page request to a Web server, and content is presented based on user request.

Preferences can be maintained on the server and linked to either a cookie on the user's machine or tied to a login.

**PHP:** Initially known as Personal Home Page Tools, PHP is an open source script language that was designed specifically to generate dynamic Web pages. PHP code is embedded within HTML of a Web document. The PHP script runs on the server side, and performs any programs and operations specified in the script when a user requests the document; a dynamically generated HTML page is then delivered to the user. PHP runs as an optional module within the Apache Web server. It is an open source alternative to Microsoft's Active Server Pages (ASP), Sun's Java Server Pages (JSP), and the like.

**Portal:** In strict technical terms, a portal is a Web site containing links to other sites. Commercial portals typically include a search engine, free e-mail, instant messaging, chat, personalized Web page, and Web hosting, and can often be personalized or tailored to the individual user's needs. Specialized library portals may include channels or a variety of information sources dealing with library news, subject guides for example, along with links to the catalog and databases. There are corporate portals, business portals, and enterprise portals. Portal technology is widely used in Web content management. A portal template, like any CMS template, contains blocks where content elements or content objects will be placed. These elements may be HTML fragments, XML converted to HTML by XSLT, news feeds including JavaScript or XML RDF, images, applets, Flash files, etc. Collectively, these content objects are sometime called portlets.

**Portlet:** A portlet is any content object that appears in some block in a portal. It comes from applets and servlets, which might be providing the portlet content via a Web service.

**PostScript:** PostScript is Adobe's original page description language. PostScript files contain images of full pages (mixed text and graphics). The black-and-white image pages are scaleable, but not searchable. PostScript files are more compressed than bitmaps, so they take up much less storage space. PostScript files retain high resolutions for printing.

**Practical Extraction and Report Language (PERL):** PERL is a script programming language designed specifically for processing text. PERL combines syntax from several UNIX utilities and languages. It is widely used to write common gateway interface (CGI) programs—one method through which developers can provide dynamic interaction between users and Web sites, such as Web forms. PERL is a popular choice for programming server-side tasks such as automatically updating user accounts and newsgroup postings, processing removal requests, synchronizing databases, and generating reports. Its text-processing prowess makes it a frequent choice for building homegrown content management systems.

**Production Server:** The production server is the active server computer that sits outside the organization firewall. Production servers are used to serve external audiences via a Web server application running on a production server. Production servers are often designed to be specialized servers serving different types of content. For example, an organization may have one server to serve all media assets and another to run all CGI scripts, and set up multiple production servers to serve different geographic regions (see also Development Server and Application Server).

# R

**Really Simple Syndication (RSS):** RSS is part of a family of XML-based communication standards along with Rich Site Summary and RDF Site Summary. RSS can be understood as a Web syndication protocol that is primarily used by news Web sites and Weblogs. RSS allows a Web developer to publish his or her Web site in a format that a computer program can easily understand and digest. This allows users to easily repackage the content on their own Web sites or blogs, or privately on their own computers. RSS simply repackages a Web site as a list of data items, such as the date of a post, a description of the post, and a link to it. A program known as an RSS aggregator or feed reader can then check the RSS-enabled Web page for the user and display any updated articles that it finds. This is more convenient than having users repeatedly visit their favorite news Web sites, because it makes sure that readers only see material that they haven't seen before. Web-based RSS aggregators are also available, sparing users the inconvenience of downloading an application to their computers. Such readers can make a user's feeds available on any computer with an Internet connection.

**Resource Description Framework (RDF):** RDF is the tool for adding semantics (meaning) to content objects in Web pages. RDF is most often sent between computers using XML as its syntax. It allows parsers and inference engines to discover the meaning. RDF is usually used for library catalogs, large directories, media asset repositories, and personal media collections like books, CDs, and digital images.

**Reuse:** Reuse describes a content element that can be propagated to more than one place in the site. Maintaining an element in one place insures uniformity and accuracy. Because style and layout are controlled by the associated template, the same information can be wholly integrated into each use. Note that a content element can be a complete templated object with many sub-elements, an RSS news feed, or simply an HTML or XML fragment from a database. SCORM (Shareable Content Object Reference Model) is a proposed standard for reusing content objects. RSS Feed

# S

**Sandbox:** A sandbox is a special Web site running a CMS that allows anyone to sign in and to test drive the application. A sandbox user normally has all the same privileges as the administrator. A sandbox does, however, restrict a program to a set of privileges and commands that make it difficult or impossible for the program to cause damage to the host's data.

**Script:** Script is a type of computer code that can be directly executed by a program that understands the language in which the script is written. Scripts can run on both the development and production servers. Scripts are written in interpreted languages that can contain English statements for commands like PERL and JavaScript. Interpreted languages execute more slowly than compiled programs written in C or C++. Scripting is usually used for simple, lightweight applications and is typically much easier to write than a standard program written in C or C++.

**Server Side Includes (SSI):** Content that sits on the server itself is dynamically included in Web pages upon page request. Server Side Includes are used to make content modular so that a content component such as page header, footer, or navigation bar can be included on multiple Web pages, and content components can be changed in one place and automatically be reflected in all Web pages.

**Staging Server:** A staging server or development server is used in content management development or Web development to test, develop, or compile content or applications before they are deployed to a production or delivery server. The staging server should have the same characteristics as the production server (see also Development Server and Production Server).

**Standard Generalized Markup Language (SGML):** SGML is an international standard. SGML is a text-based language, describing the content and structure of digital documents. It is a meta-language included in a file's document type definition. It specifies the rules for the tagging elements of a markup language, which in turn determines the formatting of the text. It tags documents as a series of data objects rather than storing them as huge files, thus it allows organizations to structure and manage information in a cross-platform, application-independent way.

**Structured Query Language (SQL):** SQL is a specialized programming language for defining, maintaining, and viewing information in a relational database. First commercialized in the early 1990s, SQL has evolved into a complete language for the management of complex data objects. It can be used for most industrial-strength and many smaller database applications. Each specific application will have its own version of SQL implementing features unique to that application, but all SQL-capable databases support a common subset of SQL.

# T

**Taxonomy:** Taxonomy, as it relates to content management, refers to either a hierarchical classification of things or the principles underlying the classification. The structure, typically highly regimented, impacts the data model, directory structure, and file naming conventions for a given implementation of a content management system.

**Template:** A template identifies the presentation or layout of information content, including style and positioning to be used by the browser when displaying specified elements. The content elements or content objects could be HTML or XML fragments, RSS news feeds and other remote server-driven applications (servlets), or client-side application programs (applets). Pages on a site using the same template present a common look and feel.

# V

**Version Control:** Version control in content management assists the administrator and users of the system in coordinating production and tracking older versions of content or code. In order to prevent files from accidentally being replaced by another user's changes, version control is typically done by requiring users to "check in" and "check out" files that they are working on. Version tracking archives track old versions of content, the content management system's source code, and other files, which can be retrieved and re-published to the live site. This is done using time and date stamping, and other data about a file to maintain it.

# W

**Wiki:** "Wiki wiki" means "super fast" in the Hawaiian language. A wiki Web site enables documents to be authored collectively in a simple markup language using a Web browser. A wiki is an organic or growing collection of Web pages with novel linking structures. Each link is the name of a page in the wiki, with a special capital letter plus medial-cap syntax that makes it a "WikiWord." The wiki builds itself when pages are added that include a WikiWord. Standard wiki pages contain no HTML. They are simple text fields in the database. All HTML is generated, turning WikiWords into hyperlinks, adding unique wiki. A wiki feels like a glossary, but it is not, since the entries are special WikiWords. It is a CMS. It manages the content in pages with its simple but powerful tools.

**Workflow:** Workflow describes a set of interdependent tasks that occur in a specific sequence. Workflow as it applies to content management describes the process of breaking down a high-level task into a series of orderly, pre-defined steps that answer these questions: What needs to be done? Who needs to do it? Who needs to approve it? And when must it be completed? *Approval-centered* and *task-oriented* constitute two types of workflow management. An approval-centered workflow tracks the approval chain of command on a piece of content, no matter what the form—from a press release to a video clip of a speech. A task-oriented workflow centers on the tasks that must be done by different resources, or people, to complete the task.

# Z

**Zope:** Zope is an object-oriented Web application server written in the programming language Python. It can be almost fully managed with a Web-based user interface. A Zope Web site is composed of objects, as opposed to files, as is usual with many other Web server systems. Zope maps URLs to objects using the containment hierarchy of such objects, and methods are considered to be contained in their objects as well.

# Endnote

\*    The glossary of terms included in this list is primarily drawn from the disciplines of content management and, by extension, Web content management. It is not intended to be a comprehensive list but a brief guide to some of the more commonly used technical terms found in the literature and in the case studies published here. Entries are listed alphabetically. Acronyms are used for entries wherever possible with the full term placed alongside in parentheses.

Many sources were used in the preparation of this glossary. Online dictionaries and encyclopedia referenced include CMSWatch (*http://www.cmswatch.com/*), Edit-x (*http://www.edit-x.com/glossary.php*), and Wikipedia (*http://en.wikipedia.org/*).

# About the Authors

**Holly Yu** is Web Administrator and Reference Librarian at the University Library, California State University, Los Angeles (CSULA) (USA). She coordinates the development and maintenance of the library's Web site, and is heavily involved in designing and testing Web interfaces for the library. She also provides curricular support, library instruction, and reference services to students and faculty. She is the author of "Web Accessibility and the Law: Recommendations for Implementation" (*Library Hi Tech*, Vol. 20, No. 4). She has presented at American Library Association conferences as well as regional conferences and Internet Librarians' conferences on the topics of Web site usability and library Web development. She is active in the Library Information & Technology Association (LITA) and the American Library Association (ALA). To contact: hyu3@calstatela.edu.

\* \* \*

**Matthew M. Calsada** is a Product Training and Software Testing Specialist at Atlas Systems, Incorporated. Previously, he was the Electronic Resources Programmer/Analyst for the University at Albany Libraries. His specialties include ASP, VB, .NET and database administration. Among his applications are WebReview discussed in this chapter, an XML-based content management system, a human resources management application and various electronic resources management systems. He can be reached at mcalsada@atlas-sys.com.

**Laura B. Cohen** is Library Web Administrator at the University Libraries, University at Albany, SUNY. In this capacity, she manages the Libraries' Web site and coordinates staff contributions to the site. She is a member of the team that maintains the Web site infrastructure hosted in the University Libraries. Her work also includes management of the Libraries' staff intranet Web site and provision of off-campus access to licensed resources through a proxy server. Her collection of Internet Tutorials are used world-wide. She has written and spoken widely about using the Web as a research tool and Web site management and technologies. She can be reached at lcohen@uamail.albany.edu.

**Diane Dallis** is currently the Instructional Services Librarian in the Indiana University Bloomington Information Commons Undergraduate Services Department (USA). She is a member of the IUB Libraries Web Team and participates in the development of the content manager and usability studies. Her role on the Web Team is to bring the library instruction point of view to the development of the Web system. She has worked with members of the team to create templates for course-specific instructional Web pages, and is planning to develop more tools and resources for library instruction in the new system. To contact: ddallis@indiana.edu.

**Anne Marie Donovan** (BA, MA, MSIS) retired from the U.S. Navy in 2000 after serving 20 years as a Naval Intelligence Officer. She received her MSIS degree in 2003 from the School of Information at the University of Texas at Austin. She presently resides in Austin, where she works as an Independent Consultant in digital records management and digital archiving. Her recent work includes the development of a digital archive program plan for the City of Austin, Austin History Center, and an assessment of e-mail and instant messaging software products for a records management consulting firm. To contact: amdonovan@austin.rr.com.

**Debra Engel** graduated with an MLS from the University of Arizona. Since 2001, she has worked as the Director of Public Services for the University of Oklahoma Libraries. In her current position, she chairs the Web Liaison Committee and has played a leadership role in the last two major revisions of the library's Web site. Prior to 2001, Ms. Engel worked as the Assistant Director for the Pioneer Library System, in Norman, Oklahoma. She is an active member of the Oklahoma Library Association and American Library Association. To contact: dhengel@ou.edu.

**Frederick J. Jeziorkowski** is Network Manager/Systems Administrator at the University Libraries, University at Albany, SUNY. Fred's primary responsibility is management of the Microsoft-based network for the University Libraries. Fred's professional experience spans the private sector, consulting and academia. His areas of expertise include network architecture and design, implementation of Microsoft's Active Directory Services, network security and data networking. He is a member of the team that maintains the Web site infrastructure hosted in the University Libraries. He can be reached at fjeziorkowski@uamail.albany.edu.

**Michelle Mach** is a Digital Projects Librarian at Colorado State University in Fort Collins, Colorado (USA). In this position she advises library staff on Web projects, teaches workshops in Web design, and designs online library instruction. Her current research interests are online tutorials, usability testing, and Web site administration. To contact: mmach@lib.colostate.edu.

**Michael Nomura** is an Information Analyst at the University of Texas Institute for Advanced Technology in Austin, Texas. Before his arrival at the University of Texas, he served as a Command and Control Officer in the U.S. Air Force. He holds an MS in Information Studies from the University of Texas and a BS in Finance from California State University. His professional interests include information design, information organization and retrieval, and business information research/competitive intelligence. To contact: nomuram@ischool. utexas.edu.

**Andy Osburn** is the Web Database/Application Developer for the Library at California State University, Sacramento (CSUS). His areas of interest include network database applications, network security, and integrating open source systems into custom solutions. Previously, he worked as a graphic artist for 10 years before switching to his current vocation. To contact: andyo@csus.edu.

**Johan Ragetli** earned his MLIS degree in 1996 from the Graduate School of Information Studies at the University of Western Ontario. He is currently working as a Library Information Analyst for Kawartha Pine Ridge District School Board in Peterborough, Ontario, Canada. He manages Library Automation and is Systems Administrator. He is also responsible for developing and implementing electronic library services for the board. He provides support and training on Internet-related issues for teachers and other employees of the board. At the ALA/CLA Joint Conference in June 2003, he spoke on the development of Web OPAC interfaces for library systems. To contact: johan_ragetli@kprdsb.ca.

**Sarah Robbins** is a recent MLIS graduate from the University of Oklahoma's School of Library and Information Studies. Since graduating in 2001, she has worked as the Electronic Services Coordinator for the University of Oklahoma Libraries. Ms. Robbins serves on several committees of the Oklahoma Library Association and is a member of the American Library Association's New Members Round Table. To contact: srobbins@ou.edu.

**Juan Carlos Rodriguez** holds an MLIS from UCLA with a specialization in Information Systems. He is currently the Director of Library Information Systems at California State University, Sacramento (CSUS). Prior to joining CSUS, he held several positions at UC Riverside including Science Reference Librarian and Coordinator of Information Technology for the Science Library. His research interests include emerging information technologies and their potential use in an academic environment, information seeking behavior in an online environment, and Web-based technologies in libraries. He is also a member of the INFOMINE (http://infomine.ucr.edu/) Development Team. INFOMINE is one of the first virtual libraries of scholarly Internet resources developed by librarians. He has presented nationally in the areas of information retrieval of Internet resources and metadata. To contact: carlos@csus.edu.

**Doug Ryner** is the Libraries Web Administrator at Indiana University. As the chief architect of the IUB Libraries Web system, he coordinates several teams contributing to the Libraries' Web presence including usability, content development, intranet, content delivery, and electronic resources. Mr. Ryner has been a recipient of five International Web Page Awards, including an International Web Page Award for "Best of Category" in 1999 for www.coachbobknight.com, beating out such sports entrants as the Web sites for Nike, USA Today, and the Miami Dolphins. In addition, his work has been recognized by the American Advertising Federation, with two Indianapolis ADDY Awards and three citations of excellence. To contact: dryner@indiana.edu.

**Stephen Sottong** was the Engineering, Technology, Computer Science, and Psychology Librarian at California State University, Los Angeles (CSULA), prior to his retirement. Before becoming a librarian, he was an electrical engineer in the aerospace industry. In addition to writing on Web page design, he has written extensively on the technical difficulties associated with e-books. During his career at the CSULA, he also designed and edited Web pages, was backup for library systems, and wrote specialized software for libraries. To contact: ssotton@yahoo.com.

**Michael D. Whang** is in charge of Web and Internet Services at Western Michigan University Libraries, Kalamazoo, Michigan. In his position, he is actively involved in technology management, Web and multimedia development, and digital archiving. His research interests focus on information architecture and human factors of online information retrieval. He received his MLIS from the University of Hawaii. To contact: michael.whang@wmich.edu.

# Index

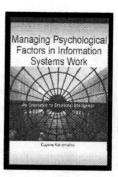